HATE CRIMES

HATE CRIMES

VOLUME 3

The Victims of Hate Crime

Barbara Perry, General Editor
and Volume Editor

PRAEGER PERSPECTIVES

Westport, Connecticut
London

Library of Congress Cataloging-in-Publication Data

Hate crimes / Barbara Perry, general editor.
    p. cm.
  Includes bibliographical references and index.
  ISBN 978–0–275–99569–0 (set : alk. paper) — 978–0–275–99571–3
(vol. 1 : alk. paper) — 978–0–275–99573–7 (vol. 2 : alk. paper) — 978–0–275–99575–1
(vol. 3 : alk. paper) — 978–0–275–99577–5 (vol. 4 : alk. paper) — 978–0–275–99579–9
(vol. 5 : alk. paper)
  1. Offenses against the person. 2. Hate crimes. 3. Violent crimes. 4. Genocide.
I. Perry, Barbara, 1962–
  K5170.H38   2009
  364.15—dc22   2008052727

British Library Cataloguing in Publication Data is available.

Library of Congress Catalog Card Number: 2008052727
ISBN: 978–0–275–99569–0 (set)
      978–0–275–99571–3 (vol. 1)
      978–0–275–99573–7 (vol. 2)
      978–0–275–99575–1 (vol. 3)
      978–0–275–99577–5 (vol. 4)
      978–0–275–99579–9 (vol. 5)

First published in 2009

Praeger Publishers, 88 Post Road West, Westport, CT 06881
An imprint of Greenwood Publishing Group, Inc.
www.praeger.com

Printed in the United States of America

The paper used in this book complies with the
Permanent Paper Standard issued by the National
Information Standards Organization (Z39.48–1984).

10 9 8 7 6 5 4 3 2 1

For "us" and "them"
who are really one and the same.

CONTENTS

ACKNOWLEDGMENTS

I thank the usual suspects: Praeger, for proposing and supporting this project; my colleagues for inspiring me; and my family for supporting me. This time around I owe unending gratitude to the contributors to this volume. I am honored to be able to include the work of people whom I have long respected for their passion and their incisiveness. Their work stimulates me and, I hope, will stimulate our readers to help change the ways we construct "us" and "them" through our perceptions and actions.

SET INTRODUCTION

Barbara Perry
General Editor

The twentieth century appeared to close much as it had opened—with sprees of violence directed against the Other. The murder of Matthew Shepard, the lynching of James Byrd, the murderous rampage of Benjamin Smith, and post-9/11 anti-Muslim violence all stand as reminders that the bigotry that kills is much more than an unfortunate chapter in U.S. history. Racial, gender, ethnic, and religious violence persist. It is a sad commentary on the cultural and social life of the United States that a series such as this remains timely as we enter the twenty-first century. The dramatic cases cited earlier are but extreme illustrations of widespread, daily acts of aggression directed toward an array of minority communities. I use the term *communities* purposefully here since these acts are less about any one victim than about the cultural group they represent. Hate crime is, in fact, an assault against all members of stigmatized and marginalized communities.

Clearly this is not a new phenomenon, even in the United States. It is important to keep in mind that what we currently refer to as hate crime has a long historical lineage. The contemporary dynamics of hate-motivated violence have their origins in historical conditions. With respect to hate crime, at least, history does repeat itself, as similar patterns of motivation, sentiment, and victimization recur over time. Just as immigrants in the 1890s were subject to institutional and public forms of discrimination and violence, so, too, were those of the 1990s; likewise, former black slaves risked the wrath of the Ku Klux Klan (KKK) when they exercised their newfound rights in the antebellum period, just as their descendants risked violent reprisal for their efforts to win and exercise additional rights and freedoms in the civil rights era; and women who demanded the right to vote on the eve of the twentieth century suffered the same ridicule and harassment as those who demanded equal rights in the workplace later in the century. While the politics of difference that underlie these periods of animosity may lie latent for short periods of time, they nonetheless seem to remain on the simmer, ready to resurface whenever a new threat is perceived—when immigration levels increase; or when relationships between groups shift for other political, economic, or cultural reasons; or in the aftermath of attacks like those on 9/11. Consequently, hate crime remains a crucial indicator of cultural fissures in the United States and around the globe. This set, then, remains similarly relevant in the current era.

Hate Crimes offers interested readers a comprehensive collection of original chapters surveying this phenomenon we have come to know as hate crime. Interestingly, the field of hate crime studies is interdisciplinary, so the contributors here represent a variety of disciplines, including law, sociology, criminology, psychology, and even public health. Moreover, since it is also a global phenomenon, we have invited not just American scholars, but international contributors as well. This comparative/cross-cultural approach adds an important element to the set. It reminds readers that hate crime is a universal problem and that approaches taken elsewhere might be of use to North Americans.

The volumes included in this set have been divided into five distinct focal areas. Volume 1, *Understanding and Defining Hate Crime*, is edited by Brian Levin of California State University, San Bernardino. He has collected a series of chapters that lay a strong foundation for the volumes that follow. The pieces here provide an introduction to what it is we mean by the term *hate crime*. There is ongoing debate about such things as whether the term is even appropriate, what behaviors ought to be included in our understanding of hate crime, and what classes of victims should be included. The relevant chapters, then, offer diverse definitions, ranging from legal to sociological approaches.

One consequence of the varied and divergent definitions used to conceptualize bias-motivated crime is that the confusion also complicates the process of gathering data on hate crime. Berk, Boyd, and Hamner (1992) astutely observe that "much of the available data on hate motivated crime rests on unclear definitions; it is difficult to know what is being counted as hate motivated and what is not" (p. 125). As a result, while both academic and media reports make the claim that ethnoviolence represents a "rising tide," the truth is that we don't know whether in fact this is the case or not (Jacobs & Potter, 1998). Thus Levin also includes a number of chapters that attempt to address the issue of data collection and measurement of hate crime.

The limitations of definition and measurement highlighted previously help to explain the limited attempts thus far to theorize hate crime. In the

absence of empirical information about bias-motivated violence, it is difficult to construct conceptual frameworks. Without the raw materials, there
is no foundation for theorizing. Additionally, the relatively recent recognition of hate crime as a social problem (Jenness & Broad, 1998) also contributes to the lack of theoretical accounts. This volume, however, includes
chapters that begin to offer compelling models to help us make sense of
hate crime.

The second volume, *The Consequences of Hate Crime*, is a particularly valuable contribution to the literature on hate crime. Editor Paul Iganski of Lancaster University in the United Kingdom has brought together a unique
collection of chapters that explore both the individual and the social impacts associated with this form of violence. Running through much of the
literature—even through court decisions on hate crime—is the assumption
that such offences are qualitatively different in their effects, as compared to
their non-bias-motivated counterparts. Specifically, Iganski (2001) contends
that there are five distinct types of consequences associated with hate crime:
harm to the initial victim; harm to the victim's group; harm to the victim's
group (outside the neighborhood); harm to other targeted communities; and
harm to societal norms and values. The first of these has been the subject of
considerable scholarly attention. Research suggests that first and foremost
among the impacts on the individual is the physical harm: bias-motivated
crimes are often characterized by extreme brutality (Levin & McDevitt,
1993). Violent personal crimes motivated by bias are more likely to involve
extraordinary levels of violence. Additionally, the empirical findings of studies of the emotional, psychological, and behavioral impacts of hate crime are
beginning to establish a solid pattern of more severe impact on bias crime
victims, as compared to nonbias victims (see, e.g., Herek, Cogan, & Gillis,
2002; McDevitt et al., 2001). Several chapters in this volume explore these
individual effects.

Additionally, however, this volume includes a number of chapters that
begin to offer insights into other often overlooked consequences of hate crime:
community effects. Many scholars point to the "fact" that hate crimes are
"message crimes" that emit a distinct warning to all members of the victim's
community: step out of line, cross invisible boundaries, and you, too, could
be lying on the ground, beaten and bloodied (Iganski, 2001). Consequently,
the individual fear noted previously is thought to be accompanied by the
collective fear of the victim's cultural group, possibly even of other minority
groups likely to be victims. Weinstein (as cited by Iganski, 2001) refers to
this as an *in terrorem* effect: intimidation of the group by the victimization of
one or a few members of that group. It is these effects that contributors such
as Monique Noelle and Helen Ahn Lim address.

Barbara Perry, editor of volume 3, *The Victims of Hate Crime*, introduces
this volume with the caveat that little empirical work has been done on the

distinct experiences of different groups of hate crime victims. Much of the literature has more or less assumed a homogeneous group known as "victims." However, this occludes the fact that the frequency, dynamics, motives, and impacts of bias-motivated violence differ across target communities. Thus the volume draws on emerging theoretical and empirical work that explores manifestations of hate crime within diverse communities. Especially novel here is the inclusion of pieces that address hate-motivated crime directed toward women and the homeless community. Consideration of these groups, in particular, forces us to expand our traditional characterization of hate crime victims, which is often restricted to race, religion, ethnicity, or sexual orientation.

Volume 4, *Hate Crime Offenders*, brings us to a consideration of the second half of the equation: perpetrators of hate crime. Randy Blazak from Portland State University has gathered an intriguing collection of chapters. The authors here have been set the task of responding to Blazak's opening question, Who are the hate mongers? Many would respond to this question by reference to members of the KKK or a skinhead group, for example. This is a very common myth. In fact, fewer than 5 percent of identifiable offenders are members of organized hate groups. Recognizing this, Blazak has asked his contributors to explore both individual perpetrators and those involved in hate groups. Thus this is an engaging and diverse collection of chapters, which explore issues ranging from women's involvement in hate crime, to typologies of hate crime offenders, to white power music. He even includes an interview with a hate offender.

Frederick Lawrence, editor of volume 5, *Responding to Hate Crime*, has solicited work from his contributors that gives us food for thought with respect to how we might respond to hate crime. Clearly there are diverse approaches available: legislation, social policy, community organizing, or education, to name just a few. In the extant scholarship, there have been relatively few concentrated analyses of such efforts to respond to or prevent bias-motivated crimes. In large part, such recommendations come by way of a conclusion and are thus not fully developed. Hence the chapters in Lawrence's volume explicitly present interventions intended to ameliorate the incidence or impact of hate crime. While the emphasis is on criminal justice responses (legislation, policing, prosecution), Lawrence also includes chapters that explore preventative measures, restorative justice initiatives, and the role of organizations like the Southern Poverty Law Center.

I speak for all of the editors when I say that we are very pleased to have been asked to develop this collection of hate crime literature. It was a unique opportunity to share emerging perspectives and analyses with a diverse audience. It is hoped that what we offer here will provide the insights that readers are seeking, but also inspiration for further explorations and interventions into this disturbing class of violence.

REFERENCES

Berk, R., Boyd, E., & Hamner, K. (1992). Thinking more clearly about hate-motivated crimes. In G. Herek & K. Berrill (Eds.), *Hate crimes: Confronting violence against lesbians and gay men* (pp. 123–143). Newbury Park, CA: Sage.

Herek, G., Cogan, J., & Gillis, R. (2002). Victim experiences in hate crimes based on sexual orientation. *Journal of Social Issues, 58*, 319–339.

Iganski, P. (2001). Hate crimes hurt more. *American Behavioral Scientist, 45*, 626–638.

Jacobs, J., & Potter, K. (1998). *Hate crimes: Criminal law and identity politics.* New York: Oxford University Press.

Jenness, V., & Broad, K. (1998). *Hate crimes: New social movements and the politics of violence.* New York: Aldine de Gruyter.

Levin, J., & McDevitt, J. (1993). *Hate crimes: The rising tide of bigotry and bloodshed.* New York: Plenum.

McDevitt, J., Balboni, J., Garcia, L., & Gu, J. (2001). Consequences for victims: A comparison of bias- and non-bias motivated assaults. *American Behavioral Scientist, 45*, 697–713.

Introduction: Filling in the Blanks

Barbara Perry

To date, hate crime literature has tended to be very broad and nonspecific in its focus. That is, little scholarship devotes attention to specific categories of victims. Extant literature has tended to discuss hate crime in generic terms, as if it were experienced in the same ways by women, by Jews, by gay men, by Latinos, by lesbians. Even racial violence is collapsed into one broad category, as if all racial and ethnic groups experience it in the same way. Consequently, we do not have a very clear picture of the specific dynamics and consequences that may be associated with victimization on the basis of different identity positions. This volume promises to lend specificity to our understanding of the discrete experiences of diverse groups, ranging from ethnic and racial minorities to homeless people. The contributors to this volume have made significant contributions to the literature in other contexts. I am honored that they have agreed to share their insights here.

In the United States, the limited data available suggest that African Americans are the most frequent victims of racial violence. Franz Fanon was no stranger to this reality: as an active and outspoken critic of Western racial politics, he often found himself accused of racial transgressions. Thus, he recalls (2000), "I was expected to act like a black man—or at least like a nigger. I shouted a greeting to the world and the world slashed away my joy. I was told to stay within my bounds, to go back where I belonged." bell hooks (1995) similarly attests to the violent potential inherent in the game of racial accountability. She observes that the daily violence experienced by so many black people is necessary for the maintenance of racial difference. Indeed, if black people have not learned our place as second-class citizens through educational institutions, we learn it by the daily assaults perpetuated by white offenders on our bodies and beings that we feel but rarely publicly protest or name . . . Most black folks believe that if they do no conform to white dominated standards of acceptable behavior they will not survive. (p. 15)

Carolyn Turpin-Petrosino's chapter in this volume goes a long way to deepening our understanding of the cumulative, ongoing nature and impact of ethnoviolence experienced by African Americans.

Few racial or ethnic groups in North America have experienced anything like the genocidal attempts to remove the American Indians from their land. However, scholarly attention to the historical and contemporary victimization of American Indians as nations has unfortunately blinded us to the corresponding victimization of American Indians as individual members of those many nations. A review of the literature on Native Americans and criminal justice, and even a similar review of the narrower literature on ethnoviolence, reveals virtually no consideration of Native Americans as victims of racially motivated violence (Nielsen, 1996, 2000). Moreover, there is no Native American equivalent to the annual audits of anti-Semitic violence or antigay violence published by the Anti-Defamation League and the National Gay and Lesbian Task Force, respectively. Perry's article in this volume adds to our understanding of Native American victimization, drawing upon a series of interviews conducted in multiple sites across the country.

Nearly as little is known about Latino victims of racially motivated crime as about Native Americans. While this population has a staggeringly high rate of victimization in general, little effort has been made to tease out the effect of racial animus in this context. Moreover, anti-Hispanic victimization is often inseparable from anti-immigrant violence, given the elision noted previously. As is the case for Native Americans, there is no uniform collection of data on anti-Hispanic violence. A recent National Council of La Raza report offers some insights here, but even that is limited. It is a one-time-only report that does not systematically replicate its inquiry on an annual basis. Silvina Ituarte's chapter here is thus a very welcome addition.

In contrast to antiblack and anti-Hispanic hate crime, anti-Asian violence accounts for a relatively small proportion of all racially motivated hate crime. However, it does represent a growing proportion. Many sources suggest that it constitutes the most dramatically and rapidly growing type of racial violence (Federal Bureau of Investigation, 2007; United States Commission on Civil Rights, 1992). The most comprehensive source of data on violence against Asian Americans is the Asian American Justice Center's yearly audit (formerly the National Asian Pacific American Legal Consortium). The audits consistently seem to confirm what anecdotal evidence and intuitive observations have suggested: riding a wave of anti-immigrant sentiments, anti-Asian violence has been on the rise since at least the mid-1990s. Asians—regardless of the longevity of their ties to the United States—are frequent victims of violence ranging from offensive bumper stickers, to verbal harassment, to assault, to murder. However, neither the dynamics of white-on-Asian violence nor Asian conflicts with other groups have been systematically examined. In the aftermath of the September 11 attacks, it is more important than ever to study and understand the animus that underlies anti-Asian violence. Two chapters in this volume shed light on anti-Asian violence: Helen Ahn Lim's chapter on anti-Asian violence, and Scott Poynting's chapter on Islamophobic hate crime.

The latter brings us to the question of religiously motivated violence. From the time European settlers landed on the shores of what is now the United States, there has been a close connection between race, ethnicity, the "immigrant experience," and religion—perhaps more so than in most countries. For many ethnic groups arriving in this new land, religion has provided the basis for continued (albeit often short-lived) solidarity and sense of community. It has often served as the glue that would reinforce group identity. At the same time, religion has been a frequent source of divisiveness between groups, where religious beliefs and practices have defined worshipers as "different."

It is ironic that a country resettled by people seeking freedom from religious persecution has had such an extensive history of religious bigotry and violence. It is equally ironic that while the First Amendment guarantees religious freedom, some religious minorities have been met with considerable legal and extralegal intolerance. Its remains the case, in spite of our popular mythology, that the United States is not a melting pot of religious "tolerance and harmony." On the contrary, "all of the ancient European hatreds based on nation and religion reappeared on this side of the Atlantic. Cities became boiling cauldrons of suspicion and hatred" (Walker, 1998). From Puritan persecutions of "heathens" and "heretics," to contemporary acts of anti-Muslim violence, religious difference has inspired periodic waves of hostility culminating in violent rhetoric and action. However, these remarks are speculative—there is virtually no literature to confirm my analysis of the contemporary contours of religiously motivated violence. This can even be said of anti-Semitic violence, which is quite likely the most frequent class of religiously motivated violence. Imagine my surprise when I was unable to locate a single scholarly piece on U.S. anti-Semitic violence. Again, this is an area in which European scholars can provide guidance to researchers in the United States. For this reason, I am very pleased to offer Paul Iganski's chapter on anti-Semitism in the United Kingdom.

Not only does religion often form the basis for hostility toward other religions, but it also informs other categories of animosity and violence. One such case is violence against gay men and lesbians, which is very often informed by narrow and particularistic readings of religious tracts. Attacks against homosexuals tend to be among the most brutal acts of hatred. They often involve severe beatings, torture, mutilation, castration, even sexual assault. They are also very likely to result in death (Levin & McDevitt, 1993). This feature of violence against gays may account for its emergence as a recognizable social problem, worthy of public attention. In this context, Ellen Faulkner offers an intriguing comparative account of antigay and antilesbian violence in Canada and the United States.

Given the depth of cultural heterosexism, it is perhaps not surprising that there has consistently been resistance to including sexual orientation as a protected class in hate crime legislation. What is, perhaps, surprising is that similar controversy has swirled around the inclusion of gender as a protected category. There is a tragic irony in the fact that, on December 6, 1989, in Montreal, Canada, Marc Lepine lined up female engineering students against a wall, opened fire and killed 14 while shouting his intent to "kill the feminists." Just four months later, on April 23, 1990, the U.S. Congress signed into law the Hate Crime Statistics Act, mandating the collection of data on crime motivated by prejudice on the basis of race, ethnicity, religion, and sexual orientation. In light of the international publicity assigned the former, the failure of the latter to include gender is telling. Perhaps more clearly than any other case, the Lepine murders demonstrate that much violence against women is indistinguishable from other hate crimes, as Walter DeKeseredy argues in chapter 8. It, too, is intended to intimidate and control the larger class of people—women—not just the victims.

The bias motivation underlying harassment and intimidation of people with disabilities also continues to be largely neglected. It was not until 1996 that the category was added to the federal hate crime legislation; few states have followed suit (see Grattet and Jenness, 2001). A bare handful of articles have explicitly addressed bias-motivated violence against persons with disability. Moreover, these have not typically been grounded in empirical investigations of such victimization. Consequently, we know very little about the extent, nature, or impact of violence against this population. Lane, Shaw, and Kim's chapter here offers a comprehensive account of what we know—empirically and theoretically—about violence against people with disabilities.

Finally, this volume includes Sandra Wachholz's intriguing analysis of violence against homeless people. This is a population that is largely invisible to the public, and one that seems to have been completely neglected in the hate crime literature until Wachholz's work in New England. We see from her chapter how the deep-rooted hostility and distrust of people living on the street conditions their daily experiences of harassment and intimidation.

Collectively, the chapters in this volume represent the most comprehensive and up-to-date analyses of the experiences of diverse victims of hate crime. I am grateful to each of the authors for their willingness to contribute to this project. I hope that their insights will be used to broaden academic and popular understanding of bias-motivated violence, so that the knowledge can be used to transform attitudes and behaviors.

REFERENCES

Fanon, F. (2000). The fact of blackness. In L. Back & J. Solomos (Eds.), *Theories of race and racism* (pp. 257–266). London: Routledge.

Federal Bureau of Investigation. (2007). *Hate crime statistics, 2006.* Washington, DC: Author.

Grattet, R., & Jenness, V. (2001). The birth and maturation of hate crime policy in the United States. *American Behavioral Scientist, 45*(4), 668–696.

hooks, b. (1995). *Killing rage: Ending racism.* New York: Henry Holt.

Levin, J., & McDevitt, J. (1993). *Hate crimes: The rising tide of bigotry and bloodshed.* New York: Plenum.

Nielsen, M. (1996). Contextualization for Native American crime and justice. In M. Nielsen & R. Silverman (Eds.), *Native Americans, crime and justice* (pp. 10–19). Boulder CO: Westview.

Nielsen, M. (2000). Stolen lands, stolen lives: Native Americans and criminal justice. In Criminal Justice Collective (Eds.), *Investigating difference: Human and cultural relations in criminal justice* (pp. 45–58). Needham Heights, MA: Allyn & Bacon.

U.S. Commission on Civil Rights. (1992). *Civil rights issues facing Asian Americans.* Washington DC: Author.

Walker, S. (1998). *Popular justice: A history of American criminal justice.* New York: Oxford University Press.

CHAPTER 1

RACIST VIOLENCE AGAINST NATIVE AMERICANS

Barbara Perry

MISSING PIECES: THE DEARTH OF SCHOLARSHIP ON ANTI-INDIAN VIOLENCE

Scholarly attention to the historical and contemporary victimization of American Indians as nations has unfortunately blinded us to the corresponding victimization of American Indians as individual members of those many nations. A review of the literature on Native Americans and criminal justice, and even a similar review of the narrower literature on ethnoviolence, reveal virtually no consideration of Native Americans as victims of racially motivated violence (Nielsen, 1996, 2000). Bachman's (1992) examination of violence on Native American reservations is silent on the question of intergroup violence. Nielsen and Silverman's (1996) anthology on Native Americans, crime, and justice likewise makes no mention of Native Americans as victims of racially motivated crime. The same can be said of Ross and Gould's (2006) more recent collection of essays on Native American criminal justice issues. Barker's (1992) journalistic account of the murders of Native Americans in Farmington, New Mexico, touches on the issue of hate crime but provides no concrete data or analysis.

To be fair, there have been a handful of Civil Rights Commission investigations into discrimination and violence against American Indian communities, but these have been largely regional studies, and the resultant reports have not been grounded in scholarly forms of analysis. Additionally, there has been some limited scholarship on the "anti-Indian movement," especially by Rudolph Rÿser and the Center for World Indigenous Studies, and/or the violence associated with the Midwest spearfishing controversy (Whaley &

Bressette, 1994). However, these have been restricted to analyses of quite specific times and places. Consequently, the research on which this chapter is based was an important endeavor.

In addition to the lack of scholarship, there is also an absence of concrete data on hate crimes against Native Americans. There is no Native American equivalent to the annual audits of anti-Semitic violence or antigay violence published by the Anti-Defamation League and the National Gay and Lesbian Task Force, respectively. As noted above, federal hate crime statistics provide little insight. The latest available report indicates that in 2004, there were 83 incidents in which Native Americans were victims of hate crime, representing far less than 1 percent of all offenses, and just 2 percent of all those motivated by race (Federal Bureau of Investigation [FBI], 2005).

The general limitations of Uniform Crime Report (UCR) hate crime data are by now well-known and well documented (see Silverman, 1996). Of particular concern at present are two issues: the narrow range of categories of crime and underreporting. The UCR data reflect only Part I Index Offenses. The report does not include other forms of violence, such as harassment; circulating racist, sexist, or homophobic literature; or the use of racial symbols or epithets, for example. Consequently, it ignores much of the daily experience of ethnoviolence, which have cumulative negative effects.

UCR data—and especially the hate crime data—are notoriously flawed by public underreporting of criminal victimization (McDevitt et al., 2000). Fewer than 25 percent of the incidents of ethnoviolence are ever reported, for a variety of reasons ranging from fear of retaliation to lack of faith in police response (Berrill & Herek, 1992). This may be particularly relevant in the case of Native Americans, thereby explaining the low rates of victimization recorded in UCR statistics. In light of the history of oppression experienced by Native Americans, it should come as no surprise that they fail to report victimization to police. As the visible and uniformed face of the "dominant society," law enforcement agents—even Native American officers—bear the brunt of this suspicion. They command mistrust rather than confidence:

> In many respects the relationship between the police and the Aboriginal community both reflects and shapes Aboriginal concerns about their relationship with government more generally. The police are the first and most frequent contact that Aboriginal people have with the justice system and as such often are seen to represent that system. (Canada, Department of Justice, 1991, p. 33)

Native peoples are not likely to freely initiate contact with officers who represent a state or a culture that has so often betrayed them.

Moreover, the involvement of police in interpersonal affairs is a notion foreign to Native interpretations of justice. To report victimization may be seen as a violation of the traditional value of noninterference with the actions of others (Dumont, 1996). Aboriginal peoples share a "reluctance to testify for or against others or him/herself, based on a general avoidance of confrontation" (Dumont, p. 32). Withdrawal, rather than confrontation, is often the response to hostile experiences. Additionally, the role of police is limited in a culture that values informal community control over formal institutions, and conciliation over retribution (Dumont).

Finally, the data that are available tend to emphasize the quantitative dimensions of ethnoviolence—that is, the incidence and prevalence. The research described here is significant in that it emphasizes qualitative insights into the dynamics and impact of victimization. Participants were questioned about—for example—the nature of the violence they have experienced, the context in which it occurred, how it affected them, and how they responded to it. The interviews also explored the extent to which the violence appears to be embedded in broader patterns of discrimination.

THE LEGACY OF COLONIZATION

It is impossible to understand the current strains of Native American racial victimization outside of their connection with colonialism. Indeed, colonialism is itself an exploitive and disempowering form of violence intended to disrupt, if not eradicate, its subjects. From first contact, British, French, and Spanish colonizers have invested great energy in the debilitation of the Aboriginal inhabitants of this continent.

It will be readily apparent from what follows that the historical patterns of colonization experienced by American Indians have followed the typical modes of conquest, including the suppression and destruction of native values and ways of life by the colonizing power, with the intent of forced assimilation of the colonized group into dominant society. The process is also associated with the surveillance and regulation of the colonized by representatives of the colonizers, as by armed forces or, more recently, by "Indian Affairs" bureaucrats or law enforcement personnel. Moreover, as will be detailed more explicitly in the following section, the associated practices of exploitation and oppression are justified by a colonizing and racist discourse that insists upon the relative inferiority of the colonized people. In short, colonial practice and discourse were intended to deprive Native Americans of their status as an independent people and reduce them to just another racialized group. In fact, one of the central projects of American colonial history vis á vis Native Americans was this very effort at racializing a distinct community (see, e.g., Saldaña-Portillo, 2001/2002). Yet it is also clear—from the strength of Native American social movements, the persistence of viable treaties, and the continued existence of an arguably depleted land base, for example—that the process was incomplete. As a people, Native Americans have managed to resist the wholesale elimination of their sovereignty.

These practices of colonization have taken slightly different forms over the years since first contact, representing a qualitative shift in emphasis from genocide to ethnocide. There is an important distinction between the two terms. The former—genocide—refers to the explicit and frequently brutal physical violence perpetrated against Native Americans in an effort to eliminate them as a people. There are those who would oppose the use of such strong terminology. Ward Churchill, for example, has come under attack for his persistence in referring to the historical treatment of Native Americans in these terms. However, there can be no disputing the facts of history. American Indians have been subject to the full array—consciously and unconsciously—of practices associated with genocide, according to the United Nations (1948) Convention on the Prevention and Punishment of the Crime of Genocide:

> any of the following acts committed with intent to destroy, in whole or in part, a national, ethnic, racial or religious group, as such:
>
> a.   Killing members of the group;
> b.   Causing serious bodily or mental harm to members of the group;
> c.   Deliberately inflicting on the group conditions of life calculated to bring about its physical destruction in whole or in part;
> d.   Imposing measures intended to prevent births within the group;
> e.   Forcibly transferring children of the group to another group. (Article 2)

It will become readily apparent over the course of the chapters to follow that each of these measures has been invoked against Native American communities—and many continue to be exercised today. These constitute the most direct and tangible strategies for the elimination of a sovereign people.

In contrast, the second term—ethnocide—refers to the much more "subtle" efforts to deculturate Native Americans, sometimes through physical violence, but more often through the social violence implied in efforts to "resocialize" or "civilize" the natives. In short, colonizing forms of violence run along a continuum and are manifest in multiple conscious acts, such as the introduction of and spread of diseases, the forced removal of children to boarding schools, deculturation, and physical punishment for engaging in traditional activities. Each of these constitutes violent means of subjection.

Whether by violence or assimilationist policy, whites have consistently exerted their energies in the ongoing effort to physically or culturally annihilate Native peoples. Indeed, American Indians were the first to suffer the impact of European religious bigotry in the United States. Initially, the decimation of the Native American population took on the appearance of unintended consequences. That is, contact inadvertently resulted in death through the introduction of diseases to which Native Americans had no natural or developed immunity—smallpox, measles, scarlet fever, and venereal diseases, for example. It has been estimated that, between 1500 and 1900, Native Americans were subject to nearly 100 epidemics of European viruses (Stiffarm & Lane, 1992). Increasingly, these epidemics became part of the arsenal of Indian extermination. That infection was official policy is evident in the correspondence of British and American officers of the day. For example, Sir Jeffrey Amherst of the British forces assured a subordinate, "You would do well to (infect) the Indians by means of blankets as well as to try every other method that can served to extirpate this exorable race"; similarly, a captain in the U.S. forces wrote in a journal that "we gave them two blankets and a handkerchief out of the smallpox hospital. I hope it will have the desired effect" (cited in Stiffarm & Lane, 1992, p. 32). Native Americans' vulnerability to disease was exacerbated by concerted efforts to deprive them of their traditional bases of nutrition, such as the destruction of their agricultural base and the decimation of the buffalo population (Stannard, 1992). Ultimately, hundreds of thousands, if not millions, of Native Americans died of starvation, and in fact, whole nations were eliminated.

This very brief synopsis nonetheless suggests that systemic forms of violence run throughout the historical processes that have characterized the colonization of America. It has been a constant weapon in the arsenal of, first, Europeans and then Americans as they have attempted to eliminate the "savages" from their homelands. Thus, the violence of conquest set the stage for later patterns of systemic violence that would continue to have far-reaching effects on Native American individuals and communities. In the section that follows, I explicitly take up the persistent patterns of stereotyping and structural constraints that contextualize contemporary forms of hate crime perpetrated against American Indians.

THE CONTEXT FOR ANTI-INDIAN VIOLENCE: NATIVE AMERICANS AND THE "FIVE FACES OF OPPRESSION"

The racial violence that is the focus of this chapter is nested in a web of everyday practices that seek to marginalize and disempower Native American communities—especially increasingly vocal and active communities. In short, the oppression of which racial violence is a part is more than the outcome of the conscious acts of bigoted individuals. It is systematic. It represents a network of norms, assumptions, behaviors, and policies that are structurally connected in such a way as to reproduce the racialized and gendered hierarchies that characterize the society in question. Iris Marion Young (1990), for example, operationalizes oppression in a way that provides a very useful framework for contextualizing ethnoviolence, especially that perpetrated against Native Americans. She articulates five interrelated "faces of oppression" by which we might characterize the experiences of minority groups: exploitation; marginalization; powerlessness; cultural imperialism; and violence. The first three of these mechanisms reflect the structural and institutional relationships that restrict opportunities for minority groups to express their capacities and to participate in the social world around them. It is the processes and imagery associated with cultural imperialism that support these practices ideologically. Together, structural exclusions and cultural imaging leave minority members vulnerable to systemic violence. As such, "the oppression of violence consists not only in direct victimization, but in the daily knowledge shared by all members of oppressed groups that they are *liable* to violation, solely on account of their group identity" (Young, 1990, p. 83).

Exploitation, from Young's (1990) perspective, refers to processes that transfer "energies" from one group to another in such a way as to produce inequitable distributions of wealth, privilege, and benefits. While typically understood in class terms, the notion of exploitation can also be extended to racial and ethnic relations. Historically, people of color, including Native Americans, have been relegated to the categories of menial laborers or even servants. Racialized job segregation persists to this day. When employed, Native Americans continue to be overrepresented in menial and low-paying jobs, and dramatically underrepresented in the professions.

Beyond the exploitation associated with underemployment, there is a lengthy history of resource exploitation (Fixico, 1998; Osborne, 1995). Native Americans have lost over 95 percent of their land base. What is left is indeed resource rich. However, consecutive abrogations of treaty rights with respect to mineral resources (Churchill & LaDuke, 1992), water (Guerrero, 1992), and fishing (Institute for Natural Progress, 1992) have largely ceded control of resources to governments and corporations, at the expense of Native economies.

Related to the exploitation of Native Americans and their lands is the *marginalization* of Native Americans—the process of pushing them to the political and social edges of society. More so than other minority groups, Native Americans have even been geographically marginalized, first through expulsion into the "frontier," and subsequently, by "relocation" onto reservations or fragmented urban communities (Bigfoot, 2000; Stiffarm & Lane, 1992). Concomitant with this physical separation have been myriad practices intended to expel them from "useful participation" in the economic and political life of society (Jaimes, 1995; Nielsen, 1996). Economically, Native Americans are among the most impoverished, with 23 percent of all Natives living below the poverty line, as compared to 12 percent of the general population. This impoverishment is even more pronounced on reservations, where poverty rates may go well over 50 percent (Housing Assistance Council, 2002). Native Americans also experience elevated rates of unemployment. At a time when national unemployment rates reached lows of less than 5 percent, the rate of unemployment for Native Americans was well over 40 percent (Center for Community Change, 2005). Similar patterns of disadvantage are apparent in the area of educational attainment, wherein Native Americans continue to experience high rates of early school dropout and low levels of participation in postsecondary education. The cumulative impact of these multiple forms of marginalization is evident in dramatically heightened rates of alcoholism, malnutrition, infant mortality, suicide, and early death by accident and disease (Bachman, 1992; Beauvais, 1996; Jaimes, 1992).

The marginality of Native Americans renders them relatively *powerless* within the context of structural and institutional relationships. Most pressing is the ongoing loss of autonomy of Native Americans (Robbins, 1992; Snyder-Joy, 1996). By virtue of being a colonized people, Native Americans were very early stripped of their right to control their own destinies. The attempt to eliminate Native sovereignty was exacerbated by the Major Crimes Act of 1885, for example, which extended federal jurisdiction over felonies to Indian territories. This legislation was followed by over 5,000 additional statutes that extended federal control to Native jurisdictions (Robbins, 1992, p. 93). This political disempowerment, coupled with Native Americans' economic marginalization, leaves them with limited power with which to exercise the right to freely determine their own political, economic, and social directions.

The federal state's rejection of Native Americans' traditions of governance is but one symptom of *cultural imperialism*. Specifically, this dimension of oppression refers to the ways in which "the dominant meanings of society render the particular perspective of one's own group invisible at the same time as they stereotype one's group and mark it as the Other" (Young, 1990, pp. 58–59). Since first contact, Europeans and then Euro-Americans have engaged in this process of deculturating Native Americans and simultaneously representing them as inferior beings (Jaimes, 1995; Mihesuah, 1996; Stannard, 1992). It is the long-lasting images of Native Americans as "savages," as "backward," as "uncivilized," or as "unintelligent" that have facilitated the injustice and oppression experienced by Native Americans (Riding In, 1998). With missionary zeal, Euro-Americans have persisted in "saving" Native Americans "from themselves" by repressing traditional folkways and attempting to assimilate them into the dominant culture.

The structural constraints on Native Americans, together with their construction as the deviant Other, provide the context for anti-Indian *violence*. The former makes them vulnerable targets; the latter makes them legitimate targets. As noted previously, the collective victimization of Native Americans is well documented. Stannard's (1992) work is an encyclopedic survey of the atrocities perpetrated against the indigenous peoples of the Americas. Similarly, the extensive works of Churchill frequently return to the theme of Native American genocide (see Churchill, 1994), as does the more recent work of Andrea Smith (2005). What these accounts fail to address, however, are the "mundane" everyday experiences of "unprovoked attacks on their person or property, which have no motive but to damage, humiliate or destroy the person" (Young, 1990, p. 61). In other words, they have failed to account for what is here referred to as hate crime: acts of violence and intimidation, usually directed toward already stigmatized and marginalized groups. As such, it is a mechanism of power, intended to reaffirm the precarious hierarchies that characterize a given social order. It simultaneously recreates the supposed dominance of the perpetrator's group and the subordination of the victim's group. Bias-motivated violence is directed not only at the individual victim, but also toward his or her community. It is a mechanism to intimidate a group of people who "hold in common a single difference from the defined norm—religion, race, gender, sexual identity" (Pharr, cited in Wolfe & Copeland, 1994, p. 203). It is important to keep in mind that the violence to which I refer runs the continuum from verbal harassment to extreme acts such as assault, arson, and murder.

NORMATIVE VIOLENCE

The analysis offered in this chapter is largely informed by a long-term project in which I conducted the first large-scale empirical exploration of hate crime against Native Americans. The project has consisted of three legs of research: a 1999 pilot study undertaken in the Four Corners region (funded by the Office of Intramural Grants at Northern Arizona University [NAU]); a campus hate crime survey of Native American students at NAU; and a 2002–2003 study in the Great Lakes and the northern plains region (funded by the U.S. Department of Agriculture [USDA]). In total, I have interviewed approximately 280 Native Americans from seven states (Colorado, New Mexico, Arizona, Utah, Wisconsin, Minnesota, and Montana), representing a minimum of seven Native American nations.

The majority of Native Americans interviewed told tales of exactly those daily onslaughts referred to above. Most had either themselves been victims, or knew of someone close to them who had been a victim, of some form of hate crime—ranging from verbal harassment to pushing and shoving to brutal assaults with knives and lighter fluid. By far the most common incidents were various types of name-calling and verbal harassment on the street and in commercial establishments. Nonetheless, there were also a small number of physical and slightly more property offenses. Among the most vicious attacks were two cases in which perpetrators bit their victims. In one of these cases, a small piece of the victim's ear was bitten off; in the other, the tip of the victim's tongue was lost. Some participants further reported that they had been victimized by police officers, a finding that might help to explain why so few victims in general reported their experiences.

For the Native American community, nothing in recent years compares to the harassment and violence they experienced at the Wisconsin boat landings in the closing years of the twentieth century. Participants shared some remarkable tales of their experiences at the time:

> I was out by the boat landing one night where there was over a thousand people chanting racial things . . . The stories that came out of that, especially the ones . . . how people would prepare themselves to be there at night. There was spearguns, there was pipe bombs, there was airguns, there was slingshots. One day we were setting the nets and they were throwing rocks and they were shooting, shooting wrist rockets, slingshots with ball bearings. One hit Sarah in her side, and knocked her to the bottom of the boat. I got hit too. (Wisconsin, female)

> We had people chase us, we had people follow us. We had threats, we had people pushing. When we would stand at the landings they would come up behind us and they would push the backs of our knees, and they would throw lit cigarettes at us. They would spit on us, throw rocks. Death threats. My son—nuts were loosened on his tires on his van. He was coming home and he thought he had a flat tire, because his car started wobbling. So he stopped and all the lug nuts were loose. A lot of them too were slashed at the landings. (Wisconsin, female)

While the tension around spearfishing has subsided, the violence and harassment have not disappeared. Rather, it continues and, to those with whom I spoke, the violence seems unremarkable. Racial violence and the potential for racial violence are in fact normative in Native American communities and reservation border towns. It has become an institutionalized mechanism for establishing boundaries, both social and physical. Violence is one means by which to remind Native Americans where they do and don't belong.

> The Crow people have it in their heart that just by walking down the street, or seeing him in the wrong place, if they're alone especially and don't know anyone, or if they've been drinking or whatever, and they see Anglos that have been drinking, they don't know if there's going to be violence. They always have it in their heart that there just might be. (Montana, male)

This observation cuts to the heart of the paramount theme that emerged over the course of the interviews. Regardless of the region, or town, or tribal community, there was a very strong sense among participants that racial violence—hate crime—was endemic. The reality that violence permeates the lives of Native Americans is, first, evident in the fact that most complained of multiple victimizations over the course of their lives. Rarely did they describe violent victimization as one-off affairs that touched them once and never again. There was always the sense, the fear, the expectation, that in the presence of non–Native Americans, they were vulnerable to harassment and attack:

> It's always there. I don't want to say it's a norm, but we get so used to it, we never know what's coming next, or where it's coming from. That's what it's like to be an Indian around here. (Minnesota, male)

Ironically, so common is the violence and harassment perceived to be that many claim to have ceased to pay attention:

> We get so used to it—some of us, most of us, just ignore it, let it wash away. (Montana, male)
>
> You don't really notice it, it's so common. It's like an itch that's always there. After a while, it's just another irritation. (Montana, male)

Perhaps one of the most telling statements in this context comes from a Lame Deer resident who observed that he is

> so used to it, when it's absent you don't know how to act. You are so used to the harassment and name calling being around, you don't notice it until it is gone. (Montana, male)

He described for me his experiences in towns and cities away from the reservation, away from the state, where his reception was much warmer than in nearby border towns. He explained that he didn't feel the same animosity, that he was able to relax without fear of harassment. It was in those situations, he claimed, that he realized how bad things were on the reservation and local communities. His story is especially revealing. It highlights how incessant and oppressive the reservation and border climate must be for so many Native Americans. While seemingly minor, the very pervasiveness of those petty actions—name-calling, being followed, and so on—is experienced as a violent form of oppression. Moreover, it is not readily apparent which of these acts might be the prelude to a more serious assault or beating.

It is also important that perceptions of the significance of harassment and violence be seen through the prism of Native Americans' social and individual histories. For them, any one incident of hate crime adds to the ledger of racism (Varma-Joshi, Baker, & Tanaka, 2004, p. 191). As Varma-Joshi et al. describe it, indigenous peoples experience racist harassment and violence within the context of the history of colonization and segregation, and within the context of their own lifelong experiences of similar incidents. The combined personal and cultural biographies cultivate a sense of intergenerational grief and trauma that, according to Bubar and Jumper Thurman (2004), "are the psychological fallout from federal policies that demeaned Native culture and used violence to force assimilation" (p. 74). It is, moreover, the correspondence of the individual and the collective experience that problematizes the treatment while at the same time rendering it normative.

To those with whom we spoke, the violence seems unremarkable. Often, when asked if they perceived racial violence to be a problem in their communities, participants would respond with an almost dismissive, "Oh yeah. Of course." One participant responded to the question by saying, "Yeah, racial attacks are common in Indian Country, and of course Indian people have become calloused over the years, and when it happens, they don't think anything of it. It's just the way life is here" (Wisconsin, male). This is eerily reminiscent of Trask's (2004) observation that "the natural, everyday presence of the 'way things are' explains the strength and resilience of racism. Racism envelops us, intoxicating our thoughts, permeating our brains and skins" (p. 10). Consequently, racial attacks are dismissed, rendered meaningless by their very pervasiveness. "The paradox," writes Scheper-Hughes (1996), "is that they are not invisible because they are secreted away and hidden from view, but quite the reverse" (p. 889). They are invisible because they are sewn into the fabric of daily life. To say that this is "everyday violence" is not to diminish its importance. Rather, it is to highlight the ubiquity and taken-for-grantedness of victimization:

> Anyway, I think race-motivated violence in the Native Americans is common in the community so, I'm not sure it's unusual there's a lot of, there's a lot of Indian bashing. I just think that um, I think people get used to it, so they don't say anything. I think I've, and all my friends and family and kids, we've all got lots of stories. You don't think about it, 'cause it's normal, you don't think about it until somebody like you comes, and you ask us. (Minnesota, female)

WHAT'S THE HARM?

Not surprisingly, the cumulative effect of anti-Indian activity takes its toll. Those I have interviewed describe an array of individual and collective reactions, many of which were indicative of the aggregate impact of normative, systemic victimization. One participant stated the impact very simply: "A lot of it is petty stuff. But it's the petty stuff that gets to you after a while, because it's all the time." This remark corresponds to Feagin's (2001) observation that

> For any given individual, repeated encounters with white animosity and mistreatment accumulate across many institutional arenas and over long periods of time . . . The steady acid rain of racist encounters with whites can significantly affect not only one's psychological and physical health, but also one's general outlook and perspective. (p. 196)

Among my Native American participants, there were many whose stories supported Feagin's (2001) contention, especially with respect to "outlook and perspective." Indeed, there was a generalized sense of feeling weighed down, oppressed by the ongoing threat of harassment and other racist actions:

> You just get tired. You don't want to have to face it anymore. After a while, you hate to go into town, 'cause ya know as soon as you cross that line, somebody's gonna do something—yell at ya, curse ya, maybe chase you back across the river. Sometimes it's just too much.
>   It wears us down, ya know? We don't have to do anything. We're just there and someone calls us a "lazy Indian," or an "Indian whore," and maybe they throw stuff, or, one time someone spit on me—I didn't do anything! It's that stuff every day or every week that gets to me. I just don't wanna have to face any white people. (Minnesota, female)

The perception of recurrent threats and harassment leaves its victims feeling disempowered. It is, as many expressed it, "overwhelming," or "tiring," or "wearing." Even those who try to ignore or deny their daily realities feel embattled by that effort. For some, the constancy of the fear is almost paralytic. At the very least, it limits their desire to interact with white people. For others, it limits their movements and their perceived options, resulting in withdrawal. It creates "more borders," said one participant, in that people become fearful of moving out of the relative safety of the reservation. They "stay here for all their lives, because they're afraid to go 'out there' because of what's going on, for all of these reasons." Very similar sentiments were expressed by others:

> That's why people don't leave, why they don't go into the towns to look for a job. They're afraid to go there, so they stay inside. They know—from their experience, or their family's, or their friends'—what can happen. There's too much risk out there. (New Mexico, female)

For too many Native Americans, the perception, if not the reality, of "what's out there" has its intended effect of keeping people in their place. It reinforces the boundaries—social and geographical—across which Native Americans are not meant to cross. It contributes to ongoing withdrawal and isolation; in short, it furthers historical patterns of segregation. Through violence, through the threat of violence, or even through the malevolent gaze, Native Americans are daily reminded that there are places in which they are not welcome:

> There were places you just didn't want to go. Like Mercer and all—that's where the head of the Ku Klux Klan lives. That's only 14 miles from here. There's just places you don't wanna go, you don't feel safe. Really you don't fell safe when you go off the rez. (Wisconsin, female)

There is just places where you get in you know you are not supposed to be in there. I guess there is, there's a kind of sense, places—for Indians and non-Indians in the communities around here—there is an idea that Indians have a certain place; that there is a certain way that they are supposed to behave when they are on the communities. And like in the South compared to this area is the deep North you know. The whole sense of maintaining one's place and one's position in society is the kind of feeling that Indian people get around here. (Wisconsin, male)

Another damaging cumulative effect of the daily threat of harassment is the cultivation of antiwhite sentiment and, ultimately, antiwhite violence. Several participants spoke of the way that their harassment exacerbates anger toward and distrust of whites.

I just get so mad sometimes. Why do they have to do that? Why do they follow me and call me names? Or try to scare me? It makes it so I don't want to have nothin' to do with them. Why would I? They hate me so I kinda feel the same way. (Montana, female)

For some, the anger spills into action. Some reported hearing of, witnessing, or engaging in retaliatory violence against whites. Again, it was the daily barrage of insults, slights, harassment, and surveillance that engendered bitterness that some were unable to contain: "For many of the Native people, we hit a boiling point of pent up frustrations and anger at the racism and ignorance and the fact that we feel powerless to fight and we explode" (Minnesota, male). One educator described her perception of retaliatory violence in the schools:

It goes both ways. The Indian kids come here, maybe from the reservation schools, or at least from the reservation. And they're already angry when they get here, so it doesn't take much for them to react when someone calls them "Chief," or tells them to go back to the reservation, or bumps into them—intentionally or not—in the hall. These kids live with it every day, and at some point, some of them turn around and give some back. (Minnesota, female)

A mother tells the story of how her daughter "gave some back":

My kids are going through the same thing, just like I did . . . My daughter got in a fight last week, and she ended up leaving because that's what the guy said, kept saying, "Ya Indian, ya fuckin' Indian," "You girls are nothin' but Indian whores," "You need to go back to your reservation where you belong," "I wish you were all dead." She just went off. She ended up fighting with him, and then I had to go to the school and she ended up being suspended. I had to take her out of that school because this is happening all the time. (Minnesota, female)

Not surprisingly, many of the reactions to the normative violence described by participants are negative. That is, they are characterized by withdrawal, anger, or even retaliation. However, there are those who react in a constructive manner. Some use harassing moments as opportunities to educate. One student in a campus hate crime survey tells this tale:

> The first incident was in a class with a professor who did not know I was Native American and made some condescending remarks about Native Americans. I immediately raised my hand and told him that I had a 4.0 GPA, was in the Honors program, never drank, smoked, or had sex and I did not appreciate his stereotype. That was the only comment he ever made. (Arizona, female)

Other examples of people standing up to and correcting bigotry were plentiful. A particularly memorable one occurred on a bus trip:

> This lady was sitting in back of the bus driver, and I was sitting in the other front seat. And they started to talk about things, and the subject of spearing came up, and about *all* those fish that are thrown in the dump and why do they take them. And he was kinda half agreeing with her. After they got through talking, I said, "Can I interject something here?" And I told them, "I don't know if people realize it or not, but those aren't fish that are thrown in the dump. It's the hide and the skeleton of the fish. The meat is taken out of it." "Oh," he says, and she didn't say nothin'. She got off in Minocqua! It's all these misconceptions, and lies—they're just ignorant. (Wisconsin, female)

Most remarkable, perhaps, is the strength and resilience of Native Americans in the face of the everyday violence described here. In fact, they currently enjoy a resurgence of numbers and of nationalist identity. As Frideres (1993) puts it, "With the emergence of Native identity, the sense of alienation experienced by many Natives has been dispelled by a new sense of significance and purpose" (p. 508). The activism that has been at the root of so much violence, and the backlash associated with it, has engendered a renewed pride in Native American identity, and with it, a recognition of the need to pursue that which is theirs by right. In short, it has mobilized Native Americans around their cultural identity and political sovereignty.

> A lot of people—this has been my experience anyway—even among Indian people there were people saying "Don't!" Because when you're told you're bad for doing something, and told a thousand times, sometimes you start to believe is. And there were others that weren't quite sure, but became supportive. People who don't go to meetings were coming to meetings. People who went about their lives—they wanted, they really needed to learn, what are these treaties about, how did they occur, you know. And

they developed the sense that it was a birthright for future generations. That was exciting. That was a very positive outcome of the conflict that will have contributions for years to come. (Wisconsin, male)

It is these sorts of reactions to the normativity of violence that will ultimately present the greatest defense. To use the moment of victimization to confront and challenge oppression speaks volumes. In particular, it says to the perpetrator that Native Americans refuse to "stay in their place," but will instead fight for a reconstructed definition of what that place is. Moreover, such resistance sends a powerful message of strength and solidarity to Native American communities as well.

REFERENCES

Bachman, R. (1992). *Death and violence on the reservation*. New York: Auburn House.

Barker, R. (1992). *The broken circle*. New York: Simon and Schuster.

Beauvais, F. (1996). Trends in Indian adolescent drug and alcohol use. In M. Nielsen & R. Silverman (Eds.), *Native Americans, crime and justice* (pp. 89–95). Boulder, CO: Westview.

Berrill, K., & Herek, G. (1992). Anti-gay violence and victimization in the United States. In G. Herek & K. Berrill (Eds.), *Hate crime: Confronting violence against lesbians and gay men* (pp. 19–45). Thousand Oaks, CA: Sage.

Bigfoot, D. (2000). *History of victimization in Native communities*. Oklahoma City, OK: Center on Child Abuse and Neglect.

Bubar, R., & Jumper Thurman, P. (2004). Violence against Native Women. *Social Justice, 31*(4), 70–86.

Canada, Department of Justice. (1991). *Aboriginal people and justice administration: A discussion paper*. Ottawa, Ontario, Canada: Author.

Center for Community Change. (2005). *Native American background information*. Retrieved August 15, 2006, from http://www.communitychangecccfiles.org/issues/nativeamerican/background

Churchill, W. (1994). *Indians are us?* Monroe, ME: Common Courage Press.

Churchill, W., & LaDuke, W. (1992). Native North America: The political economy of radioactive colonialism. In A. Jaimes (Ed.), *The state of Native America* (pp. 241–266). Boston: South End Press.

Dumont, J. (1996). Justice and Native Peoples. In M. Nielsen & R. Silverman (Eds.), *Native Americans, crime and justice* (pp. 20–33). Boulder, CO: Westview.

Feagin, J. (2001). *Racist America: Roots, current realities and future reparations*. New York: Routledge.

Federal Bureau of Investigation. (2005). *Hate crime statistics, 2004*. Washington, DC: Author.

Fixico, D. (1998). *The invasion of Indian Country in the twentieth century: American capitalism and tribal natural resources*. Boulder: University Press of Colorado.

Frideres, J. (1993). *Native Peoples in Canada: Contemporary conflicts*. Scarborough, Ontario, Canada: Prentice Hall.

Guerrero, M. (1992). American Indian water rights: The blood of life in Native North America. In A. Jaimes (Ed.), *The state of Native America* (pp. 189–216). Boston: South End Press.

Housing Assistance Council. (2002). *Taking stock of rural people, poverty, and housing for the 21st century.* Washington, DC: Author.

Institute for Natural Progress. (1992). In usual and accustomed places: Contemporary American Indian fishing rights struggles. In A. Jaimes (Ed.), *The state of Native America* (pp. 217–240). Boston: South End Press.

Jaimes, A. (1995). Native American identity and survival: Indigenism and environmental ethics. In M. Green (Ed.), *Issues in Native American cultural identity* (pp. 273–296). New York: P. Lang.

Jaimes, A. (1992). Introduction: Sand Creek: The morning after. In A. Jaimes (Ed.), *The state of Native America* (pp. 1–12). Boston: South End Press.

McDevitt, J., Balboni, J., Bennett, S., Weiss, J., Orschowsky, S., & Walbot, L. (2000). *Improving the quality and accuracy of bias crime statistics nationally.* Washington, DC: Bureau of Justice Statistics.

Mihesuah, D. (1996). *American Indians: Stereotypes and realities.* Atlanta, GA: Clarity Press.

Nielsen, M. (1996). Contextualization for Native American crime and justice. In M. Nielsen & R. Silverman (Eds.), *Native Americans, crime and justice* (pp. 10–19). Boulder, CO: Westview.

Nielsen, M. (2000). Native Americans and the criminal justice system. In Criminal Justice Collective (Eds.), *Investigating difference: Human and cultural relations in criminal justice* (pp. 47–58). Needham Heights, MA: Allyn & Bacon.

Nielsen, M., & Silverman, R. (Eds.). (1996). *Native Americans, crime and justice.* Boulder, CO: Westview.

Osborne, S. (1995). The voice of the law: John Marshall and Indian land rights. In M. Green (Ed.), *Issues in Native American cultural identity* (pp. 57–74). New York: P. Lang.

Riding In, J. (1998). Images of American Indians: American Indians in popular culture: A Pawnee's experiences and views. In C. R. Mann & M. Zatz (Eds.), *Images of color, images of crime* (pp. 15–29). Los Angeles: Roxbury.

Robbins, R. (1992). Self-determination and subordination: The past, present and future of American Indian governance. In A. Jaimes (Ed.), *The state of Native America* (pp. 87–122). Boston: South End Press.

Ross, J., & Gould, L. (Eds.) (2006). *Native Americans and the criminal justice system.* Boulder, CO: Paradigm Publishers.

Saldaña-Portillo, M. (2001/2002). On the road with Che Guevara and Jack Kerouac: Melancholia and colonial geographies of race in the Americas. *New Formations, 47,* 87–108.

Scheper-Hughes, N. (1996). Small wars and invisible genocides. *Social Science and Medicine, 43*(5), 889–900.

Silverman, R. (1996). Patterns of Native American crime. In M. Nielsen & R. Silverman (Eds.), *Native Americans, crime and justice* (pp. 58–74). Boulder, CO: Westview.

Smith, A. (2005). *Conquest: Sexual violence and American Indian genocide.* Boston: South Side Press.

Snyder-Joy, Z. (1996). Self-determination and American Indian justice: Tribal versus federal jurisdiction on Indian lands. In M. Nielsen & R. Silverman (Eds.), *Native Americans, crime and justice* (pp. 38–45). Boulder, CO: Westview.

Stannard, D. (1992). *American holocaust*. New York: Oxford University Press.

Stiffarm, L., & Lane, P. (1992). The demography of Native North America. In A. Jaimes (Ed.), *The state of Native America* (pp. 23–54). Boston: South End Press.

Trask, H. (2004). The color of violence. *Social Justice, 31*(4), 8–16.

United Nations. (1948). *United Nations Convention on the Prevention and Punishment of the Crime of Genocide*. New York: Author.

Varma-Joshi, M., Baker, C., & Tanaka, C. (2004). Names will never hurt me? *Harvard Educational Review, 74*(2), 175–209.

Whaley, R., & Bressette, W. (1994). *Walleye Warriors: An effective alliance against racism and for the earth*. Philadelphia: New Society Publishers.

Wolfe, L., & Copeland, L. (1994). Violence against women as bias motivated crime: Defining the issues in the United States. In M. Davies (Ed.), *Women and violence* (pp. 200–213). London: Zed Books.

Young, I. (1990). *Justice and the politics of difference*. Princeton, NJ: Princeton University Press.

CHAPTER 2

BLACK VICTIMIZATION: PERCEPTIONS AND REALITIES

Carolyn Turpin-Petrosino

Black people have been attacked by skinheads across the country for no other reason than their being black.
L. Christensen, *Skinhead Street Gangs* (1994, p. 98)

Hate crime first gained public attention during the 1980s. It was during that time period that law enforcement and media reported an apparent increase in neo-Nazi skinheads as well as other like-minded extremist groups in the United States. Some of these groups were organized and possessed internal structure, a chain of command, an established philosophy, a distinct culture, and the motivation to network with similar groups (Hamm, 1993). Not surprisingly, this growth in hate groups mirrored an increase in bias-motivated criminal activity.

As a result of these developments, Congress enacted the Hate Crimes Statistics Act (HSCA) of 1990. Representative John Conyers, founder of the Congressional Black Caucus, was instrumental in introducing the bill to the House of Representatives. The HCSA requires the Federal Bureau of Investigation (FBI) to annually publish hate crime statistics provided by local and state law enforcement agencies in the United States. Specifically, the statutory language of HCSA requires data collection on crimes that "manifest prejudice based on race, religion, sexual orientation, or ethnicity" (U.S. Department of Justice HCSA, 2004, Appendix A, ¶ (b)(1)). Following the enactment of this seminal law, several states, as well as the federal government, began to pass hate crime laws. Today, most states have hate crime statutes.

The federal government defines hate crime as a "criminal offense committed against a person or property motivated in whole or in part by an offender's bias against a race, religion, disability, ethnic/national origin or sexual orientation" (U.S. Department of Justice, 2007, Hate Crimes, Overview section, ¶ 1). Since the enactment of hate crime statutes and the availability of related data, practitioners, policymakers, and academics are better able to examine various aspects of this social problem. Hate crime studies are wide-ranging and include topics such as the constitutionality of hate crime laws, the social and political aims of the hate movement, and the impact of victimization, to name a few.

Despite the broad categories of bias motivated crime identified in the HCSA, many individuals perceive hate crime laws as primarily protecting the rights of racial and ethnic minorities. While this perception is incorrect, it is undeniable that racially motivated hate crimes against minorities occur with regularity. Generally speaking, racially motivated hate crimes account for more than half of all reported hate crime incidents. Moreover, within the category of racial motivation (see Table 2.1), antiblack rates are the most pronounced (Saucier, Brown, Mitchell, & Cawman, 2006; Torres, 1999; U.S. Department of Justice, 2000, 2001, 2002, 2003, 2004b, 2005). Additionally, blacks are among those who have been victimized by bias-motivated crime and other acts of bigotry since their first appearance in the new world (Petrosino, 1999; Shenk, 2001; Torres). Even so, there are few studies that focus solely on anti-black-motivated hate crime.

Table 2.1   Prevalence of Antiblack Hate Crime

Reporting year	Total bias incidents	Racially motivated (number)	Racially motivated (%)[a]	Antiblack (number)	Antiblack (%)[b]
1995	7,947	4,831	61	2,988	62
1996	8,759	5,396	62	3,674	68
1997	8,049	4,710	59	3,120	66
1998	7,755	4,321	56	2,901	67
1999	7,876	4,295	55	2,958	69
2000	8,152	4,368	54	2,904	66
2001	9,726	4,366	45	2,900	66
2002	7,462	3,642	53	2,486	68
2003	7,489	3,844	51	2,548	66
2004	7,649	4,042	53	2,731	68
2005	7,163	3,919	55	2,630	67

Source: Department of Justice Statistics retrieved from http://www.fbi.gov/hq/cid/civil rights/hate.htm

[a]Percent of total bias incidents. [b]Percent of racially motivated incidents.

Although not explicitly stated in hate crime studies, there may be a presumption that the nature of antiblack hate crime is the same as the nature of antiwhite, anti-American Indian/Alaskan Native, anti-Asian/Pacific Islander or anti-Multiple Races hate crime (i.e., the remaining racial bias categories stated in the U.S. Department of Justice hate crime data). But the question must first be asked, are they the same? Are crime and offender effects similar across all racial bias categories? Or are there distinguishing aspects about antiblack hate crime? This chapter explores such questions and identifies potential areas in which answers might be discovered. I will describe what is known and what might be inferred about antiblack hate crimes based on published accounts of relevant crimes, reported bias incidents, and hate crime studies.

PICTURES OF ANTIBLACK HATE CRIMES

Some of the most notorious hate crimes ever committed have targeted blacks. Among those most publicized are the cases in Howard Beach, New York; Bensonhurst, New York; Fayetteville, North Carolina; and Jasper, Texas. Following are brief synopses of each of these infamous antiblack hate crimes.

- *Howard Beach, New York, December 20, 1986*—Three black men were driving in the predominately white area of Howard Beach when their car broke down. They were soon attacked by a group of white youth carrying baseball bats. Evidence of antiblack motivation included verbal statements made by attackers prior to the actual confrontation (i.e., they expressed racial animosity). Codefendant John Lester was overheard saying to others, "There's niggers on the boulevard. Let's kill them" (Levin & McDevitt, 2002, p. 11; Pinkney, 1994). Michael Griffith, the single fatality, was hit by a car and killed as he attempted to flee from his attackers. Cedric Sandiford was severely beaten; Timothy Grimes was able to escape with few injuries. Four defendants (17-year-olds Scott Kern, Jon Lester, and Jason Ladone, and Michael Pirone, age 16) were all charged with manslaughter, first-degree assault, and second-degree murder. Ladone, Kern, and Lester were convicted of second-degree manslaughter and first-degree assault, but were acquitted of the second-degree murder charges. Pirone was acquitted of all charges.
- *Bensonhurst, New York, August 23, 1989*—Looking for a used car listed in an ad, 16-year-old Yusef Hawkins and three other black youth went to the Italian neighborhood of Bensonhurst in Brooklyn. They were accosted by approximately 30 white youth armed with baseball bats (and at least one with a gun). The mob believed that Hawkins had committed an unacceptable act—dating a white girl from Bensonhurst. During the encounter, Hawkins was beaten and suffered two bullet wounds to the chest. He was pronounced dead upon arrival at a local hospital. As in the Howard

Beach incident, evidence of antiblack motivation was determined by the mind-set of the attackers, including racial slurs made before and during the assault. According to court testimony, one of the leaders of the mob "boasted that he would 'blow the heads off the nigger bastards'" hours before Hawkins was shot to death (Glaberson, 1990, ¶ 1). Joseph Fama was convicted of second-degree murder and received a sentence of 32 and one-third years. Keith Mondello was convicted of riot, menacing, unlawful imprisonment, and criminal possession of a weapon and was sentenced to 5 and one-third to 16 years. Convicted of the same charges as Mondello, John Vento was sentenced to 2–8 years (Lubasch, 1991). Joseph Serrano was convicted of riot and unlawful possession of a weapon and received a sentence of 300 hours community service (McFadden, 1990).

- *Fayetteville, North Carolina, December 7, 1995*—Jackie Burden and Michael James, two African Americans, were shot to death on the streets of Fayetteville by two white Fort Bragg soldiers, who were also neo-Nazi skinheads. Witness statements indicated that the codefendants sought a "dimly lit place where, they could victimize blacks" ("Ex-G.I. . . . ," 1997, ¶ 15). Court testimony indicated that some skinhead groups use a spider-web tattoo to signify that the wearer has murdered a black person. One of the soldiers involved in the killings, Private James Burmeister, remarked that he might be "earning his spider web tattoo" that very night ("Ex-G.I. . . . ," ¶ 14). He achieved his objective and qualified for the tattoo. Burmeister and Private Malcolm Wright shot six bullets into the heads of the victims that they happened upon as they entered a black neighborhood in Fayetteville.

- *Jasper, Texas, June 7, 1998*—James Byrd Jr. fell victim to one of the most infamous racially motivated murders in recent U.S. history. Prosecutors believed the killers sought to use the Byrd murder to spark new membership in their nascent hate group, the Texas Rebel Soldiers. Byrd was beaten, and some accounts state that his face was also sprayed with black paint. He was then chained about the ankles to the back of a truck and dragged until his body tore into pieces ("A Murder . . . ," n.d., ¶ 2; Babineck, 2004). All three defendants—John William King, Lawrence Brewer, and Sean Berry—were found guilty of murder. King and Brewer received death sentences, and Berry received a life sentence. The Byrd murder received enormous media attention. Many were repulsed over the ferocity and violence of this crime; but not everyone was outraged about Byrd's murder. Two white men, Joshua Talley and John Fowler, were arrested and charged with desecrating the grave of Byrd (Barnes, 2004).

These high-profile cases involved aggravated assaults and murders, the most violent of hate crimes. But the overwhelming majority of antiblack hate crimes are for offenses less serious than those just described. They typically receive less media attention but are nevertheless serious and harmful to victims and their communities.

Hate crime statistics reported by the FBI from 1995 to 2005 consistently show that victims more often experience threats of bodily harm or actual assaults than the destruction of their property. In these data, offenses are reported in three categories: "crimes against persons," "crimes against property," and "crimes against society." On average, 63 percent of all hate crimes fall into the "crimes against persons" category, which comprises murder, nonnegligent manslaughter, forcible rape, aggravated assault, simple assault, and intimidation offenses. Since "crimes against persons" is the dominant category, we expect to find the same pattern in anti-black-motivated hate crimes. Table 2.2 reports 2005 data for "crimes against persons" by racial motivation (U.S. Department of Justice, 2005).

These data use the terminology antiblack, antiwhite, anti-American Indian, and so on, to describe the motivation that instigated the attack. However, the data should not be interpreted as meaning that all victims of anti-black-motivated hate crime are in fact black individuals. For example, a perpetrator may perceive a dark-skinned Pakistani as black and assault him or her; thus, the motive is antiblack, even though the victim is an Asian Indian. For the purpose of this chapter, it is assumed that those targeted for antiblack hate crime in the United States are more than likely to be black. Table 2.2 indicates that there is 3.4 times as many antiblack than antiwhite victims; the number grows to 5.5 times more when compared to other racial minority victims. Antiblack victims experience simple assault 2.3 times more often than antiwhite victims and 6 times more often than all other racial minority victims. For the more serious assault category, aggravated assault, there are 2.3 times as many antiblack victims as antiwhite victims and 9.6 times more antiblack victims than the combined minority group. Antiblack victims experience intimidation and the destruction of property at approximately the same rate (see Table 2.2). But antiblack victims experience intimidation offenses almost 7 times as often as the other two victim categories and property-damage offenses about 5.5 times more often.

Table 2.2   The Nature of Antiblack Hate Crime (2005 UCR Data)

Racial bias category	Number of victims	Simple assault	Aggravated assault	Intimidation	Property destruction damage vandalism
Antiwhite bias	975	242	179	172	161
All other minority bias[a]	598	92	44	174	214
Antiblack bias	3,322	554	425	1,180	1,016

[a]This category includes Anti-American Indian/Alaskan Native; Anti-Asian/Pacific Islander; and Anti-Multiple Races (http://www.fbi.gov/ucr/hc2005/table7.htm).

ANTIBLACK HATE CRIME ABROAD

It is more complicated to discern the rate of antiblack hate crime in Europe and elsewhere outside of the United States. This difficulty is due in part to how other nations expand the term "black" beyond the customary reference to those of African descent to include other ethnic groups. For example, East Asians, Arabs, and Gypsies (Roma) are referred to as "black" in a pejorative sense by hate crime perpetrators. To further complicate this picture, international media may also identify victims of bias crime as blacks, when the victims are not necessarily people of African descent. Caution must be taken, therefore, in considering antiblack-motivated bias crime outside of the United States. The following section describes examples of these offenses.

Great Britain

In England, blacks mostly consist of black Caribbeans. These are individuals from the West Indies, primarily Jamaica, Trinidad, and Barbados. Individuals from various African nations are also included in this racial category. Generally speaking, the steady influx of immigrants from Pakistan, India, and the West Indies corresponds with British hate crime rates (Bleich, 2007). England experiences an antiblack crime rate that differs from that of the United States. There, it is anti-Asian victimization rates that exceed those of any other category of racially motivated hate crime (Bowling, 1994 cited in Hamm, 1994; Seagrave, 1989, cited in Hamm, 1994). However, both the 1981 British Home Office Study and a report by Sampson and Phillips (1992) describe antiblack motivated crime as a serious and repetitive problem, "families of . . . Somali [African] origin on one estate in East London suffered (multiple) incidents in a six-month period" (Bowling, 1994, cited in Hamm, p. 3).

The Home Office Study also reports the frequency of racial harassment of African and black Caribbean women as one in five reporting abuse (Bowling, 1994). These acts were mostly carried out by groups of white males near the home or workplace of victims. Likewise, African and black Caribbean men reported similar rates of racial harassment, but more experiences of threatened violence and the actual destruction of property. Although these findings are alarming, it is important to note that in Britain, antiblack hate crime is sometimes intertwined with anti-immigrant sentiments.

Germany

Levin and McDevitt (2002) give several accounts of hate crimes that have occurred across the globe. Many of these acts targeted blacks and Jews as well as immigrants and guest workers from developing nations. The authors describe the following incidents: "Some racist skinheads have proudly proclaimed certain neighborhoods in German cities to be 'national liberated zones,' off-limits to blacks, Jews, and immigrants who are beaten senseless or killed if they are caught there" (p. 143). Black Africans from Mozambique have been the frequent targets of neo-Nazi German youths. "In September 1991, six hundred right-wing German youths firebombed a home for foreigners and then physically assaulted two hundred Vietnamese and Mozambicans in the streets of Hoyerswerde" (p. 144).

The VOICE Refugee Forum, a German-based human rights advocacy group, contends that Africans are subject to racially motivated attacks on a daily basis, which are encouraged by apathetic police and courts. According to The VOICE Refugee Forum (2007, ¶ 8): "The common man on the streets sees an African or a black as an object of ridicule. We are afraid that the next pogrom in Germany will be against the blacks."

During soccer tournaments black soccer players are frequently subject to ugly racist taunts and harassment in Germany and throughout Europe. This phenomenon is sometimes referred to as "football racism." These games are attractive opportunities for neo-Nazi skinheads to engage in these ugly racist behaviors. Samuel Eto, a well known African football player, endured many racist chants, called "monkey chants," while being showered with peanuts. Similarly, DaMarcus Beasley, a black American playing on European teams, was the target of racial slurs and monkey noises, and was tossed banana skins as he played in various tournaments (Zirin & Cox, 2007).

Indicative of the dangerous climate that exists in some parts of Germany, Uwe-Karsten Heye of the Social Democratic-Green coalition government made the following statement: "There are small and mid-sized towns in Brandenburg, Germany and elsewhere where I would advise anyone . . . with a different skin color not to go. They might not make it out alive" (Zirin & Cox, 2007, ¶ 5). This perception is also supported by *The Berliner Zeitung*, a major daily newspaper, which reported that "there are indeed many places in Germany which nobody can in all honesty recommend to a black African as a destination for an outing" (Morley, 2006, ¶ 7).

OTHER NATIONS

Similar acts have occurred in France. Due to antiblack and xenophobic attitudes, North Africans and black sub-Sahara Africans have been the targets of hate crimes. However, according to several print and online media sources, North African Arabs and Jews, not blacks, are more often the targets of hate crime in France (BBC News, 2003; Smith, 2006; Tagliabue, 2005). The National Consultative Commission for Human Rights, an independent body instituted by the Prime Minister to report on xenophobic, anti-Semitic, and racist activity in France, also reported this trend. According to the Commission, a 90 percent increase in bias crimes occurred in 2004. The majority of these offenses (60%) were motivated by anti-Semitism and targeted Jews. The perpetrators were primarily "people of Arab-Muslim origin" ("Racist Attacks . . . ," 2005, ¶ 1; "Special Report . . . ," 2004, ¶ 1). However, the second-largest category of bias crimes was anti-Muslim attacks. Thus, it is more likely that in France, blacks may be targeted for their immigrant status or for being Muslim, rather than for a purely racial motive.

In China, reports indicate the existence of racial animus toward black African students attending universities. Particularly noted are the Nanjing anti-African demonstrations that occurred during 1988–1989. As a result of the mounting resentment of Chinese students regarding the resources allocated to African university students, the cultural differences between the two groups, and the inevitable prospect of interracial dating, thousands of Chinese students rallied in large numbers, issuing taunts and threatening violence against African students ("Unbeautiful Black," 1989). It is reported that the demonstrating students "screamed racial slogans like 'Beat the blacks'" (Levin & McDevitt, 1993, p. 152).

WHAT IS KNOWN ABOUT ANTIBLACK HATE CRIME?

A Developing Literature

The history of black mistreatment, both criminal and noncriminal, is compared to modern-day hate crimes and commonalities are identified (Petrosino, 1999). In Petrosino's analysis, both slavery and lynching, as well as other events, are examined as historical antiblack events. These brutal acts committed upon blacks (which would qualify as hate crime if they occurred today) were justified by the public attitudes of that time. Petrosino points to the common existence of cultural beliefs and social practices that fomented both past and present acts of bigotry. Today, it is recognized that racial attitudes and cultural norms impact the occurrence of antiblack hate crime (Feagin, 2001; Higginbotham, 1978; Perry, 2001; Petrosino, 1999).

Torres (1999) prepared one of the earliest examinations of antiblack hate crime. Primarily descriptive, Torres uses FBI hate crime statistics to show trends in black victimization. He argues that the increase in antiblack hate crime between the years 1992 and 1996 reflected resentment about the changing demographics in the United States. He further suggests that cultural and economic factors foster a climate that facilitates attacks on blacks and other "suitable" targets.

Torres' reference to changing demographics can be found in other studies as well. The concept of "defended neighborhoods" is often used to describe racially motivated hate crimes that occur as a result of racial change in neighborhoods that were previously all white (Bell, 2002; Green, Strolovitch, & Wong, 1998; Levin & McDevitt, 2002; Lyons, 2006). These acts frequently occurred as blacks migrated from the south to northern metropolitan areas (Massey & Denton, 1993). Green and his colleagues studied patterns of racially motivated crime occurring from 1987 to 1995 in New York City and concluded that demographic change was more associated with these behaviors than economic stress.

There are several competing theories regarding racially motivated crimes and demographic patterns. The two theoretical approaches frequently referred to in this research are the "power threat" hypothesis and the "power differential" hypothesis. Power threat hypothesis predicts the likelihood of attacks on minorities when whites believe that incoming minority groups threaten their economic, social, and political security (Blalock, 1967; Eitle, D'Alessio, & Stolzenberg, 2002; Tolnay, Beck, & Massey, 1989). The flash point—that is, when whites feel sufficiently threatened and begin to target minorities (primarily blacks) for harassment, intimidation, or worse—can occur at different points during the community-change process (Bobo, Schuman, & Steeh, 1986; Horowitz, 1985). Power differential hypothesis asserts that when whites dominate a given neighborhood by sheer numbers, and control its political institutions, they are less constrained from committing racially motivated acts (Green et al., 1998; Levin & McDevitt, 1993).

These theories suggest that antiblack hate crime may be a product of conflict dynamics in which hate crime perpetrators act out to protect white hegemony.

Current studies on antiblack hate crime provides some important insights, but further examination about the nature and scope of these offenses is clearly needed. The next section reviews the dynamics of antiblack offenses and incidents.

THE SCOPE AND CHARACTERISTICS OF ANTIBLACK HATE CRIME

Federal hate crime data are presented in grouped aggregate form. Categories include the type of offenses, bias motivation, crime location, race or ethnicity of victim and offender, and jurisdiction. Missing from these data are further details about the offenses, surrounding circumstances, victims, and offenders. The National Incident-Based Reporting System (NIBRS), an additional crime database maintained by the Bureau of Justice Statistics, addresses this deficiency. Its purpose is to provide more in-depth crime data, exceeding that which is reported in the Uniform Crime Reports (UCR). Hate crime data is reported in NIBRS, but only about 20 percent of law enforcement agencies participate in the program (Nolan, Mencken, & McDevitt, n.d., ¶ 1).

There are several publications by nonprofit organizations, such as the Southern Poverty Law Center and the Anti-Defamation League, that provide *contextual* information about reported antiblack and other hate crimes.

The Intelligence Report and *The Race Relations Reporter* (hereafter referred to as *The Reporter*) are two that describe hate crime incidents reported in various media sources. *The Reporter* is a weekly publication currently distributed electronically to subscribers of the *Journal of Blacks in Higher Education.* It maintains a record of race-related incidents that occur throughout the United States. While this and other similar sources of reported hate crimes are informative and useful, such accounts, which mostly come from newspaper articles, do not always report the legal status of reported incidents. So, although an incident might have been reported and an arrest occurred, the media (and subsequently *The Reporter*) might not indicate whether charges were subsequently dropped or that a conviction was obtained. Nevertheless, *The Reporter* categorizes and publishes all racially motivated incidents as reported in the nation's newspapers. As such, it does gauge alleged racially motivated acts in the United States, of which many are likely legitimate criminal acts. For the purposes of this chapter, *The Reporter* is used to obtain additional information on the dynamics of antiblack hate crime.

After a review of the print versions of *The Reporter* issued during the years 1994–2002, the most frequently appearing types of antiblack bias incidents were selected in order to make observations and discern common features. The following section describes the most consistent factors among the 88 incidents that comprise the sample.

Observations and Inferences

Attacks Occurred In or Around the Residence of the Victim

Forty-four percent of the sample incidents (39 of 88) took place in or around the victim's home—the largest category for offense location. Although antiblack hate crime is often triggered when blacks move into predominately white neighborhoods (Bell, 2002; Crump, 2004), it is less known that blacks are also targeted in predominately black neighborhoods. Levin and McDevitt (1993) state that some hate crime perpetrators enter the environs of the targeted group to carry out attacks. (This phenomenon is particularly evident in Europe where residential areas are maintained primarily for guest workers.) Such attacks may have greater consequences for victims who are not able to point to any behavior they committed to trigger their victimization. Even in their own neighborhoods, safety is not guaranteed. *The Reporter* also describes a number of recent incidents in which Hispanic gangs attacked random blacks, in predominantly black and black/Hispanic neighborhoods, for *racial* reasons. Although it is speculated that some of these attacks may have been initially interpreted as rival gang warfare, they are now viewed as primarily racially motivated attacks. Currently, four Hispanic men face life sentences in California following their conviction on a variety of federal charges in 2007 involving racially motivated offenses, including murder. Prosecutors described their actions as "a chilling racial cleansing plot against African Americans and their Latino friends by Latino gang members" (Stark, 2006, ¶ 4).

Antiblack Hate Crimes Occurred in Every Geographic Region of the United States

Antiblack hate crime is a large percentage of the racially motivated hate crimes that occur across the country, even in states where few blacks live. In 2000, blacks numbered 36.4 million, or roughly 12.9 percent of the nation. The majority live in the South (54.8%), 17.6 percent live in the Northeast, and another 18.8 percent live in the Midwest. The area with the lowest percentage of African Americans is the West, at 8.9 percent (U.S. Census Bureau, 2000). States with disproportionately low numbers of black citizens underscore the pervasiveness of antiblack hate crime. From 1992 through 2006, Arizona reported a total of 50 racially motivated hate crimes; 37 (74%) were antiblack incidents. However, blacks make up only about 3.6 percent of the population in Arizona (U.S. Census Bureau). A state with similar data is Idaho. There were a total of 10 racially motivated hate crimes recorded in 2003; six (60%) of them were antiblack, but blacks are only 0.6 percent of Idaho's population (U.S. Census Bureau). The *Reporter* sample included incidents that occurred throughout the United States (e.g., Maine, Florida, Michigan, Colorado, Kentucky, and California), but a disproportionately high rate of antiblack hate crime appears to be constant, regardless of geographical region. When racially motivated crime occurs, the likelihood is that a black person, or one who is perceived to be black, is the target.

Attackers Communicated the Motivation for Their Actions to the Victims

The sample of incidents also reveals the consistency of perpetrators communicating the motivation for their actions to the victims. This usually took the form of racial epithets or the use of hate symbols that historically are associated with violent antiblack acts in the United States (e.g., an actual hangmen's noose or writing *KKK*). These powerful symbols and their meaning are clearly recognizable to blacks; the victims understand they were targeted for racial reasons. Eighty-three of the 88 sample incidents (94%) demonstrated this characteristic.

Destructive Acts Alone Are Not Sufficient: Racist Branding Is Consistently Included

Regardless of whether the act targeted an individual or property (Bell, 2002), the application of racial branding—the use of racist symbols and/or slurs—is part of the harmful act. So that the point is not lost on the victim, attackers harm them by destroying their property and/or causing them bodily injury and including racist branding or the use of racial slurs. Interestingly, attackers readily used symbols that originated with hate organizations, even though most hate crimes are committed by unaffiliated individuals. The power of such symbols and their affect on victims should not be underestimated. As demonstrated in the Jena, Louisiana, incident (referred to as the "Jena Six" incident), the triggering event involved white students placing a hangman's noose from a tree on school grounds. The antiblack sentiment of this message, along with its injurious impact, was not lost on black students.

Perpetrators Do Not Refrain from Victimizing Young Black Children

The following incident appeared in *The Reporter* (1994):

A complaint was filed by the Colorado Civil Rights Commission that alleges racial harassment against a black family residing in Aurora. The complaint alleges that two men grabbed one of the children by the back of the collar and shouted racial slurs at him. Reportedly the verbal abuse by the two men against the black family continued for several days. (p. 4)

Another incident that highlights the targeting of black children: "Racial slurs have been directed at a mixed race child by neighbors in Sanford, Maine, according to the child's mother. Neighbors referred to the child as 'nigger,' 'black dog,' 'brown dog,' and 'brown spot on the road'" (*The Reporter*, 1995b, p. 4).

Since black families are sometimes targeted in their homes, there is greater likelihood that children will witness and experience the racially motivated attack. Cross burnings, acts of arson, racist graffiti, and racial epithets painted on homes and cars, along with verbal or physical threats, can have extraordinary effects on anyone, but particularly on children. Such acts can rob children of their sense of security and safety, especially with the recognition they were targeted because of their race. In the *Reporter* sample, 13 of the cases (15%) indicate that children were present during the incident. Eleven of these cases are incidents that targeted children 17 years of age and younger. In addition to children, black women are also victimized. In the sample, 8 cases (9%) specifically targeted women. In these instances, the perpetrators did not hesitate to harm women or black children who were present during attacks.

The next section reviews a variety of settings that are less recognized as areas where antiblack hate crime incidents occur.

AMERICAN PRISONS: AN UNEXPECTED SETTING FOR ANTIBLACK HATE CRIMES

Although rarely included in discussions about hate crime, antiblack offenses committed within correctional settings have also been reported. These occurrences may be viewed with some skepticism due to the well known fact that there is a disproportionate number of blacks incarcerated in jails and prisons. So how are blacks targeted in prisons? Inmates tend to segregate themselves along racial lines and often affiliate with prison gangs, such as the Aryan Brotherhood, Mexican Mafia, and the Black Guerilla Family (DeLisi, Berg, & Hochstetler, 2004). These groups commit acts of violence to further their illegal enterprises, such as drug trafficking, rather than committing crimes for purely racial motives. Nevertheless, one of the worst examples of antiblack hate crime committed by inmates occurred inside the Marion, Illinois, federal penitentiary in 1997. Leaders in the Aryan Brotherhood—a white-supremacist prison gang—allegedly declared war on all black inmates in the federal prison system. Synchronized attacks followed, resulting in the deaths of two black inmates (Holthouse, 2005).

Racially motivated acts committed by correction officers may also be unexpected, but occur nonetheless. Multiple civil suits have been filed by black correctional officers and black inmates alleging acts that range from racial harassment to aggravated assaults by white officers. In California's Corcoran prison, white officers carved Nazi swastikas into the butts of their rifles, gave preferential treatment to members of the Aryan Brotherhood, and participated in the periodic beatings of black inmates. Federal criminal and civil rights charges were subsequently filed against eight Corcoran correctional officers in 1998 (Intelligence Report, 2000, Lawsuits section, ¶ 2). In the Florida correctional system, black officer Roy Hughes witnessed racist signage in a supervisor's office: "He [Hughes] noticed the following 'hunting license' on his walls: OPEN SEASON ON PORCH MONKEYS . . . Daily kills limited to ten" (Intelligence Report, 2000, p. 28).

ARSON AND BLACK CHURCHES

During the 1990s, there was a spate of bombings and burnings of places of worship in the United States. Due to the disproportionate number of black churches that were destroyed and the history of white supremacists targeting the black church and its leaders, federal authorities oversaw the investigations of these crimes. In 1996, President Clinton signed the Church Arson Prevention Act (Title 18 U.S.C. Section 247), providing federal prosecutors more resources and latitude in bringing these cases to justice. The National Church Arson Task Force (hereafter referred to as the Task Force) spearheaded the federal government's response to address these crimes.

An excerpt of the 1996 testimony of Ozell Sutton, then chair of the Church Burning Response team, before Congress, captured the concern of many regarding these incidents:

> The attack on African American churches is more than just an act of terrorism against a place of worship. A black church to the African American community is far more than a place of worship. It is an attack on the very soul of the African American community. It is the source of their sense of humanity, their sense of self-worth, their fight for dignity and equality, their leader and trainer in the struggle for freedom and justice. (National Church Arson Task Force, 2000, p. 3)

Ultimately the Task Force found that not all of the burnings of black churches were due to racial motives, but some were (see also Figure 2.1). For the 162 incidents involving black churches, 136 individuals were arrested for these crimes (85 were white, 50 were black, and 1 was Hispanic). But

Figure 2.1 National Church Arson Task Force: Racial Makeup of Subjects Arrested for Church Arson/Bombings in the South, January 1, 1995, to August 15, 2000

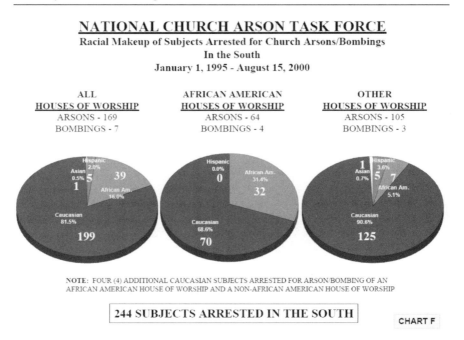

Source: National Church Arson Task Force Fourth Year Report for the President, September 2000.

how many of these crimes were motivated by racial animus? The Task Force report indicated that "of the 79 defendants convicted of federal charges, 46 were determined to be bias motivated which resulted in 37 convicted on hate crime charges" (National Church Arson Task Force, 2000, p. 5). Federal authorities obtained criminal civil rights convictions against defendants who committed antiblack church arsons (National Church Arson Task Force, 1997, Multiple Motives section, ¶ 1).

School Settings and Antiblack Hate Crimes

Racial harassment as well as hate crimes occur in the public school system (Anti-Defamation League [ADL], 1993; Ehrlich, Pincus, & Morton, 1987; Magner, 1989; Morris, 1991; Southern Poverty Law Center [SPLC], 1998, 2000). As many as 25 percent of the nation's youth in grades 8 through 11 have been victimized by racial or ethnic incidents (U.S. Department of Education, 1999). Bias incidents and hate crimes are also reported among the United States' most prestigious universities and colleges, such as Harvard University, the University of Michigan, Cornell University, and Boston College (Petrosino, 2002; The Reporter, 1997, 1998). The Higher Education Extension Service of New Rochelle, New York, conducted survey research on hate crime violence on American college campuses and found that black students are most frequently targeted ("Racism on Campus . . . ," 1995). Following are accounts of antiblack hate crimes that have occurred on various campuses.

> Harvard—Last fall a black tutor who lived at a residence hall at Harvard University found the word "nigger" scrawled on the nameplate of his door. In December, students living in one dormitory awoke to find racist posters on their doors denouncing "minority parasites" who live off the money of "ordinary, straight white Americans." ("Racism on Campus . . . ," 1995, p. 38)
> University of California, Berkley—In December, black students at Boalt Hall found a poster stuffed in their campus mailbox. The poster had a picture of a gorilla and the words: "Affirmative Action Sucks!!! Don't Flunk Out!!!" ("Racism on Campus . . . ," 1995, p. 39)
> Minnesota—Returning to her car after school, a black high school student in Anoka, Minnesota, found the words "nigger" and "KKK" scrawled on her car's windshield and the interior. Several burn marks were also found on the car's upholstery. Minneapolis Star Tribune, November 23, 1994. (The Reporter, 1995a, p. 3)

Many public school systems address the problem of racism and intolerance among students by incorporating multicultural topics in curricula and providing special programs to commemorate diversity (Chesler, Lewis, & Crowfoot, 2005; DeLeon & Reyes, 2007; SPLC, 2007, Teaching Tolerance section, ¶ 1). Even with such well-meaning educational aims, black students, as well as others, continue to be victimized by bias-motivated crimes.

Thus far we have identified characteristics that may be unique to antiblack hate crimes and reviewed the various settings in which these acts have occurred. The next section considers possible explanations for antiblack hate crime and why it occurs more frequently than other racially motivated categories.

REASONS FOR ANTIBLACK HATE CRIME: SCAPEGOATING, BLACKS ARE THE CAUSE OF MY PROBLEMS!

Scapegoating is among the more pragmatic explanations for hostilities toward blacks. It is the practice of inappropriately blaming others (either individuals or groups) for personal and/or general social problems and conditions. It reflects a devaluation of the individual or group deemed responsible by those engaged in this practice. Blacks are among those groups that are often blamed for a host of social problems (Allport, 1954; Dollard, Doob, Miller, Mowrer, & Sears, 1939; Feagin, 2001). For example, some white males perceive the advent of affirmative action, equal-opportunity initiatives, political correctness, and multiculturalism as threats to their status quo. Add to this picture fears and anxieties resulting from an uncertain economy, shifting job markets, and ebbing political capital, and some of them begin to search for someone to blame. Some identify blacks (and also women) as the source of their problems and thereby deserving of punishment.

BLACK STEREOTYPES ARE TRUE: THEY ARE THREATENING

All ethnic and racial groups in the United States are subject to stereotypes. One of the more typical and persistent stereotypes is that blacks, especially black males, are violent and dangerous, and therefore pose a real threat to white society (Perlmutter, 1992). Blacks are stereotyped as crime-prone, sexual predators, violent, indolent, and less intelligent (Russell-Brown, 2004). Considering these portrayals, it is no wonder that some feel that their lifestyles, values, property, and lives are threatened when blacks move into their neighborhoods. A racially integrated neighborhood may present the alarming prospect of interracial dating. One of the most powerful historical triggers of antiblack hate crime is the threat of interracial relationship. Even today, given the right circumstances, black males who date white females are at risk for violent confrontation (Glaser, Dixit, & Green, 2002; Perry, 2001). Agreement with black stereotypes exacerbates white anxiety, which may be managed by maintaining social boundaries between racial groups (Perry,

2001). Antiblack hate crimes are acts committed by some to fortify racial boundaries (Crump, 2004).

PROSELYTIZING VIA THE INTERNET: SPREADING ANTIBLACK MESSAGES

The Internet is utilized by those in the hate movement to reach thousands with its messages of anti-Semitism, racism, ethnocentrism, and white supremacy. Some have even drafted the enormously popular YouTube as a means to influence others. A video produced by a National Socialist group presents the following antiblack message:

> Los Angeles blacks are destroying property and attacking white people as a soft, pitiful ballad plays in the background. Then, about two minutes into the video, the words "Whose Freedom?" appears as a still frame of a young, smiling German girl at a Third Reich rally suddenly replaces the footage of the 1992 Rodney King riots. A man wearing a swastika armband stands protectively behind her, his head cropped from the frame, while the words, "A paradise lost," scroll down beneath her chin. Finally, a message, "Save the White Race," fills the screen before dissolving into a Celtic cross encircled by the phrase, "White Pride World Wide." (Mock, 2007, ¶ 1)

Recently, the FBI investigated several hate Web sites after it was reported that the names and addresses of the black teenagers referred to as the "Jena 6" (from the Jena, Louisiana, incident mentioned previously) were found on them along with a call for the teens lynching. Generally speaking, hate Web sites are used to promote the beliefs and agenda of the radical right. Antiblack messages are consistently included in the content on these sites. A review of www.Stormfront.org. or www.resist.com, for example, illustrates the explicitness of these messages. The White Aryan Resistance (WAR) utilizes racist cartoons to disseminate antiblack messages. They provide a link to a cartoon page entitled "Nigger." The National Alliance provides a comprehensive statement of organization goals; it is replete with antiblack communication:

> *White Living Space*—In spiritually healthier times our ancestors took . . . all of Europe and . . . the Americas, . . . Australia and the southern tip of Africa. This was our living area . . . and it must be so again. After the sickness of "multiculturalism," . . . we must again have a racially clean area of the earth for the further development of our people. We must have White schools, White residential neighborhoods and recreation areas, White workplaces, White farms and countryside. We must have no non-Whites in our living space . . . We will do whatever is necessary to achieve this White living space and to keep it White. The long-term demographic trend toward a darker world . . . must be reversed. (National Alliance, 1998, National Alliance Goals/White Living Space section, ¶ 1–2)

The famous "14 Words" motto, coined by now deceased white supremacist David Lane, continuously fuels the efforts of whites to seek out their own territories (Perry & Blazak, 2006); "We must secure the existence of our people and a future for White children" (ADL, 2007, Extremism section, ¶ 4). This motto is frequently found on many Web sites of the extremist right.

Some Ku Klux Klan Web sites contain more subtle antiblack messages. One site states the following:

> In the 1960s, there was a real comeback for the Ku Klux Klan. This was attributed to the south being forced to open their schools and public places to blacks. Nobody in the south wanted that to happen, so a new resistance was born and the Ku Klux Klan began to increase their membership once again . . . During this time, the Klan flourished.
>
> WE BELIEVE: that the current of pure American blood must be kept uncontaminated by mongrel strains and protected from racial pollution.
>
> WE BELIEVE: that the perpetuity of our nation rests upon the solidarity and purity of our native-born, white, Gentile men and women. (Brotherhood of Klans, International, n.d., History of the KKK section, ¶ 10)

BLACK PROGRESS AND ZERO-SUM THINKING: IF THEY GAIN, WE LOSE!

White superiority is the foundation of the hate movement. Central to the idea of white supremacy is the belief in the inherent inferiority, inadequacy, and incompetence of nonwhites. When racial minorities, particularly blacks, achieve economically, educationally, and/or politically, white supremacists view these gains as not credible. They see black progress as the result of preferential treatment or the lowering of standards to accommodate black inferiority. Attitudes of resentment are part of this perspective, in addition to the idea that when blacks gain, whites lose—a zero-sum perspective. Such ideas also fuel antiblack hate crime (Levin & McDevitt, 2002). A good example of how zero-sum thinking relates to antiblack hate crime is reflected in an article by human rights activist Loretta Ross (1995) entitled "White Supremacy in the 1990s": "FBI statistics report that 65 percent of America's hate crimes are committed by whites against Blacks. A good portion of these crimes are what we call 'move-in' violence, when neighborhoods, schools, churches, or jobs become . . . (integrated)" (¶ 13). When blacks "gain" by moving into better appointed neighborhoods—where whites are the majority—whites lose. There are instances in which calculating extremists exploit fears that arise from changing demographics in predominately white workplaces and neighborhoods. In January, 2003, the World Church of the Creator (WCOC), a white supremacist group, targeted Lewiston, Maine, as a rally site in hopes of drawing support for their cause. Their rationale was to encourage whites to reject the increasing presence of Somali refugees in the area (MacQuarrie, 2002).

THE WORLDWIDE APOCALYPTIC RACIAL WAR

The term "Racial Holy War" (RAHOWA) is touted in the literature of many extremist groups. It represents an objective in the hate movement to facilitate the all-important "race war," which will cause whites to wake up and join in a violent uprising against blacks, Jews, other "undesirable" groups, and the Zionist-controlled government. This violent racial purging is expected to usher in Aryan rule. The following is an excerpt from the Creativity Movement Web site entitled "RAHOWA! Its Full Ramifications":

> (with) this one word we sum up the total goal and program of not only the Church of the Creator, but the total . . . challenge. We gird up for total war against the Jews and the rest of the goddamned mud races . . . we regard it as the heart of our religious creed . . . —a racial holy war. Rahowa! is INEVITABLE. It is the Ultimate and Only solution. No longer can the mud races and the White Race live on the same planet and survive. It is now either them or us. We want to make damn sure it is we who survive. RAHOWA! This Planet is All Ours. (The Creativity Movement, n.d., ¶ 13)

This radical solution goes well beyond the idea of racially segregated living, the development of a "white living space," or even the ideas represented by the 14 Words motto. RAHOWA calls for the racial genocide of non-Aryans. Clearly this rhetoric could well inspire antiblack and other racial violence.

PAN-ARYANISM

Pan-Aryanism is the viewpoint of white supremacists that their struggle is a global one. At its core is the belief that those dedicated to the hate movement must see that all whites are in the midst of a shared crisis (a threat to their existence) and must employ the same solution to the crisis (nothing short of a total social, political, and violent revolt) to achieve the survival and ordination of Aryans as the master race. This philosophy, by definition, encourages and justifies global antiblack hate crime. The former leader of the National Alliance, William Pierce, described pan-Aryanism in the following way: "We must understand that we are in a planet-wide race war, and survival of our race depends on our winning this war" (Intelligence Report, 2001, p. 6). Mark Cotterill, a leader in the British National Party, affirmed the importance of pan-Aryanism in an Internet communication: "It is not an American fight or a British fight or a German fight. It is a white fight, and we have got to win it" (Intelligence Report, 2001, p. 18).

CONCLUSION

The purpose of this chapter is to gain a better understanding of the nature and scope of antiblack hate crime. Both media and scholarly sources were examined and observations are offered regarding distinguishing characteristics of antiblack hate crime. These observations are preliminary in nature and suggest areas for future research.

Following are three generalizations that summarize characteristics of antiblack hate crime.

First. Antiblack hate crime is historical, pervasive, and global.

Racism is deeply rooted in American culture and helps to explain why antiblack-motivated acts, in particular, have persisted over 300 years. Since before the institutionalization of black slavery, blacks have been socially constructed to symbolize the antithesis of white superiority; as a result, they are devalued as a group, which bolsters the impression of white supremacy (Feagin, 2001; Perry, 2001; Petrosino, 1999). With this history and the current racial stratification in the United States, it is no surprise that antiblack hate crime outpaces all other categories of racially motivated hate crime and that it occurs in every quadrant of the United States. Antiblack hate crime also occurs globally. People of African descent are victimized in Europe, China, Russia, and elsewhere; black vulnerability is a global phenomenon.

Second. Antiblack hate crimes have an omnipresent quality and a depravity reflected in the willingness to identify black children (and women) as legitimate targets that are as threatening as black males.

What adds to the malicious nature of antiblack hate crime is the absolute need to racially debase the victim, in addition to committing the base crime (i.e., malicious damage, aggravated assault, etc.). For example, one incident described in the *Reporter* sample—an assault with a deadly weapon—involved the shooting of a black male as the perpetrator screamed racial epithets. Another incident involved perpetrators destroying the black victim's car, urinating on it, and then writing racial slurs on the vehicle. The use of universal symbols of hate and racial slurs terrorize the black community and reflect their vulnerability not only to hate crime perpetrators but also to indifferent law enforcement agencies or apathetic local governments.

Blacks are often targeted in or around their residences and when black children are present, they are not spared during such attacks. Their presence does not seem to provide an opportunity for second thoughts. For the perpetrator, black children, women, and men are viewed as equally threatening. Finally, the omnipresent quality of antiblack hate crime is reflected in the diversity of locations in which blacks have been victimized. including their homes, workplaces, schools, churches, and even in prisons.

> Third. The viewpoint that minorities and the poor are responsible for the social ills of society can be found in the dominant culture as well as the hate movement. Ideological convergence between mainstream culture and the radical right may embolden hate crime perpetrators.

It appears that antiblack hate crime fulfills a social need. It enforces a racial hierarchy and ensures white hegemony. Functionalist perspectives suggest that because black animus is inherent to American culture, antiblack hate crimes work to maintain society's norms. It therefore serves a purpose. Hate movement ideology asserts that blacks and other racial minorities must be restrained or perhaps eliminated so that the white race can thrive. We therefore see a convergence between racial attitudes that are found in the dominant culture and views within the hate movement regarding the threat of blacks. This element of commonality may be largely responsible for the ubiquitous and persistent nature of antiblack hate crime.

This examination identifies several directions for future research: (1) Continued efforts to discern trends within the categories of racially motivated hate crime; (2) Investigation of the impact of hate crime victimization on racial minority victims in light of their continued subjugation to cultural discrimination; (3) Additional focus on the social and political mechanisms that promote the globalization of antiblack hate crime; and finally, (4) Examine those social processes that permit the assimilation and/or adoption of extremist perspectives into mainstream culture.

Research on antiblack hate crime is in its infancy. It is hoped that the observations and questions raised here will prompt further attention to this understudied area.

REFERENCES

A murder in Jasper, Texas, brings back haunting memories. (n.d.). *San Francisco Chronicle in Education*. Retrieved September 7, 2007, from http://www.kqed.org/ programs/tv/niot/KQEDCIC-NIOT4.pdf

Allport, G. (1954). *The nature of prejudice*. Reading, MA: Addison-Wesley.

Anti-Defamation League. (1993). *The 1992 audit of Anti-Semitic incidents*. New York: Author.

Anti-Defamation League. (2007). Extremism: David Lane, white supremacist terrorist and ideologue, dies in prison. Retrieved April 22, 2007, from http://www.adl. org/main_Extremism/david_lane_dies.htm

Babineck, M. (2004). Byrd killing still touchy subject. Chron.com. Retrieved September 13, 2007, from http://www.chron.com/disp/story.mpl/special/jasper/latest news/1931474.html

Barnes, S. (2004, May 12). Teenagers charged in grave desecration. *New York Times.* Retrieved September 13, 2007, from http://query.nytimes.com/gst/fullpage.html?res=9F0DE6D8103CF931A25756C0A9629C8B63

BBC News. (2003, November 17). France vows to fight hate crime. Retrieved August 15, 2007, from http://news.bbc.co.uk/2/hi/europe/3275519.stm

Bell, J. (2002). *Policing hatred: Law enforcement, civil rights, and hate crime.* New York: New York University Press.

Blalock, H. M. (1967). *Toward a theory of minority-group relations.* New York: John Wiley & Sons.

Bleich, E. (2007). Hate crime policy in Western Europe: Responding to racist violence in Britain, Germany, and France. *American Behavioral Scientist, 51,* 149–166.

Bobo, L., Schuman, H., & Steeh, C. (1986). Changing racial attitudes toward residential integration. In J. M. Goering (Ed.), *Housing desegregation and federal policy* (pp. 152–169). Chapel Hill: University of North Carolina Press.

Bowling, B. (1994). Racial harassment in East London. In M. Hamm (Ed.), *Hate crime: International perspectives on causes and control* (pp. 1–36). Cincinnati, OH: Anderson Publishing.

Brotherhood of Klans, International. (n.d.). History of the KKK. Retrieved May 26, 2007, from http://www.bok33.org/KKKhistory.html

Chesler, M. A., Lewis, A., & Crowfoot, J. (2005). *Challenging racism in higher education: Promoting justice.* Lanham, MD: Rowman & Littlefield.

Christensen, L. (1994). *Skinhead street gangs.* Boulder, CO: Paladin Press.

Crump, J. R. (2004). Producing and enforcing the geography of hate: Race, housing segregation, and housing-related hate crimes in the United States. In C. Flint (Ed.), *Spaces of hate: Geographies of discrimination and intolerance in the U.S.A.* (pp. 227–244). New York: Routledge.

DeLeon, W., & Reyes, X. A. (2007). Multicultural education is good for the United States beyond sensitivity training. In T. A. Osborn (Ed.), *Language and cultural diversity in U.S. schools: Democratic principles in action.* New York: Rowman & Littlefield Education.

DeLisi, M., Berg, M. T., & Hochstetler, A. (2004). Gang members, career criminals and prison violence: Further specification of the importation model of inmate behavior. *Criminal Justice Studies, 17*(4), 369–383.

Dollard, J., Doob, L. W., Miller, N. E., Mower, O. H., & Sears, R. R. (1939). *Frustration and aggression.* New Haven, CT: Yale University Press.

Eitle, D., D'Alessio, S. J., & Stolzenberg, L. (2002). Racial threat and social control: A test of the political, economic, and threat of black crime hypotheses. *Social Forces, 81*(2), 557–576.

Ehrlich, H. J., Pincus, F. L., & Morton, C. (1987). *Ethnoviolence on campus: UMBC study.* Baltimore: National Institute Against Prejudice and Violence.

Ex-G.I. at Fort Bragg is convicted in killing of 2 blacks. (1997, February 28). *New York Times.* Retrieved September 16, 2007, from http://query.nytimes.com/gst/fullpage.html?res=9A02E3DB1331F93BA15751C0A961958260&n=Top/Reference/Times%20Topics/Subjects/H/Hate%20Crimes

Feagin, J. R. (2001). *Racist America: Roots, current realities and future reparations.* New York: Routledge.

Glaberson, W. (1990, April 17). Murder trial is told of boast in Bensonhurst. *New York Times*. Retrieved May 22, 2008 from http://query.nytimes.com/gst/fullpage

Glaser, J., Dixit, J., & Green, D. P. (2002). Studying hate crime with the Internet: What makes racists advocate racial violence? *Journal of Social Issues, 58*, 177–193.

Green, D., Strolovitch, D. Z., and Wong, J. S. (1998). Defended neighborhoods, integration, and racially motivated crime. *American Journal of Sociology, 104*(2), 372–403.

Hamm, M. S. (1993). *American skinhead. The criminology and control of hate crime*. Westport, CT: Praeger.

Hamm, M. S. (Ed.). (1994). *Hate crime: International perspectives on causes and control*. Cincinnati, OH: Anderson Publishing Co.

Higginbotham, A. L. (1978). *In the matter of color*. London: Oxford University Press.

Holthouse, D. (2005, November, 21). Hate crimes in prison. *AlterNet*. Retrieved September 21, 2007, from http://www.alternet.org/story/27723/

Horowitz, D. L. (1985). *Ethnic groups in conflict*. Berkeley: University of California Press.

InsidePrison.com. (n.d.). California State Prison, Corcoran: History & news. Retrieved September 21, 2007, from http://www.insideprison.com/california-state-prison-corcoran.asp

Intelligence Report. (2000, Fall). Behind the wire, Issue 100, pp. 24–29.

Intelligence Report. (2001, Fall). The ties that bind: The WEB of associations between European and American right-wing extremists has thickened. Issue 103, p. 6.

Levin, J., & McDevitt, J. (1993). *Hate crimes. The rising tide of bigotry and bloodshed*. New York: Plenum Press.

Levin, J., & McDevitt, J. (2002). *Hate crimes revisited: America's war on those who are different*. Boulder, CO: Westview Press.

Lubasch, A. H. (1991, January 12). Minimal sentences are given to Bensonhurst defendants. *The New York Times*. Retrieved October 10, 2008, from http://query.ny times.com/gst/fullpage.html?res=9D0CE4DF1231F931A25752C0A967958260

Lyons, C. J. (2006, November). *Racial threat and defense of turf: Antiwhite and antiblack hate crime in Chicago communities*. Paper presented at the annual meeting of the American Society of Criminology, Royal York, Toronto, Ontario, Canada.

MacQuarrie, B. (2002, November 25). Racist group eyes protest of Somalis in Maine. *The Boston Globe*, p. B3.

Magner, D. K. (1989). Blacks and whites on the campus: Behind ugly racist incidents, student isolation and insensitivity. *Chronicle of Higher Education, 35*(1), A28–A31.

Massey, D. S., & Denton, N. A. (1993). *American apartheid: Segregation and the making of the underclass*. Cambridge, MA: Harvard University Press.

McFadden, R. D. (1990, November 30). Judge drops some charges in racial case. *New York Times*, p. 8.

Mock, B. (2007). Sharing the hate: Video-sharing websites become extremist venue. Intelligence Project, Issue 125. Retrieved September 16, 2007, from http://www.splcenter.org/intel/intelreport/article.jsp?aid=756

Morley, J. (2006). Racism shadows Germany's World Cup party. *Washington Post.com*. Retrieved June 10, 2007, from http://blog.washingtonpost.com/worldopin ionroundup/2006/05/racism_shadows_germanys_world_1.html

Morris, J. R. (1991). Racial attitudes of undergraduates in Greek housing. *College Student Journal, 25,* 501–550.

National Alliance. (1998). National Alliance Goals. Retrieved October 13, 2007, from http://www.natall.com/what-is-na/na2.html

National Church Arson Task Force. (1997). First year report. Retrieved October 15, 2007, from http://www.atf.gov/pub/gen_pub/arsonrpt.htm

National Church Arson Task Force. (2000). Fourth year report. Retrieved October 15, 2007, from http://www.atf.treas.gov/pub/gen_pub/report2000

Nolan, J. J., Mencken, F. C., & McDevitt, J. (n.d.). The FBI's UCR hate crime data collection program and NIBRS. Retrieved May 17, 2007, from http://www.as.wvu.edu/~jnolan/aboutnibrs.html

Perlmutter, P. (1992). *Divided we fall: A history of ethnic, religious, and racial prejudice in America.* Ames: Iowa State University Press.

Perry, B. (2001). *In the name of hate. Understanding hate crimes.* New York: Routledge.

Perry, B., & Blazak, R. (2006, November). *Places for races: The white supremacist movement's organization of US geography.* Paper presented at the annual meeting of the American Society of Criminology (ASC), Los Angeles Convention Center, Los Angeles, CA. Retrieved April 9, 2007, from http://www.allacademic.com/meta/p125432_index.html

Petrosino, C. (1999). Connecting the past to the future: Hate crime in America. *Journal of Contemporary Criminal Justice, 15*(1), 22–47.

Petrosino, C. (2002). Hateful sirens: Who hears their song? An examination of student attitudes toward hate groups and affiliation potential. *Journal of Social Issues, 58*(2), 281–301.

Pinkney, A. (1994). *Lest we forget—White hate crimes: Howard Beach and other racial atrocities.* Chicago: Third World Press.

Race Relations Reporter. (1994). Residential terrorism. Vol. 2, No. 3.

Race Relations Reporter. (1995a). Racism in education. Vol. 2, No. 11.

Race Relations Reporter. (1995b). Residential terrorism. Vol. 3, No. 7.

Race Relations Reporter. (1997). Racism in education. Vol. 5, No. 10.

Race Relations Reporter. (1998). Racism in education. Vol. 6, No. 7.

Racism on campus: Are the strongest institutions the most vulnerable? (1995). *Journal of Blacks in Higher Education, 7,* 38–39.

Racist attacks in France up. (2005, March 23). *The Hindu.* Retrieved May 7, 2007, from http://www.thehindu.com/2005/03/23/stories/2005032303671401.htm

Ross, L. (1995). White supremacy in the 1990s. *The Public Eye.* Retrieved September 4, 2007, from http://www.publiceye.org/eyes/whitsup.html

Russell-Brown, K. (2004). *Underground codes. Race, crime, and related fires.* New York: New York University Press.

Sampson, A., & Phillips, C. (1992). Multiple victimization: Racial attacks on an East London estate. Police Research Group Crime Prevention Unit Series Paper 36. In M. Hamm (Ed.), *Hate crime: International perspectives on causes and control.* Cincinnati, OH: Anderson Publishing.

Saucier, D. A., Brown, T. L., Mitchell, R. C., & Cawman, A. J. (2006). Effects of victims' characteristics on attitudes toward hate crimes. *Journal of Interpersonal Violence, 21*(7), 890–909.

Seagrave, J. (1989). Racially motivated incidents reported to the police. Home Office Research and Planning Unit Paper 54. In M. Hamm (Ed.), *Hate crime: International perspectives on causes and control*. Cincinnati, OH: Anderson Publishing.

Shenk, A. H. (2001). Victim-offender mediation: The road to repairing hate crime injustice. *Ohio State Journal on Dispute Resolution, 17*, 185–217.

Smith, C. S. (2006, March 26). Jews in France feel sting as Anti-Semitism surges among children of immigrants. *New York Times*. Retrieved September 19, 2007 from http://www.nytimes.com/2006/03/26/international/26antisemitism.html?_r=1&oref=slogin

Southern Poverty Law Center. (1998, Fall). Hate crime alarms college campuses. *Intelligence Report, 92*, pp. 37–39.

Southern Poverty Law Center. (2000, Spring). Hate goes to school. *Intelligence Report, 98*, pp. 10–13.

Southern Poverty Law Center. (2007). Teaching tolerance—Pioneering anti-bias education. Retrieved May 11, 2007, from http://www.splcenter.org/center/tt/teach.jsp

Special report: France. Attacks against Muslims and Jews are soiling France, says Chirac. (2004, July 9). *Guardian Unlimited*. Retrieved September 17, 2007, from http://www.guardian.co.uk/france/story/0,11882,1257445,00.html

Stark, A. (2006, August 31). Gang crimes as hate crimes. *Los Angeles City beat*. Retrieved August 4, 2007, from http://www.lacitybeat.com/article.php?id=4277&IssueNum=169

Tagliabue, J. (2005, March 22). France: Hate crimes double. *New York Times*. Retrieved March 28, 2007, from http://query.nytimes.com/gst/fullpage.html?res=9C06EFDB1F3CF931A15750C0A9639C8B63

The Creativity Movement. (n.d.). RAHOWA! This planet is ours. Retrieved October 10, 2008, from http://www.creativitymovement.net/documents/RAHOWATH.PDF

The VOICE Refugee Forum. (2007, June 1). Oury Jalloh: African Community Conference in Dessau. Retrieved August 4, 2007, from http://www.thevoiceforum.org/node/411

Tolnay, S. E., Beck, E. M., & Massey, J. L. (1989). The power threat hypothesis and black lynching: "Wither" the evidence? *Social Forces, 67*, 634–641.

Torres, S. (1999). Hate crimes against African Americans: The extent of the problem. *Journal of Contemporary Criminal Justice, 15*(1), 48–63.

Unbeautiful black. (1989, January 7). *The Economist*.

U.S. Census Bureau. (2000). Retrieved May 19, 2007, from http //quickfacts.census.gov/qfd/states/04000.html

U.S. Department of Education. (1999). *Protecting students from harassment and hate crimes: A guide for schools*. Washington, DC: Author.

U.S. Department of Justice Hate Crime Statistics Act. (2004). Retrieved October 6, 2007, from http://www.fbi gov/ucr/hc2004/appendix_a.htm

U.S. Department of Justice. (2000). Uniform Crime Reports. Hate crimes 2000. Retrieved October 6, 2007, from http://www.fbi.gov/ucr/cius_00/hate00.pdf

U.S. Department of Justice. (2001). Uniform Crime Reports. Hate crimes 2001. Retrieved October 6, 2007, from http://www.fbi.gov/ucr/01hate.pdf

U.S. Department of Justice. (2002). Uniform Crime Reports. Hate crimes 2002. Retrieved October 6, 2007, from http://www.fbi.gov/ucr/hatecrime2002.pdf

U.S. Department of Justice. (2003). Uniform Crime Reports. Hate crimes 2003. Retrieved October 6, 2007, from http://www.fbi.gov/ucr/03hc.pdf

U.S. Department of Justice. (2004a). Hate Crime Statistics Act 2004, Appendix A. Retrieved October 6, 2007, from http://www.fbi.gov/ucr/hc2004/appendix_a.htm

U.S. Department of Justice. (2004b). Uniform Crime Reports. Hate crimes 2004. Retrieved October 6, 2007, from http://www.fbi.gov/ucr/hc2004.hctable1.htm

U.S. Department of Justice. (2005). Uniform Crime Reports. Hate crimes 2005. Retrieved October 6, 2007, from http://www.fbi.gov/ucr/hc2005.hctable1.htm

U.S. Department of Justice. (2007). Hate crimes overview, 2007. Retrieved October 12, 2007, from http://www.fbi.gov/hq/cid/civilrights/overview.htm

Zirin, D., & Cox, J. (2007, May 22). *Racism stalks the Cup*. Africaresource. Retrieved October 19, 2007, from http://www.africaresource.com/content/view/291/202/

CHAPTER 3

LEGITIMIZED ANTI-LATINO SENTIMENT: BREEDING THE PREJUDICE THAT PERPETUATES VIOLENCE

Silvina Ituarte

In Texas, in April 2006, two young men shouting "white power" remarks stripped 18-year-old David Richardson of his clothing, "burned his skin with cigarettes, poured bleach on his wounds, rammed the end of the patio umbrella into his anus, kicked it with steel toe boots deep enough to rupture internal organs . . . and started to carve a swastika on his chest" (Kovach, 2007). Consequently, the Mexican American student required over 30 surgeries and endured three months of hospitalization before he was permitted to remove his colostomy bag and before he was able to walk again. Richardson had been a popular football player who, prior to his victimization, had served as homecoming king during his freshman year. His struggle to overcome the emotional and physical trauma from the attack, coupled with the pressure of speaking before a Congressional hearing regarding the passage of the Law Enforcement Hate Crime Act of 2007, was determined to be the cause of David's fatal leap from a Carnival Cruise ship in July 2007.

LATINO IDENTITY AND DEMOGRAPHICS

Anti-Latino[1] sentiment is not a new phenomenon; examples of abuse and violence directed at Latinos are sprinkled throughout the history of the United States. In the examination of bias crimes against Latinos, it is imperative to recognize the continuum of bias-motivated behaviors that begins with name-calling and harassment and extends into the realm of serious injury and even murder. According to the Pew Research Center (2004), approximately one-third of Latinos residing in one of the five states possessing the largest Latino populations—California, Florida, New Jersey, New York, and Texas—have experienced discrimination, and 30 percent report having been called names or being insulted (p. 3). When searching for the underlying causes of these varied forms of name-calling and other bias-motivated offenses, scholars are well advised to attend to the social messages conveyed about Latinos through media constructions, political rhetoric, legislative precedents, and social norms.

Latinos consist of individuals from diverse countries and backgrounds, thus forming a multiracial grouping that varies "by class, culture, national origin, and even religion and language, given the large numbers of indigenous peoples in Latin America" (Alcoff, 2005, p. 537). The primary characteristic commonly shared among all Latinos is a connection by ancestry to Latin America. As a matter of fact, Latinos trace their "origins to many countries with varied cultures, and while some Latinos have family histories in the United States that date back centuries, others are recent arrivals" (Pew Research Center, 2005, p. 73).

In the United States, the geographic distribution of Latino/a(s) varies according to region. Approximately 80 percent of Latinos reside in Arizona, California, Colorado, Florida, Illinois, New Jersey, New Mexico, New York, and Texas (Pew Research Center, 2005). Most descendants of Mexico live in southwestern states, including Arizona, California, Colorado, New Mexico, and Texas, while Cuban Americans largely reside in Florida (Marin & Marin, 1991; Pew Hispanic Center, 2004). Puerto Ricans, 61 percent of whom reside in the New York/New Jersey Metropolitan areas, are considered the privileged subgroup among Latinos, since their status as United States citizens guarantees them certain rights, protections, and privileges from birth (Adler, 2006, p. 64).

Bias crimes, commonly referred to as hate crimes, have been the subject of scholarly inquiry for over two decades, yet little academic attention has focused on bias-motivated attacks targeting Latino victims. In compiling its bias crime data, the FBI designates "white," "black," "American Indian/Alaskan Native," "Asian/Pacific Islander," and "Multiple Races" for their racial designations and simply divides the categories "Hispanic" and "Other Ethnicity/National Origin" to account for the ethnic designations (Uniform Crime Report, 2005).

Nationally, anti-Latino attacks account for 50 percent or more of the ethnic-based attacks throughout the past decade except the years 2001–2003, when the attacks shifted to include much larger numbers of Middle Eastern victims as a result of the terrorist attacks of September 11 and the commencement of the Iraq War. In California, the state with the largest Latino population, ethnically motivated offenses against Latinos account for 16 percent to 18 percent of the total number of bias-motivated crimes in the state, with 147 anti-Latino attacks in 2005 and 160 in 2007 (California Department of Justice, 2007).

Table 3.1 indicates the number of ethnically based bias offenses reported nationally to the FBI for data available from the past 10 years. Despite the public's lack of awareness regarding bias-motivated attacks against Latinos, the FBI has recorded over 3,600 anti-Latino offenses since 2000.

Research on bias-motivated offenders has largely rested on the foundational examination conducted by Levin and McDevitt in 1993. Their research determined that the majority of offenders do not comprise unstable and extreme hate mongers belonging to organized hate groups, but rather ordinary citizens who release their boredom, distrust, zeal, and vengeance by targeting those perceived to be "the other." Levin and McDevitt originally proposed three bias-offender profiles demarked by the categories "thrill seekers," "reactionists," and "missionary offenders." Upon later review of additional data, a revised version of the bias-motivated offender typology resulted in the construction of a fourth category: "retaliatory offenders" (Levin & McDevitt, 2002). Levin and McDevitt identified the largest group of bias-motivated offenders as thrill seekers composed of youthful offenders who pursue a sense of excitement, strength, and dominance through shared camaraderie. For thrill seekers who characteristically travel outside

**Table 3.1   Anti-Ethnicity/Anti-Latino Bias Motivation
United States: 1996–2006**

Year	Total anti-ethnicity incidents	Anti-Latino incidents	Percent anti-Latino
1996	940	564	60%
1997	836	491	58%
1998	754	482	64%
1999	829	466	56%
2000	911	557	61%
2001	**2,098**	**597**	**28%***
2002	1,102	480	44%
2003	1,026	426	42%
2004	972	475	49%
2005	944	522	55%
2006	984	576	59%

Source: Federal Bureau of Investigation Uniform Crime Report (1996–2006).

*In 2001, the number of bias-motivated attacks against Latinos remained consistent with the number of attacks in previous and following years. Due to the additional number of anti-ethnic attacks against persons of Middle Eastern descent taking place after September 11, 2001, the percentage of attacks against Latinos appears skewed.

their neighborhoods to commit their offenses, publicly accepted antagonism toward Latinos can be perceived as a legitimizing factor that justifies bias-based attacks against marginalized groups.

Reactionist offenders, on the other hand, consist of residents or employees protecting their neighborhoods or jobs in a defensive stance against the "invasion" of outsiders. Upon examination of the conditions under which racially and ethnically motivated crimes occurred in New York neighborhoods, Green, Strolovitch, and Wong (1998) uncovered that "demographic change, not economic hardship or inequality, predicts racially motivated crime directed at minorities" (p. 373). The findings affirmed Levin and McDevitt's (1993) typology given that racially and ethnically motivated attacks were found to escalate in predominantly Caucasian neighborhoods undergoing demographic shifts when residents took a protective stance to guard their perceived exclusive resources from African Americans, Asians, and Latinos (Green et al., 1998).

Extensive research has confirmed that "the extent to which individuals perceive a particular group as a threat to their own group's position in the social strata has a large impact on their attitudes toward that group" (Houvouras, 2001, p. 140). As the number of reported bias-motivated attacks against Latino/a(s) has remained consistently high for the past decade (see Table 3.1), one must recognize the need for examining Levin and McDevitt's (1993) reactionist offender within the context of the changing United States demographics. For Latino/a(s), who will comprise an estimated 29 percent of the United States population by the year 2050 (Passel & Cohn, 2008), this poses a critical concern. Currently, Latino/a(s) represent the largest minority group in the United States and account for 13 percent of the workforce, second only to Caucasian employees (Pew Research Center, 2005). As with thrill seekers, reactionists may be influenced by how they perceive Latinos: perceptions that are often formed by exposure to the media and awareness of legislative parameters that define and constrain the role of Latinos within mainstream culture.

Missionary offenders are the smallest group of offenders; they are composed of individuals committed to a superior loyalty, such as organized hate groups seeking to promote racial supremacy. While these offenders often receive the bulk of the media attention, missionary offenders represent the least common category of bias-motivated attackers. Finally, retaliatory offenders rationalize their attacks against members of marginalized groups as a consequence or payback for a negative experience in which a member of a minority group caused them harm (Levin & McDevitt, 2002).

What this model—and the literature on bias-motivated offenders in general—does not address is the opportunist offender who preys on oppressed groups who are unlikely to report their victimization to the police for fear of the social repercussions they may have to endure. These offenders are not opportunist in their seizing of situational factors such as a single Latino day laborer standing on a corner waiting for work, but rather sociopolitically opportunist offenders who seize the sociopolitical climate of the culture to attack members of marginalized groups who are most vulnerable, and who are also targets of other social prejudices whether through media portrayals, discriminatory legislation, or prejudiced police practices.

The lack of research probing violence against Latinos undoubtedly represents a substantial limitation in the expansion of criminological knowledge regarding racial and ethnic disparities in violent crime (Martinez, 2007). The chapter provides a contextual overview of the history of anti-Latino intolerance in the United States and takes an optimistic vision by suggesting recommendations on how to begin undertaking the fight to reduce bias attacks directed at Latinos. Additionally, this chapter examines the ways in which Latinos are dehumanized through media images and left unprotected by legislative actions, serving to legitimize anti-Latino hostility, and identifies examples of how certain law enforcement practices cultivate a social climate conducive for anti-Latino violence and in the process reduce the willingness of Latinos to report victimizations.

ANTI-LATINO HOSTILITY: A HISTORICAL CONTEXT OF DISCRIMINATORY LEGISLATION AND SOCIAL ALIENATION

As with all other immigrant groups, Latinos have endured many obstacles in establishing a home in the United States. After the Mexican–American War of 1848, California, Nevada, Utah, and segments of Arizona, Colorado, New Mexico, and Wyoming were relinquished by the Mexican government, resulting in the expansion of the United States. The occupation of the southwest region left the social sensitivity of the American populace with the subconscious perception of Mexicans as "foreigners" despite Mexico being the original owner of large regions of the United States territory (Romero, 2006, p. 449). For Latinos, and specifically Latinos of Mexican ancestry who were the predecessors to the formation of the region, the history of the United States is filled with bias-motivated discrimination, hostility, and cruelty.

In large part, the relationship between Latinos and the United States has been defined by government policies used to exclude and embrace Latinos according to the labor demand of the nation during a specific era. During the Great Depression of the 1930s, the United States government sponsored the Mexican Repatriation Program in which Latinos of Mexican descent were persuaded to relocate to Mexico. The request was often quite forceful, and many were required to leave the homes they had established in the United States. In the 1940s, members of the mainstream, and particularly soldiers involved in combat in Europe, viewed persons of Asian and Latino descent as "foreigners" to be distrusted—even those who were

American born (Mahan, 2002). Persons of Japanese ancestry were detained in internment camps, and a social climate of cultural paranoia became the norm in which everyone was viewed as the "other" (Mahan, 2002).

When significant numbers of Americans were fighting abroad in World War II and a shortage of labor was taking place, the Bracero Program was established to reverse deportation policies and supplement the workforce in the United States with Mexican immigrants. Laborers from Mexico were brought into the United States as needed in times of crisis, whether to replace the labor formerly held by soldiers fighting abroad or for completion of agricultural labor. According to Hoffman (1981),

> From 1942 to 1964, United States immigration policy toward Mexico was molded by the economic and political concerns of Southwestern growers. Determined to keep labor costs down, these growers insisted that only Mexican farm labor could provide the necessary number of workers at a wage they could afford to pay. The Mexican government attempted to secure guarantees of equitable treatment for its braceros[2] but was seldom successful in doing so. (p. 1174)

At the same time, media portrayals of Latinos as "zoot suiters" who were untrustworthy triggered hostility between servicemen and Latinos, which spread racialized violence throughout Los Angeles neighborhoods (Mahan, 2002). According to Mahan, the Zoot Suit/Sailor Riots of June 1943 exemplified the use of violence as a means of maintaining social control since police rarely intervened in the attacks to assist the victims, and often stood by without taking any action. Newspapers referring to Latinos as the "Mexican crime wave" and the "rising tide of Mexican juvenile delinquency" delivered misperceptions about juvenile delinquency despite crime statistics negating these claims. Americans seeking to protect a sense of entitlement to specific resources, services, and rights sought defense mechanisms including denial and rationalization to legitimize discrimination against "foreigners," and therefore focused on fabricated media misrepresentation and stereotypes to justify their attacks and oppression (Mahan, 2002). Historical data contend "police took more than 600 Chicano youth into custody without just cause, [and] . . . rationalized the arrests as preventive measures" (p. 288). The Zoot Suit/Sailor Riots, as well as other riots, were typical reflections of the outcome of oppressed groups seeking access to resources including housing, employment, and education. According to Mahan,

> Fanned by media rumors, hundreds of military men, often accompanied by the police, invaded Mexican American neighborhoods, wrenched patrons of Mexican descent from various establishments, beat them, and tore off their zoot suits . . . police frequently arrested the assault victims and allowed the perpetrators to remain free. (p. 293)

It was within such a context that multiple lynchings occurred as well. Especially in contrast to lynchings of African Americans, the lynching of Latinos, specifically those of Mexican descent, has been underexamined among scholars. It is possible to trace a long history of "lynch mobs" terrorizing individuals of Latino descent through the exploration of memoirs, folk culture, newsprint articles, and government documents (Carrigan & Webb, 2003). Researchers document evidence of at least 597 lynchings of Latinos between 1848 and 1928, and confirm the systematic abuse of power used by the Texas Rangers, an early law enforcement group established in the southern region of the United States (Carrigan & Webb, 2003).

Other realms of public social life also discriminated against Latinos. Children were ethnically segregated in the schools, and Latinos were often refused service at public businesses (e.g., restaurants and hair salons) at which merchants exhibited signs asserting "No Dogs or Mexicans Allowed" (Mahan, 2002). As hostilities grew during the summer of 1954, Attorney General Herbert Brownell announced the implementation of "an intensive and innovative law enforcement campaign designed to confront the rapidly increasing number of illegal border crossings by Mexican nationals" (Hernandez, 2006, p. 421). "Operation Wetback," as the program was called, placed 800 United States Border Patrol officers along the U.S.–Mexico border to conduct a series of raids and road blocks with the goal of deporting over one million persons (Hernandez, 2006).

The historical patterns of legislative discrimination continue in the present era. Throughout the country, several high-profile examples of legislative action aimed at curtailing the rights of Latino/a(s) have served to foster hostilities and ethnic tension. "For Latinos living in California in the mid-1990s the climate was politically charged and polarized as a result of two controversial initiatives" (Pantoja & Segura, 2003, p. 266). In November 1994, California voters approved Proposition 187, the Save Our State Initiative, with 59 percent of residents voting in favor of limiting public services for undocumented immigrants. The initiative denied social services including education and nonemergency healthcare to undocumented immigrants "and required various state and local agencies to report persons who were suspected undocumented immigrants" (Michelson, 2001, p. 58). Shortly after, "Congress passed and President Clinton signed welfare reform legislation that increased border security and deportations" (p. 57). During this time period, "there was a pervasive anti-immigrant, anti-Latino mood in the country" (p. 57). These policies conveyed a sentiment of hostility, which permeated into other social aspects of the culture, thereby producing a climate conducive for bias-motivated offenses.

Two additional measures, Proposition 209 and Proposition 227, continued to constrict the rights of Latinos in California. According to Santa Ana (2002), the 1996 endorsement of Proposition 209, which ceased Affirmative

Action in educational settings, was skillfully framed as an "antiracist measure" through designating Affirmative Action as the racist practice. Moreover, in 1998, California Proposition 227 ended bilingual education in the schools for 1.3 million non-English-speaking children (Santa Ana, 2002, p. xiii). These measures revealed the recurring resentment directed at Latino/a(s) as indicated by Houvouras' (2001) claims that "individuals who express prejudice against Latino/a(s) through negative stereotyping are more likely to oppose bilingual education than people who do not express prejudice against Latinos" (p. 148). According to Green and colleagues (1998), "Crimes directed against Asians, Latinos, and blacks are most frequent in predominantly white areas, particularly those experiencing an in-migration of minorities" (p. 372).

Glassner's (1999) account of American fears as detailed in his book, *The Culture of Fear: Why Americans Are Afraid of the Wrong Thing*, describes how Americans obsess about catastrophic misfortune rather than focus on the realistic social problems as such economic, ethnic, and social injustice. Glassner claims that

> Americans live in a culture of fear in which they are constantly anxious about unlikely calamitous events, such as killer bees, plane crashes, flesh-eating bacteria, and violent crime. Meanwhile, those things that are legitimately scary, such as poverty, racism, and social inequality, are not viewed as realistic threats. (Adler, 2006, p. 50)

Glassner's insights are even more relevant in a post-September 11 world in which the Patriot Act and Homeland Security measures have increased suspicion of every nationality and ethnic group. Since the September 11 attacks on the United States, fear and trepidation of all immigrants has increased:

> Although Americans do live under a legitimate threat of terrorism, there are those who seem to take advantage and play on these fears to achieve their own goals. It appears that the linkage between immigrants and terrorism is emphasized by those who for either political or economic reasons, want to reduce immigration. Scape-goating immigrants is also a convenient way for the US government to show a frightened public that they are winning the war on terror: detained and deported immigrants, frequent raids, and highly visible militarized border security are concrete evidence that the government is protecting its constituency. (Adler, 2006, p. 50)

Government officials throughout various regions have conducted raids and mass arrests of undocumented immigrants with the intention of fostering intimidation (Robinson, 2006). Immigration raids and intentional acts of race-related police harassment of Latino/a(s) serve to "establish, maintain, and reinforce second-class citizenship and limit civil, political, economic, and cultural rights and opportunities" (Romero, 2006, p. 469) for all Latino/a(s), whether legal residents or undocumented. In these instances, "racialized citizens and legal residents become subjects of immigration stops and searches, and pay the cost of increased racism—sometimes in the form of hate crimes or the decrease of government funding and services to their communities" (Romero, 2006, p. 450). In many cases, these governmentally enforced actions reduce the willingness of Latino/(s) victims to report crimes committed against them for fear of repercussions from police or other government agency. KBR, a subsidiary of Vice President Dick Cheney's former company Halliburton, was awarded a contract of $385 million in 2006 "to build large-scale immigrant detention centers in case of an emergency influx of immigrants" (Robinson, 2006, pp. 80–81).

The actions of traditional "street" police are also characterized by apparent antipathy toward Latinos, further contributing to a social climate that fosters suspicion and hostility toward them as outsiders. Oddly, however, research examining the ways in which police officers and Latinos interact and perceive one another is scarce. Yet, according to Martinez, the fact that Latinos are so dramatically overrepresented in arrest statistics "requires researchers to consider whether Latinos respond to police tactics in the same manner as non-Latino blacks and whites" (Martinez, 2007, p. 58). After conducting an extensive case study of the five-day immigration raids known as the Chandler Roundup of the summer of 1997, Romero (2006) asserts that "immigration raids serve as a policing practice that maintains and reinforces subordinated status among working class Latino citizens and immigrants" (p. 447) while also reinforcing mainstream suspicions of oppressed groups.

Romero (2006) found that, for Latino/a(s), immigration inspections "were intimidating and frightening, particularly when conducted with discretionary use of power and force by law enforcement agents . . . [who profiled] 'Mexicanness' as indicated by skin color, bilingual speaking abilities, or shopping in neighborhoods highly populated by Latinos" (p. 468). Romero claims immigration raids and intentional acts of race-related police harassment of Latino/a(s) serve to "establish, maintain, and reinforce second-class citizenship and limit civil, political, economic, and cultural rights and opportunities" (p. 469).

RECURRING SIGN OF THE TIMES: CONVENTIONALIZING EXPLOITATION, HARASSMENT, AND VIOLENCE

Public action and sentiment mirrors the political climate. Thus, the time period from 1999 to 2007 witnessed increased assaults on immigrants, particularly Latino/a(s), in many regions. In 2000 in Farmingville, New York, residents organized a local group called the Sachem Quality of Life (SQL) to force Latino immigrants out of the community. During this time, two men in their twenties, who convinced day laborers to escort them to an abandoned warehouse with the promise of work, brutally attacked the two victims with shovels and knives (Swarns, 2006). Although the two attackers were convicted, external consultants were brought into Farmingville in efforts of regaining community harmony. Subsequently, in 2003, five teenagers in the same community were convicted of throwing firework rockets that burned the residence of a Latino family, including their two children, while they were asleep. The following year, another wave of robberies against day laborers in Farmingville resumed (Healy, 2004).

In other areas, similar attacks were also occurring. A series of 27 armed robberies targeting day workers in Jacksonville, Florida, resulted in the death of two day laborers (Sewell, 2005). In some cases, Latinos were killed along the Mexican border by white vigilantes (Santa Ana, 2002), while others were attacked in communities such as Bloomington, Minnesota, for speaking Spanish while in the workplace (Santa Ana, 2002).

Day workers, or day laborers who are commonly Latino, are often the victims of bias-motivated offenses as well as the targets of assorted forms of exploitation. They are most vulnerable to discrimination, abuse, and mistreatment since they frequently stand on designated corners waiting for potential employers to seek them for a day of labor. The mistreatment of day laborers often entails various forms of employer harassment, wage theft,[3] and an array of bias-motivated offenses. Surveys of 481 immigrant day laborers at nearly 90 hiring sites throughout southern California revealed that laborers experienced employer abuse as well as poor working conditions that jeopardized their safety (Valenzuela, 2000, p. 1). According to Valenzuela and Theodore (2007):

> Employer violations of day laborers' rights and violations of basic labor standards are an all too common occurrence in the day-labor market. Wage theft is the most typical abuse experienced by day laborers . . . In California, nearly half of all day laborers (45%) have been completely denied payment by an employer for work they completed in the months prior to being surveyed. Similarly, one in two (48%) have been underpaid by employers during the same prior. (p. 166)

Latino workers "provide almost all farm labour and much of the labour for hotels, restaurants, construction, janitorial and house cleaning, child care, gardening and landscaping, delivery, meat and poultry packing, retail, and so on" (Robinson, 2006, p. 84). In these positions, they are paid poorly, endure employer abuses, suffer workplace injuries, and even bear mistreatment from business owners and police officials. In describing the conditions of their work setting during the two months preceding the survey, day laborers recounted an environment in which the employer deprived them of food, water, and breaks in 48 percent of the cases; threatened or insulted the workers 26 percent of the time; abandoned 29 percent of workers at the worksite; and experienced violence from the employer in one in five circumstances (Valenzuela & Theodore, 2007). Valenzuela and Theodore's research also found that 8 percent of California's day laborers had been arrested for seeking work, 10 percent received citations from police for waiting at employment sites, 16 percent were asked to provide evidence of their immigration status, and 9 percent recounted having "been insulted, harassed, or threatened by security guards in the two months prior to being surveyed" (Valenzuela & Theodore, 2007, p. 166). Of those surveyed, 19 percent had been "insulted or verbally harassed by merchants and 9 percent were threatened by business owners" (Valenzuela & Theodore, 2007, p. 166). Moreover, surveys of 286 domestic workers in Maryland, a state with several of the best labor laws in the nation, also revealed that 75 percent of the workers were denied overtime pay, while approximately 50 percent earned below the state minimum wage (CASA of Maryland, 2007).

Many day laborers are legal United States residents searching for employment, yet they are still forced to subscribe to documentation checks. As Romero (2006) discovered, Immigration and Naturalization Services (INS) gathers statistics regarding 'the number of individuals apprehended but the agency does not collect data on the number of individuals stopped and searched who were citizens or legal residents" (Romero, 2006, p. 453). Since these abuses are the result of abusive police practices, Latino/a(s) are often left without any recourse when they are victimized because the police are also a part of the abusers.

THE QUEST FOR EQUALITY AND THREAT (DEFENSIVE) THEORIES

As with all immigrant groups who have prevailed in the United States, for Latino/a(s) "cultural citizenship encompasses a broad range of everyday activities as well as the more visible political and social movements" (Flores, 2003, p. 89). Latino/a(s) seek opportunities to create a home, find sustainable employment, and live securely and comfortably. Yet, in mid-March 2006, the House of Representatives sought to pass HR4437, a bill which would

> criminalise undocumented immigrants by making it a felony to be in the US without documentation. It also stipulated the construction of the first 700 miles of a militarised wall between Mexico and the US and . . . would apply criminal sanctions against anyone who provided assistance to undocumented immigrants, including churches, humanitarian groups and social service agencies. (Robinson, 2006, p. 79)

In response, marches and rallies throughout major United States cities culminated in The Great American Boycott of 2006/A Day Without an Immigrant (Robinson, 2006, p. 78). The new millennium began with a renewed sense of empowerment among Latino/a(s), who generated unprecedented momentum through the use of purchase boycotts and mass demonstrations to protest the creation of legislation that would criminalize and deport millions of Latino workers (Robinson).

While the momentum toward a new civil rights movement had begun, the "blatantly racist public discourse that, only a few years ago, would have been considered extreme ha[d] become increasingly mainstream and aired in the mass media" (Robinson, 2006, p. 80). Public figures, including radio hosts, added fuel to the anti-Latino hostilities with comments directing their listeners to prepare their weapons and "do what has to be done" (Ressner, 2006). While ordinary individuals espoused intolerance without recognizing the extent of the prejudice they were promoting, others joined the paramilitary organization "the Minutemen," composed of self-appointed vigilantes who patrol the United States–Mexican border and sometimes publicly wear T-shirts declaring "Kill a Mexican Today?" or "Human Safaris" (Robinson, 2006, p. 80).

Similarly, at New York University, a small group of student members of the Republican Club established a game called "Catch the Illegal Immigrant," in which some students wearing a name tag labeling each as an "illegal immigrant" would be "hunted" by other students in an effort to accumulate the most points. The event drew many protestors, but event organizers claim they were seeking to promote awareness and generate discussion about the issue of illegal immigration rather than to offend anyone (Arenson, 2007).

When investigating prejudice toward immigrant workers among Dutch employees, Curseu, Stoop, and Schalk (2005) analyzed a model using the integrated threat theory to examine the four main threats that shape how groups interact and relate with one another. These threats include (1) anxiety of anticipating contact with a member of a different group; (2) fear that marginalized persons will alter the prevailing group's political and economic power; (3) concern over perceived group differences with regards to values, beliefs, and attitudes; and (4) negative stereotypes that influence perceptions of traits and expectations associated with members of the marginalized group (Curseu et al., 2005, pp. 125–126). Clearly, historical events have demonstrated evidence for these theories "when women for the first time enter male-dominated occupations, military organizations, or universities, or when interracial or same sex couples challenge social boundaries concerning inter-group contact" (Green et al., 1998, p. 399). For Latino/a(s), California history has shown clear evidence of how legislation and other means of subordination have been used to stifle and suppress strives toward equality.

Occurrences of discrimination against Latino/a(s) are not unusual, and have the potential to escalate into bias-motivated crimes. Bias crimes communicate a message of hate and intolerance, but so do policies and practices that socially sanction discrimination against Latino/a(s). These practices and policies communicate to Latino bias-crimes victims that their victimizations are not important. Additionally, societal inaction to cease discriminatory policies imparts a message of acceptance toward anti-Latino hostilities and therefore lessens the likelihood of victims reporting crimes. For criminal justice professionals and scholars, victim underreporting of all crimes, and particularly bias-motivated offenses, remains a challenge.

In the media, Latino/a(s) have endured numerous negative media stereotypes that perpetuate discrimination, exploitation, and bias-motivated attacks. In *Brown Tide Rising*, Otto Santa Ana (2002) identifies prevalent metaphors used within popular discourse to represent Latino/a(s). Additionally, he investigates the ways in which these metaphors are commonly manipulated to gain support for anti-immigrant measures and to justify exploitation. Subtle words and images commonly portrayed through media outlets serve to dehumanize Latino/a(s) and foster a cultural climate of hostility often perceived to socially sanction acts of exploitation, abuse, harassment, and violence.

The portrayal of Latino/a(s) in the media is not only powerful in its ability to promote or challenge stereotypes, but also in its ability to sculpt the social consciousness of mainstream society. In his comprehensive work regarding the portrayals of Latino/a(s) in mass culture, Santa Ana (2002) examined over 4,485 instances of metaphors depicted in 671 *Los Angeles Times* articles from 1992 to 1998. He uncovered three major recurring metaphors used to describe Latino/a(s) within American culture. In 58 percent of the instances, the terms "flood," "tide," or "dangerous waters" were used to refer to the influx of Latino/a(s) residing in the United States. Twenty-three percent of the metaphors made reference to a "war" or "invasion," while 32 percent of articles utilized "animal references."

While stereotypical portrayals of marginalized groups does not necessarily lead to bias-motivated attacks, one must begin to question the impact of these portrayals since research indicates that "people automatically devote more attention to negative information than to positive information" (Smith et al., 2006, p. 210). World history contains ample examples of the dehumanization of marginalized people with "visual depictions [that] caricature physical features to make 'ethnic others' look animal-like" (Haslam, 2006, p. 253). For many individuals, the metaphors communicated through the media represent the basis for how viewers assess the world. This communication conveys images and metaphors that shape, reinforce, and sustain discriminatory attitudes and behaviors. Mize and Leedham's (2000) examination of 146 articles from four northern Colorado newspapers also yielded largely negative portrayals of Latino/a(s), suggesting "that immigrants take jobs from US citizens, depress native wage levels, and drain resources from the economy" (Briggs, 1994; Curtis, 1993; Huddle, 1993, as quoted in Mize & Leedham, 2000, p. 89). While attacks against Latinos are on the rise, and limited awareness regarding victimizations persists, many members of society continue to perceive Latino/a(s) as mostly criminal.

In their analysis of randomly selected television news stories aired in Los Angeles and Orange County in California, Dixon and Linz (2000) attempted to assess the representations of Latino/a(s), African Americans, and Caucasians with regard their portrayals as either victims or perpetrators of crimes. Their findings showed that both Latino/a(s) and African Americans were less likely to be portrayed as victims on the television news than Caucasians, and more likely than Caucasians to be portrayed as perpetrators of violence. The analysis suggests that Latino/a(s) are underrepresented as either victims or offenders, yet the study also illustrated examples of instances in which "Latinos appear to be framed as the source of the nation's immigration problem" (Dixon & Linz, 2000, p. 566).

When volatile issues are introduced, organized hate groups seize opportunities to propagate mainstream ignorance, fear, and misinformation in hopes of misguiding ordinary citizens into a continued polarization of "us" versus "them." Through the use of various modes of communication, including Internet Web sites, books, and videos, "members of white supremacist groups often refer to Latino/a immigrants as a 'cultural cancer', as a 'wildfire', as a 'gang of illegals,' that is making 'America less beautiful,' as people with the plan to 'reconquer' the United States" (Santa Ana 2002, p. xi). Recently, both the Anti-Defamation League (2008) and the Southern Poverty Law Center (2008), two leading antibias organizations, proclaimed that organized hate groups are using immigration as a pretext to incite violence against Latino/a(s), regardless of legal status or country of citizenship.

Other media outlets incorporate the ever-expanding world of virtual space. Border Patrol, a video game that encourages players to shoot at Mexican immigrants crossing the United States–Mexican border, opens with a screen that states, "keep them out . . . at any cost" (Silverstein, 2006). The images of immigrants portrayed in the game are "caricatured as bandolier-wearing 'Mexican nationalists', tattooed 'drug smugglers' and pregnant 'breeders' who spring across with their children in tow" (Robinson, 2006, p. 80). Border Patrol, like many other video games based on prejudiced ideals, perpetuates stereotyped caricatures of Latino/a(s) under the guise of fun and entertainment. While the game itself cannot be blamed for the intolerance experienced by Latino/a(s), it is obvious that one cannot deny the sentiment communicated in the game's opening message.

CONCLUSIONS AND RECOMMENDATIONS

For those seeking to understand bias-motivated offenses, it is imperative to attend to social norms and policies that legitimize the exclusion of marginalized individuals from protection, services, and equality. Careful attention must be placed on the social-sanctioning effect of discriminatory policies that limit protections for Latino/a(s) while fostering a sentiment of hostility and acceptance of intolerance through governmental policy. This climate supports exploitation in the form of wage theft and unfair practices among employers who exploit their laborers simply because they are able to get away with it. As a result, Latino/a(s) are vulnerable to the discriminatory and often violent practices of their employers as well as other ordinary attackers.

Bias crimes communicate a message of intolerance, yet so do socially accepted norms that permit, and perhaps promote, hostilities against any disenfranchised group. The historical experience of Latino/a(s) in the United States is a turbulent one. While the examples of anti-Latino attacks cited throughout this chapter may be appalling, these represent only a small number of acts of abuse and violence that occur daily. In the case of Latino/a(s), it is not possible to decipher the number of attacks that go unreported due to fear of mistreatment from the police or because of possible language barriers.

Bias-motivated offenses continue to present a challenge for legislators, criminal justice professionals, and communities. While it is unrealistic to expect to eliminate all bias-motivated offenses, improvements in curbing anti-Latino attacks are possible. The following represent the suggestions of the author, who is optimistic about the possibility of making great strides in the fight to reduce anti-Latino bias.

It is not only reasonable but absolutely necessary that attacks against Latinos be reduced. The history of Latinos in the United States is marked with exploitation, abuse, and violence, but small changes can begin to make a significant difference:

1. establish a national organization charged with the task of monitoring anti-Latino attacks and also serving as a public relations organization to educate the populace;
2. educate the public by dispelling the myths that portray Latino/as as taking American resources and producing a crime wave;
3. repair the current immigration system by substituting outdated policies and instituting nondiscriminatory procedures for immigrants seeking to legally reside in the United States;
4. ensure that criminal justice agencies enforce laws in an equitable manner and evaluate the manner in which raids are implemented;
5. demand that legislators propose fair and just policies that protect and benefit every member of society without encouraging exploitation;
6. insist on balanced media portrayals of all members of society.

It is unrealistic to expect that all portrayals and images of Latinos will reflect the positive nature of the diverse Latino cultures, yet it is not unrealistic to expect a balanced representation, one that neither ignores Latino/a images nor criminalizes Latinos by depicting only images of gang members. Although several national Latino organizations exist, none has the sole responsibility of documenting bias-motivated actions against Latinos and tracking bigoted portrayals in mass culture. Such a watch group would serve to monitor anti-Latino legislative action, track bias-motivated offenses against Latinos, and regulate media images that appear to be unbalanced across all forms of dissemination. This group would also have the role of serving as a public relations organization that dispels myths about Latinos to the general populace in an effort to reduce anti-Latino attacks. Additionally, this group could raise awareness of anti-Latino attacks and promote awareness of bias-crime legislation that excludes protections for Latinos. In David Richardson's case, his attack could not be prosecuted as a bias-motivated crime because his attack did not fit federal hate crime statutes and because first-degree felonies are exempt from hate crime stipulations in the state of Texas.

Addressing the issue of immigration in the United States will require not only legislative reform but also improvements in the proficiency of the Department of Naturalization and Immigration Services. Currently, outdated policies and congested immigration offices fail to meet the needs of immigrants seeking legal entrance and residency in the United States. Rather than focusing energy on authoritarian efforts that promote ethnic hostilities, efforts would be better served to correct antiquated and ineffective immigration policies.

In 2007, Latinos united as a group to protest unfair legislative action. This type of unity not only empowers members of disenfranchised groups, but also serves to exhibit strength in the demand for fair, equal, and just policies. More importantly, it sends a message that the mistreatment of Latinos will not be tolerated and that through a unified effort, changes to inequities and bias-motivated offenses can be achieved.

NOTES

1. While the terms "Latino" and "Hispanic" are often used interchangeably despite their distinct historical and political undertones, the author of this chapter will use the term "Latino" to address all persons of Latin descent, including those with ancestors from Spain, Latin American countries, and indigenous cultures originating in Central and South America.

2. *Bracero* was the term used to describe workers transported into the United States from Mexico to work in agriculture for a designated period of time.

3. "Wage theft" is a term used to refer to either an employer's failure to pay a day laborer for his or her work, or the robbery of a day laborer's wages by an attacker who perceives the cash earnings as an easy target for theft.

REFERENCES

Adler, R. H. (2006). 'But they claimed to be police, not la migra!": The interaction of residency status, class, and ethnicity in a (Post-Patriot Act) New Jersey neighborhood. *American Behavioral Scientist, 50*(1), 48–69.

Alcoff, L. M. (2005). Latino oppression. *Journal of Social Philosophy, 36*(4), 536–545.

Anti-Defamation League. (2008). *Immigrants targeted: Extremist rhetoric moves into mainstream.* Retrieved July 12, 2007, from http://www.adl.org/civil_rights/anti_immigrant/

Arenson, K. W. (2007, February 23). Immigrant game at N.Y.U. draws protesters. *New York Times.* Retrieved July 12, 2007, from http://www.nytimes.com/2007/02/23/nyregion/23illegal.html

Briggs, V. M. (1994). *Still an open door? U.S. immigration Policy and the American economy.* Washington, DC: American University Press.

California Department of Justice. (2007). *Hate crime in California 2007.* Sacramento, CA: Attorney General's Office.

Carrigan, W. D., & Webb, C. (2003). The lynching of persons of Mexican origin or descent in the United States, 1848 to 1928. *Journal of Social History, 37*(2), 411–438.

CASA of Maryland. (2007). *How Maryland fails to protect the rights of low-wage workers.* Takoma Park, MD: Author.

Curseu, P. L., Stoop, R., & Schalk, R. (2005). Prejudice toward immigrant workers among Dutch employees: Integrated threat theory revisited. *European Journal of Social Psychology, 37,* 125–140.

Curtis, G. (1993). Immigration R.I.P.? *Population and Environment, 14*(6), 495–502.

Dixon, T. L., & Linz, D. (2000). Race and the misrepresentation of victimization on local television news. *Communication Research, 27*(5), 547–573.

Federal Bureau of Investigations (2005). Uniform Crime Report 2005. Washington, DC: Author.

Flores, W. V. (2003). New citizens, new rights: Undocumented immigrants and Latino cultural citizenship. *Latin American Perspectives, 3*(2), 87–100.

Glassner, B. (1999). *The culture of fear: Why Americans are afraid of the wrong things.* New York: Basic Books.

Green, D. P., Strolovitch, D. Z., & Wong, J. S. (1998). Defended neighborhood, integration, and racially motivated crime. *American Journal of Sociology, 104*(2), 372–403.

Haslam, N. (2006). Dehumanization: An integrative review. *Personality and Social Psychology Review, 10*(3), 252–264.

Healy, P. (2003, November 26). Second Suffolk teenager pleads guilty in fire at Mexicans' home. *New York Times.* Retrieved July 12, 2007, from http://query.nytimes.com/gst/fullpage.html?res=9503E6D9163AF935A15752C1A9659C8B63

Healy, P. (2004, July 27). Latest crimes against migrants on L.I. have a familiar ring. *New York Times.* Retrieved July 12, 2007, from http://query.nytimes.com/gst/fullpage.html?res=9806E7D3153DF934A15754C0A9629C8B63

Hernandez, K. L. (2006). The crimes and consequences of illegal immigration: A cross-border examination of Operation Wetback, 1943 to 1954. *The Western Historical Quarterly, 37*(4), 421–444.

Hoffman, A. (1981). [Untitled book review of *Operation Wetback: The mass deportation of Mexican undocumented workers in 1954*]. *American Historical Review, 86*(5), 1174.

Houvouras, S. K. (2001). The effects of demographic variables, ethnic prejudice, and attitude toward immigration on opposition to bilingual education. *Hispanic Journal of Behavioral Sciences, 23*(2), 136–152.

Kovach, G. C. (2007, July 5). The wages of hate. *Newsweek*, Web Exclusive. Retrieved July 7, 2007, from http://www.newsweek.com/id/33291

Levin, J., & McDevitt, J. (1993). *Hate crimes: The rising tide of bigotry and bloodshed.* New York: Plenum Press.

Levin, J., & McDevitt, J. (2002). *Hate crimes revisited: America's war against those who are different.* New York: Westview Press.

Mahan, V. J. (2002). Focusing on the events of 1943, particularly the Zoot Suit/Sailor. *Journal of Hispanic Higher Education, 1*(4), 283–297.

Marin, G., & Marin, B. V. (1991). *Research with Hispanic populations.* Thousand Oaks, CA: Sage.

Martinez, R. (2007). Incorporating Latinos and immigrants into policing research. *Criminology and Public Policy, 6*(1), 57–64.

Michelson, M. R. (2001). The effect of national mood on Mexican American political opinion. *Hispanic Journal of Behavioral Sciences, 23*(1), 57–70.

Mize, R. L., & Leedham, C. (2000). Manufacturing bias: An analysis of newspaper coverage of Latino immigration issues. *Latino Studies Journal, 11*(2), 88–107.

Pantoja, A. D., & Segura, G. M. (2003). Fear and loathing in California: Contextual treat and political sophistication among Latino voters. *Political Behavior, 25*(3), 265–286.

Passel, J. S., & Cohn, D. (2008, February 11). *U.S. population projections: 2005–2050* [Pew Hispanic Center] (pp. 1–55). Washington, DC: Pew Research Center.

Pew Hispanic Center. (2004). *Latinos in California, Texas, New York, Florida, and New Jersey.* Washington, DC: Author.

Pew Research Center. (2005). Hispanics: A people in motion. In *Trends 2005* (pp. 71–89). Washington, DC: Author.

Ressner, J. (2006, Monday, May 29). How immigration is rousing the zealots. *Time.* Retrieved July 12, 2007, from http://www.time.com/time/magazine/article/0,9171,1198895,00.html

Robinson, W. I. (2006). "Aqui estamos y no nos vamos!" Global capital and immigrant rights. *Race & Class, 48*(2), 77–91.

Romero, M. (2006). Racial profiling and immigration law enforcement: Rounding up of usual suspects in the Latino community. *Critical Sociology, 32*(2–3), 448–473.

Santa Ana, O. (2002). *Brown tide rising: Metaphors of Latinos in contemporary American public discourse.* Austin: University of Texas Press.

Sewell, A. (2005, March). Violence against day laborers grows. *The Portland Alliance.* Retrieved July 12, 2007, from www.theportlandalliance.org/2005/mar/daylaborviolence.htm

Silverstein, J. (2006, 1 May). Racist video game incites anger: Internet game lets players take shots at immigrants. *ABC News.* Retrieved August 20, 2007, from http://abcnews.go.com/technology/Story?id=1910119&page=1

Smith, N. K., Larsen, J. T., Chartrand, T. L., Cacioppo, J. T., Katafiasz, H. A., & Moran, K. E. (2006). Being bad isn't always good: Affective context moderates the attention bias toward negative information. *Journal of Personality and Social Psychology*, *90*(2), 210–220.

Southern Poverty Law Center. (2008). *Immigrant Justice Project*. Retrieved January 14, 2008, from http://www.splcenter.org/legal/ijp.jsp

Swarns, R. L. (2006, February 4). Halliburton subsidiary gets contract to add temporary immigration detention centers. *New York Times*. Retrieved July 12, 2007, from http://www.nytimes.com/2006/02/04/national/04halliburton.html

Valenzuela, A. (2000). *Working on the margins: Immigrants day labor characteristics and prospects for employment*. San Diego, CA: University of California San Diego, The Center for the Comparative Immigration Studies.

Valenzuela Jr., A., & Theodore, N. (2007, 25 June). Searching and working: California's day laborers and worker centers. In *UCLA School of Public Affairs. California Policy Options. Paper 2007*. Retrieved July 12, 2007, from http://repositories.cdlib.org/uclaspa/cpc/2007J

CHAPTER 4

RACE, BIGOTRY, AND HATE CRIME: ASIAN AMERICANS AND THE CONSTRUCTION OF DIFFERENCE

Helen Ahn Lim

The study of hate crime is complex. Researchers continue to express con-
cerns over a range of issues related to hate crimes: definitions of hate crime
(Dillof, 1997; Wang, 1999); causes of hate crime (see Gerstenfeld, 2003;
Levin & McDevitt, 2002; Levin & Rabrenovic, 2004); hate crime offenders
(Hamm, 1993; Levin & McDevitt, 2002); whether hate crime laws violate
speech rights (Jacoby, 2002; Lawrence, 1999); the efficacy of hate crime laws
(Anti-Defamation League [ADL], 2004; Iganski, 2002; Jacobs & Potter, 1998;
Lawrence, 1999; Wang, 2000); impact of hate crimes (Herek & Berrill, 1992;
Iganski, 2001; Levin, 2002b); and the challenges of policing, prosecuting, and
punishing perpetrators of hate crimes (Bell, 2002; Garofalo & Martin, 1993;
Lawrence, 2002). In spite of these studies, little is known about the extent
of harm that hate crimes cause targeted communities. Researchers seldom
ask how racial minorities define, experience, and cope with hate crimes and
the threat of hate crimes. It is not surprising that these kinds of questions
are rare, since the preoccupation with racial minorities has to do with their
profile as offenders rather than as victims. It is in this way that this chapter
departs from conventional ways of studying hate crime and minorities and
crime.

This chapter presents Asian American perspectives on racial bigotry
and hate crime as a stigmatized group. In doing so, it exposes the myriad untruths about Asian Americans, specifically the belief that they are
no longer targets of racial bigotry and violence. This belief results from
misperceptions arising out of a lack of media coverage about Asian American victimization, and that as "model minorities," Asian Americans have

achieved enormous groupwide success and therefore no longer face racial antagonism experienced by other stigmatized minority groups (National Asian Pacific Legal Consortium [NAPALC], 1999). The fact that hate crimes are drastically underreported by victims also exacerbates this misperception.

It is important to recognize that the group referred to as "Asian American" covers a colorful and vast group of peoples with distinct immigration histories, political backgrounds, cultures, religions, and languages that make up the ever-expanding meaning of the American experience. Indeed, to describe Asian Americans with a word other than "diverse" would be inaccurate. Asian Indians, Cambodians, Chinese, Filipinos, Hmong, Japanese, Koreans, Samoans, Thai, and Vietnamese are just some of the different ethnic groups that belong to the category of Asian American. Since the focus of this chapter is about the treatment of Asian ethnics in America, based on their perceived racial distinctiveness as nonwhite rather than on their unique intragroup qualities, all Asian ethnics in America will be referred to as Asian Americans, and these terms will be used interchangeably.

This chapter is divided into five main sections. The first section introduces research, data collection, and Asian American narratives. Here, emphasis will be put on the importance of narrative research in understanding the impact of racial bigotry and hate crime on stigmatized populations. The second section reveals Asian American perspectives and how Asian Americans define and experience the problem of bigotry and hate crime as the distinct "other." The third section expands on this discussion by demonstrating how, for Asian Americans, the perpetual foreigner and the model minority images function as sources of racial stigmatization. Stereotypes and popular images do not cause bias incidents or bias crimes, but they do serve to justify harm against targeted groups, including serious forms of violence (*Harvard Law Review*, 1993). In the fourth section, some Asian Americans' responses to the threat and reality of racial violence will be demonstrated. The chapter concludes with final thoughts on how the stigmatization of difference affects the treatment of Asian Americans.

INTERVIEWS AND THE IMPORTANCE
OF NARRATIVE RESEARCH

The narratives in this chapter are based on 45 in-depth interviews with Asian Americans conducted in New Jersey between September 2002 and July 2003. According to the 2000 U.S. Census data, "Asian persons" made up approximately 3.6 percent of the population in the United States, and 5.7 percent in New Jersey (U.S. Census Bureau, 2000). According to that same report, Asian Americans in New Jersey were concentrated in Somerset County (8.4%), in Jersey City (16.2%), and in the Fort Lee borough

(31.4%). The enclaves and the presence of Asian-owned businesses in these cities support a concentration of Asian Americans. The interviews averaged 2.5 hours in length and took place in a variety of settings, including my place of residence, respondents' homes, restaurants, coffee shops, and bookstores, all dependent on the interviewee's preference. I analyzed each interview by carefully observing the emerging and overlapping themes within and across the subjects' responses. Highlighted are what were determined to be key elements of each interview.

The respondents in this study identify themselves as members of the following Asian ethnic groups: Chinese, Korean, Japanese, East Asian Indian, Vietnamese, Chinese Indonesian, Chinese Filipino, Chinese Malaysian, Japanese Caucasian, and Korean Caucasian. They include 23 women and 22 men who are legal permanent residents, and naturalized and natural-born U.S. citizens. They also represent a range of occupational backgrounds. Each interviewee was assigned a pseudonym in this study in order to protect his or her identity. The "snowball" method was used to locate the interviewees for this study. Snowball sampling relies on the initial contacts to obtain further referrals for the researcher. This method is widely used for exploratory studies of little-known or hard-to-obtain participants (Champion, 1993, p. 108; Hagan, 1997, p. 138). Given that snowball sampling begins with contacts known to the researcher, nearly all of the interviewees lived near the interviewer's place of residence, in New Jersey and New York. Five of the interviewees resided in California, Indiana, and Texas. I decided to interview these subjects based on personal travel convenience and the conviction that they had important experiences to share.

During the interview I was guided by the following questions: How do Asian Americans define hate crime? What do they believe to be the contributing factors? How do they manage and respond to the threat? In what ways do hate crimes affect the way they view themselves and the offender population? The responses to these kinds of questions provide an understanding of how hate crimes affect targeted communities and intergroup relations.

The pervasive role of whites as perpetrators of bias-motivated attacks is consistent in the narratives. Although hate crimes also include attacks between racial minorities, such as offenses that arise between African Americans and Asian Americans, that warrant further study (Abelmann & Lie, 1995; Asante & Min, 2000; Kim, 2000; Levin & McDevitt, 2002; Yamamato, 1999), this study concentrates on what is overwhelmingly reflected in its narratives—hate crimes committed against Asian Americans by the racial majority, herein referred to as whites. For this reason, this study and the narratives in this chapter largely address the Asian American perspective on race, bigotry, and hate crime in the context of how they experience and speak about the dominant, white majority.

The importance of Asian American narratives became increasing apparent throughout these interviews. These narratives are particularly important in demonstrating the impact of bias and racial violence on targeted communities. Bowling (1993) articulates the ways in which local and national surveys have helped prioritize legislative and procedural issues related to racial violence, but argues that criminology and the criminal justice system are severely limited in capturing the problems of certain crimes and patterns of victimization, and in their approaches to remedying victimization and rendering justice (p. 67). His major criticism rests on an illogical and inconsistent criminal justice system that counts crime and racial violence as incident-based when racial victimization, like other social processes, is dynamic, is in constant motion, and involves a number of social actors (p. 67) and multiple perspectives.

Delgado (2001) articulates the importance of narrative as a mechanism for understanding the impact of racial discrimination (cited in Delgado & Stefancic, 2001). He explains that critical-race theorists have relied on victims' day-to-day experiences, perspectives, and viewpoints, and the power of stories and persuasion in order to offer a more comprehensive understanding of how Americans see race through the use of parables, autobiographies and "counterstories" (p. 38). According to Delgado, stories conveyed through narratives can help people understand what life is like for some, and also serve as a powerful function for minority communities because many victims of racial discrimination suffer in silence or blame themselves for their trouble (pp. 39–43). Delgado argues that narratives also give voice to the victim, reveal similar hardships, and name discriminatory experiences that, once named, can ultimately be combated; moreover, narratives can draw attention to neglected areas of evidence that ultimately influence policies and formal laws (p. 43).

DEFINING HATE CRIMES AND UNDERSTANDING ASIAN AMERICANS AS THE "OTHER"

Barbara Perry (2003a) argues that though legalistic definitions of hate crime are narrow and necessary for the law enforcement community, their narrowness is less useful from a social science perspective (p. 7). Furthermore, she contends that the study of hate crime can be improved by a definition that demonstrates how hate crimes facilitate construction of identities within a power structure, and as acts against those who are defined as the "other." In defining hate crime, Perry (2001) refers to "acts of violence and intimidation, usually directed toward stigmatized and marginalized groups . . . it is a mechanism of power and oppression, intended to reaffirm the precarious hierarchies that characterize a given social order . . . it is a means of marking both the Self and the Other in such a way as to reestablish their 'proper' relative positions, as given and reproduced by broader ideologies and patterns of social and political inequality" (p. 10). Responding to this dilemma, I asked the interviewees in this study to define hate crime and to talk about their related experiences. Although some of the incidents the interviewees discussed may not fulfill the legal criteria of a hate crime or meet the requirements for successful prosecution, the respondents articulate these offenses in their stories as hate crimes for the ways that they stigmatize, marginalize, and reaffirm racial hierarchy.

Many of the respondents perceived hate crimes as offenses against those who are "different." Their definitions of hate crime focus thematically on the issue of racial distinction. They stress the significance and impact of racial stigmatization, and the social construction of difference. Scholars continue to express concern over the meanings of race, the stigmatization of difference, ways that race serves as a form of social identification and stratification, and ways in which the social construction of race structures society (see Delgado & Stefancic, 2001; Lopez, 1997; Omi & Winant, 1994; Pincus & Ehlrich, 1999; Smedley, 1998). The narratives below, taken from interviews conducted for this study, also emphasize hate crimes as attacks against those who are "different" in a socially significant way:

> Any crime that hurts anybody . . . the main idea is to hurt them because of their difference in beliefs, race, sexism, any ism. (Kelly, second-generation Filipino American, Parsippany, New Jersey)

> It is a crime against people of different races, faith, and beliefs . . . It's just taking a group of people and generalizing them as specific types. Because of that generalization, they get attacked physically and mentally. (Mike, second-generation Korean American, Rahway, New Jersey)

> I think it's an ignorant crime. People are really feeling threatened either because they may feel that their security is threatened, their jobs, or their women. It comes from seeing different cultures and not being able to understand it. So, they automatically hate it. (Heather, second-generation Korean American, Hackensack, New Jersey).

According to these respondents, hate crimes are acts against those who are "different." They are offenses committed against those who are different from a standard held by an offender who perhaps thinks that he or she constitutes the norm (see Perry, 2003b, p. 9). The targeted individual or group member is punished by the perpetrator for his or her perceived distinguishing factor.

What makes the racialized "other" distinct from white America? What is the source of such exclusionary concepts? The answers to these kinds of questions are found by examining the impact of stereotypes and popular images.

I think we should break down stereotypes because they generalize people and put them into one category . . . I always thought it is always based on the person and who you are, not your skin color. That's part of it but not the main way you see people. I see stereotypes as very negative because you categorize people before you know them. (Jerry, second-generation Korean American, Jersey City, New Jersey)

Stereotypes can be harmful mainly because others will view us in a very narrow way; a view where they are to see us in the way they have been exposed to . . . It may take more time to diminish or clear all the stereotypes before that person takes me seriously or engages in serious dialogue by saying first that this isn't who I am and then reveal who they really are. (Jamie, second-generation Korean American, Bound Brook, New Jersey)

The two narratives above illustrate a clear concern for the ways that stereotypes can function as mechanisms to marginalize a person's individuality. Stereotypes are also characterized by the following qualities: they are judgmental; they tend to be absolute categories; they do not change with new evidence; and they are highly oversimplified, exaggerated views of reality (Charon, cited in Adler & Adler, 2001).

Stereotypes are also compatible with essentialist philosophies of racial classification. Wu (2002) discusses the impact of stereotypes on blacks (p. 75). He warns his readers against buying into the idea that blacks are "innate athletes" because it diminishes their individual talent and reduces African Americans to brute animals. As historian John Hoberman argues, racialized theories that suggest blacks as having instincts that are superior, like better hand–eye coordination, resonate to a kind of belief that slave owners bred them for strength (cited in Wu, 2002, p. 73). Wu argues that what falls in line with this kind of thinking is that African Americans are also dim-witted. It's the perception that, in the sports arena, blacks with their muscular physiques are ready-made linebackers on a football team, but only recently have they become starting quarterbacks, a position that is more cerebral and that also requires leadership. African Americans can entertain the fans as athletes but still are underrepresented as managers and owners who develop key strategies and make high-impact decisions for the organization. If they are deficient at dribbling a basketball or cannot sing or dance, the individual is not perceived as someone who is "really black."

No racial minority group is free from the application of group labels (Perry, 2001, p. 63). These stereotypes also include deviant and criminal images (Levin & Rabrenovic, 2004, p. 47). Most communities of color are characterized as dishonest and deceitful, and, in some cases, males especially are labeled as criminal, violent, thieving, sexual predators (Perry, 2001, p. 63). Specific labels are also attached to specific groups. African Americans are thought to be intellectually inferior to whites (Levin, 2002, p. 26); African American males are portrayed as dangerous criminals (Levin & Rabrenovic, 2004, pp. 48–49). Native Americans and Mexican Americans are labeled as lazy and unambitious (Perry, 2001, p. 63). These images persist in the minds of many who may be unaware of enforcement and sentencing disparities, and of structural employment constraints. Racial stereotypes also shape the societal views of Asian Americans (Espiritu, 1997; Fong, 1998; Okihiro, 1994). For Asian Americans, the "perpetual foreigner" and the "model minority" images function as a source of racial marginalization. These racial stereotypes or popular images not only distinguish Asian Americans from white Americans as the "outside other" but also underlie the racial antagonism against this group.

ASIAN AMERICANS AS PERPETUAL FOREIGNERS AND MODEL MINORITIES

The "foreigner image" has long been a source of racial antagonism for Asian Americans (Takaki, 1998). One way Asian Americans have tried to diminish the harsh treatment against them as the perceived "outsider" is by changing their birth name to an "American" one.

> I changed my name too because it always has been such a stress for me . . . I try not to think about it as much, but if you're not thinking about it, it might just pass right by you and not notice that these people are treating you in a certain way because we are colored . . . Now that I'm older I wish I didn't change it . . . I thought I would become more a part of the society if I changed my name, that I would feel less as an outcast . . . I was hoping that others would perceive me as an American and that I would see myself more as one. (Kim, second-generation Korean American, New Brunswick, New Jersey)

The respondent's father wanted Kim to change her name to an "American" one after hearing that "bad things happen" to Asian immigrants with "foreign" names. The interview also revealed that the respondent's father was concerned that, as his daughter was an aspiring journalist, her job prospects would be slim if her American employers perceived her as a foreigner. For Kim, it was very clear that her first name was more about acknowledging a person's identity or individuality than about a means of identification. As Kim said, "I think calling people by name it gives you an identity . . . it means that you matter because someone knows your name . . . if you say *you*, or *he* or *she*, it doesn't give me an identity or address me as a person." Throughout the interview Kim insisted that her birth name had tremendous significance, and that she considered her birth name to be a part of her heritage since it was given to her by her grandparents. Her father was so concerned about the discrimination her daughter would face that she decided to change her name to one "that has no meaning, since I just came up with it on my own."

Unfortunately, according to Kim, this name change has done little to improve her treatment as an American or help her feel more like one.

Hwang (2001, p. 44) argues that what Asian ethnics do have in common is the way they look to the larger community and the way they are treated based upon their physical appearance. This commonality begins with a recognition that whether you are a first-generation Vietnamese American or a third-generation Chinese American, Asian Americans are constantly barraged with the question, "No really, where are you from?" (p. 44). Regardless of how long an Asian American has lived in America or whether he or she is an American-born citizen, the perception of Asian Americans as "perpetual foreigners" impacts their treatment and continuing potential for racial discrimination and violence.

> As an adult, I've been stared at, nothing physical or threatening. Actually, they even called out, "Chink, go back to your country" as they drove by really quickly . . . Then there was an incident a couple months ago where some driver almost hit my car . . . She rolled down the window and yelled, "Go back to your country" . . . She is white, Anglo, probably in her early 40s . . . I just felt angry, emotionally. In my head I was like, wow, not like surprised but how they still think that America is white people's country, some of them, and they totally ignore what they did to the American Indians by slaughtering them and exploiting them. Not only American Indians but also African Americans, and to tell Asians to go back to their country is very sad. (Jamie, second-generation Korean American, Bound Brook, New Jersey)

> There are people who see us as foreigners in this country even though we are all really foreigners. They have a certain mentality of us not belonging here or thinking that we are not as good as them. There is a certain tendency for them to follow up with this by being a little more degrading or speaking with certain words. I think they think of us as foreigners . . . When I hear ignorant responses like that, it is usually from the Caucasian race . . . Friends have told me that they were called similar stuff. (Lisa, second-generation Korean American, Cherry Hill, New Jersey)

> I remember when we first moved to California we were living in Long Beach and my dad got his car windshield bashed in two or three times within two months . . . It was probably a racial hate crime thing. This happened in front of our home, and it was the car on the street. We were only living there for only a couple of months. And I don't see any other reason . . . it [the neighborhood] was almost all Caucasian . . . That definitely made my family leave right away. It was a matter of months that we moved. (Ray, second-generation Vietnamese American, Hackensack, New Jersey)

These vignettes illustrate the treatment of Asian Americans as perceived foreigners. The verbal remarks and attacks show a standard for belonging based upon race. Ray and his family were viewed as foreigners who did not belong in that neighborhood. According to the U.S. Commission on Civil Rights (1992), harassment and vandalism were the most common forms of "move-in violence." These assaults occurred in a range of neighborhoods, including suburban communities where middle-class and professional Asian Americans resided in low-income homes that recent Southeast Asian refugees found affordable (Fong, 2002, p. 165). Incidents ranged from egg-throwing, to shattering windows with rocks or BB guns, to more serious acts of vandalism, including firebombings (Fong, 2002, p. 165).

More than a century after their initial arrival in the United States, the image of Asian Americans as perpetual foreigners persists. The treatment of Asian Americans as perpetual foreigners can be traced to federal immigration policies. The Chinese Exclusion Act of 1882 was the first major victory for exclusionists to rid the Chinese from the United States (U.S. Commission on Civil Rights, 1992). During the Supreme Court's approval of the Chinese Exclusion Act in 1889, the justices characterized Chinese immigration as "aggression and encroachment" because the Chinese individuals were "foreigners of a different race" (Wu, 2002, p. 92).

Asian Americans are also stereotyped as "model minorities." What does the term imply? The term "model" suggests that Asian Americans are in a better class position than other racial minority groups, or it could also be directed at other racial minority groups for emulation (Gotanda, 1995). The Asian immigrant who exceeds expectations and achieves unimaginable success also vindicates the American dream. Such triumphs demonstrate the payoffs of hard work, prove the power of the free market, and cover up racial discrimination. The latter part of the term, "minority," imposes a racial hierarchy by placing Asian Americans in a subsidiary position, distancing them from the Caucasian majority. The term "model," in conjunction with "minority," emphasizes a three-tier racial order with the Caucasian majority at the top, the Asian American "model minority" in the middle, and other minority groups at the bottom. For the Asian American who is depicted as a "four-eyed honor student," the image is positive compared to the stereotype of an African American "street thug." The three-tier model not only perpetuates racial discrimination, it also creates animosity among racial minority groups (Wu, 2002, p. 67).

> In some of the readings that I read, the reading says that Asians are the model minorities in the U.S. . . . Actually, there was an article in *Reader's Digest* 20 years ago. They were asking whether or not Asians are smarter than the white kids because most of the Asians excel in music. They found out that Asians aren't more superior but that the Asian culture emphasizes discipline. Parents are more involved and children are more disciplined than Americans [Caucasians]. (Elisa, first-generation Chinese Filipino, Warren, New Jersey)

In terms of job security, I know I will not get fired, but pretty certain I will hit a glass ceiling . . . I was told I was not qualified at my company for a promotion, even though I have three years of experience and received a promotion in the past, and I have a great track record . . . These glass walls serve as a barrier to prevent ethnic minorities to gaining an entrée to line-management positions. Minorities are good enough only to be in support positions as opposed to being a decision maker . . . I do feel that in certain circles job opportunities are limited, like at my company . . . There are many companies that talk very loudly of ethnic ranking. For some companies it is true, for some it is not. If you put everyone in a pecking order, ethnic minorities will be in the bottom half in support roles. The majority [white] are in decision-making roles and a few token blacks are in line management, the decision-making roles. (Peter, second-generation Korean American, East Brunswick, New Jersey)

These respondents are well aware of the popular portrayal of Asian Americans as "model minorities." The model-minority concept became popular in the 1960s with the appearance of several articles in major news media that discussed the success of Asians in America (Fong, 1998, p. 56). The initial articles emphasized Asians overcoming adversity and hardship. Two and a half decades later, the model-minority image focuses on the economic success of Asian Americans achieved through an extremely hard work ethic and strong family ties (Fong, 1998, p. 70).

As Elisa's narrative above suggests, some Asian Americans have enjoyed enormous academic and financial success; they are overrepresented in some of the nation's elite universities and in certain specialized sectors of the labor force. The problem, however, is that these successes have become exaggerated and distorted.[1] Although someone may have good intentions in calling an Asian American a "model minority," Asian Americans believe the myth is neither true nor flattering. The model-minority stereotype is a gross simplification of the multiplicity of Asian ethnic groups because it perpetuates a misleading image of groupwide economic, educational, and professional successes, as well as images of political passivity and submissiveness to authority (Takaki, 1998). It also hides within the statement an inflammatory taunt against other racial minority groups for not "making it" or sharing the same kinds of success.

Peter's statement also demonstrates an understanding that the messages of the model-minority myth are condescending toward racial minorities (Wu, 2002). According to the respondent, the line-management positions are managers who handle the most important jobs, such as sales and marketing. Line managers steer a company in a specific direction. The support-management roles include research and development, sales support, and administrative work. To him, these are secondary positions in the company that only minimally affect its direction. Although the respondent is a graduate of two of the most prestigious American universities, Harvard and Columbia, he believes that the model-minority stereotype, the belief that Asian Americans are good, subservient followers but not leaders, will limit his full potential in the company.

Wu (2002) poignantly draws attention to the fact that there are also two sides to the model-minority myth. Every good attribute matches up with a bad side. For example, to be successful in entrepreneurship is to be inscrutable, cold, and calculating; to be hardworking is to be an unfair competitor; to be analytical (strong in math and sciences) is to lack interpersonal and managerial skills; to be law-abiding is to be inflexible and legalistic. During periods of widespread economic turmoil or military crises, the negative aspect of the stereotype becomes emphasized. The stereotype of hardworking Asian Americans can lead to resentment on the part of non–Asian Americans who have just lost their jobs, and who might view the gains of Asian Americans as their own loss. In this case, Asian Americans are no longer portrayed as hardworking individuals, but as cold, unfair competitors. Through the justification of the model-minority myth, humiliation and physical attacks directed against Asian Americans become compensatory and retaliatory (Wu, 2002, p. 70).

> If something happens to North Korea and America then I think that some Caucasians will treat us differently. If there is a war, then they won't treat us like an American, but not like the Japanese internment times; but some people might resent me if they think that I'm South Korean or North Korean . . . then I think it will be different. I did hear from a co-worker telling me that, "Why did you come from Asia and take away our jobs?" I told him that you immigrated from another country, this was where the Indians lived and it's not your country . . . I got hired later than him and promoted before him, so he got upset and to my face he said, "I don't know why you Asians come over here and take over all the jobs." I told him it's not only your country, but my country. I told him that you have a lot more advantages than me—you're a Caucasian male, and it's because you are lazy that you didn't get a promotion. I told you I like to speak my mind and I did. He kept quiet. I'm not like most Asians who keep quiet. (Mary, second-generation Korean American, Yorba Linda, California)

These examples illustrate how the model-minority perception can justify blame or ill-treatment. The perception of Asian Americans as model minorities also serves as a catalyst for the most dangerous types of assaults against them, including murder (see *Harvard Law Review*, 1993). In Detroit during the recession of 1982, Vincent Chin, a 27-year-old Chinese American, was brutally murdered with a baseball bat. Two white men—Ronald Ebens, an auto plant supervisor, and his stepson Michael Nitz—had been recently laid off and blamed Japan for problems in the U.S. auto industry. Ebens and

Nitz—thinking that Chin was Japanese—called him a "Jap" and cursed: "It's because of you motherfuckers that we're out of work" (cited in Takaki, 1998, p. 481). Ebens provoked Chin in a bar, yelling at him, and, afterward, Ebens and Nitz chased Chin to a nearby McDonald's and beat him into a comatose state.[2] Two days later, Chin was removed from life support. Even if Ebens and Nitz believed that their unemployment was a result of unfair Japanese government trade practices, when they singled out Chin and attacked him, they transferred blame not only from the Japanese government to the Japanese people, but also to all people in American bearing Asian features (see *Harvard Law Review*, 1993). Ebens and Nitz were arrested at the scene; both men were convicted of homicide without premeditation and manslaughter. The Michigan judge sentenced each man to only three years' probation and a fine of $3,780. Outraged at the senselessness of the killing and at the light sentence, Asian Americans viewed Chin as a martyr whose death "galvanized the Asian American community and led to a nationwide call for federal intervention" (Fong, 1998, p. 140).

At the time of Chin's murder, American automakers were experiencing unprecedented competition from Japanese imports and blaming them for the mass layoffs. Tensions during this period made race central to everything about the Chin case (Wu, 2002, p. 70). The only association Chin had with Japan was his presumed race. The frustration and hostility targeted toward individuals of Asian descent or Asian governments transferred to an entire American population through the concept of race. This is not an uncommon experience for racial minorities and demonstrates how stereotypes can quickly expand the Asian American victim class.[3] This phenomenon, repeated again and again, ensures that individuals are attacked because they are assumed to be nonwhite members of a certain racial group.

Helen Zia (2000), a leading activist during the Vincent Chin trial, recalls that union officials believed that Chin's brutal murder would have been understandable if he was actually Japanese. Zia emphasized that foreign competition was not the cause for mass unemployment, but poor designs and inferior quality in building fuel-efficient cars were. She also stressed that American automakers relocating assembly plants overseas significantly reduced jobs in the United States. While American manufacturers were running television commercials and campaigns to "buy American," these same American automakers were investing in Japanese auto companies themselves—General Motors owns 34 percent of Isuzu, which builds the Buick Opel; Ford 25 percent of Mazda, which makes transmissions for the Escort model; and Chrysler 15 percent of Mitsubishi, which produces the Colt and Charger models (cited in Takaki, 1998, p. 483). The message that American automakers were conveying to frustrated employees was that foreign imports were taking away their jobs (Takaki, 1998, p. 483). Local car dealers also supported this sentiment by holding raffles for the honor of taking a baseball bat to a Toyota to bash it to pieces (Wu, 2002, p. 71). According to Wu, other individuals responded to the instigation by keying Hondas and bashing Toyotas to pieces.

Stereotypes that are grounded in identifying features of racial minorities consequently provide motive and rationale for verbal and physical assaults against minority groups (Perry, 2001, p. 63). These racial differences are frequently demonized and are, at the very least, the ingredients used to categorize groups in a subordinated place (Ogawa, 1999). Acting upon these stereotypes allows dominant group members to reaffirm their race as superior while simultaneously ostracizing the "other" for their presumed traits and behaviors.

RESPONDING TO THREAT: PROTECTING ONESELF FROM THE PENALTIES OF DIFFERENCE

The two narratives below illustrate how some Asian Americans may act in order to protect themselves from being singled out as nonwhite, different, or worse from a racially motivated attack. These narratives demonstrate how Asian Americans integrate the threat of hate violence into their lives, and how it affects intraracial or intragroup harmony among Asian Americans by dividing Asian interethnic groups in the process.

> In elementary school, I was picked on by the "stupid elements." I didn't speak any English so I was put in the stupid class . . . I felt picked on for those circumstances and by other Asians who felt like they were better because they were in America longer. They formed alliances with whites and felt some compulsion to pick on new immigrants. They wanted to prove they were Americans and wanted to prove that they belonged. They wanted to prove that they were different from the "FOBs" [fresh-off the boat, or newly arrived Asian immigrants], so they had to physically alienate themselves; language was not enough. (Peter, second-generation Korean American, Rahway, New Jersey)

At times, minorities attempt to move up the hierarchy by adopting the ways of those at the top who perpetuate it in order to maintain their privileged status. Mathur (2001, p. 100) might call this phenomenon internalized racism. He points out that certain communities of color try to distance themselves from other communities of color in order to benefit from white-supremacist institutions; on an individual level, this practice means that people of color will sometimes try to pass for white. If that is not possible physically, then other methods of becoming white are favored, including the adoption of racist values and judgments (Mathur, 2001, pp. 100–101).

This pursuit of becoming "white" reflects not only the oppressive nature of racial hierarchy, but also the inherent privileges of being white and the penalties for "not belonging." The response among those who experience hate by rejecting their own identity as a victim-group member can involve an effort to disassociate themselves from those who are "different" through the adoption of acceptable "white behavior," such as befriending whites, eating similar foods as whites, and speaking English free from an Asian accent. Protection from racial hatred and potential violence is gained through separating or disassociating oneself from the victim group, even to the point of rejecting that group (Matsuda, Lawrence, Delgado, & Crenshaw, 1993). This self-protective behavior superficially places Asian Americans as "near whites" and socially distances them from the "foreigner image." Chow (2001), who speaks of his experience growing up as an immigrant, writes that "language demarcates the places of my 'not belonging' as much as my flat nose, and my wide cheeks" (p. 105). Asian immigrant Cao O (1992), in reflecting on his status in the United States, writes, "No matter how many years I am here—even till I die—I will always speak English with an accent . . . That is a fact that I cannot escape from. And people would never see me as an American because the conventional wisdom is that if you are American you should speak with no accent" (p. 127, in Lee, 1992).

Physically separating oneself from being perceived as an "FOB" is another maneuver used to distance oneself from those who are viewed as different and therefore part of the "victim group." *FOB* is a derogatory term related to a newly arrived Asian who speaks broken English and is unfamiliar with the "American ways." Condemning an FOB is portrayed as another "white behavior" that places Asian Americans on the side of whites and further from the "foreigner image." Fong (2002) writes that there are serious conflicts between native-born and foreign-born students of the same racial and/or ethnic group. American-born Asian Americans often look down on and want to disassociate themselves from immigrant students (p. 98).

> Most of the emotional scars I have are from high school. I'm 33 years old and I'm still trying to get over them . . . I was dumb; I decided to join the cheerleading squad, which was the biggest mistake for me because I stood out in a white cheerleading squad. The girl I bumped off was white and the other cheerleaders weren't nice to me. They weren't nice to me and would make racial comments . . . I only made it for a one-year term, and I quit after that. I didn't want to deal with it anymore. I literally injured myself to try and get out of cheerleading before the year ended. We were doing an illegal pyramid and I decided to pick the hot spot, and the hot spot is the position you are most prone to get injured. I landed the wrong way, tore up the ligaments in my knee and couldn't cheer anymore for the rest of the year. I still have problems with my knees . . . So I guess I did go through my hate crime . . . I was the only racial minority on the team . . . One of the girls said, "You deserved it," and the other girls said, "I'm sorry." But I never really befriended anybody from the squad. (Mari, second-generation Japanese American, Bridgewater, New Jersey)

As the "other" who does not belong and who supposedly does not deserve to be on the cheerleading squad and, even worse, who replaced a white girl who did belong, the Asian woman who made the above statement described the terror she experienced as a "racial outcast." According to Mari, the continual taunting and teasing was so severe at school and among her cheerleading peers that the impact is still felt today. Mari states that "my friends think maybe I was molested when I was a child, but, at age 30, I realized it has to do with the silly emotional scars that I had in high school." Although she approached her coach for help, she did so knowing that she would not be able to discuss the real "race problems." According to Mari, "I didn't tell my coach why I didn't want to be on the team because that means there would be repercussion from the other girls." Although making the varsity cheerleading squad, especially as a young sophomore, is generally a reason for celebration, making the varsity team was a primary reason why she dreaded and hated attending school. Mari was terrorized by these circumstances and found that the only options she had were to hurt herself and endure the physical injury, or deal with the persistent taunting and intimidation. Feeling despondent and with no other solution in mind, protecting herself meant injuring herself and removing herself from this hostile environment.

Although Asian Americans vary in their responses in how they cope with racial bias and the threat of violence, the respondents in the narratives above are soberly aware of the harmful consequences of racial stigmatization. This awareness can powerfully shape how Asian Americans think and behave, even to the point of jeopardizing interethnic group relations and inflicting self-injury. Racial bigotry and the threat of violence permeate the minds of Asian Americans; whether through social distancing or de-accentuating what is "different," Asian Americans must find ways to protect themselves from harm.

FINAL DISCUSSION

Asian Americans now make up one of the fastest-growing ethnic minority groups in the United States. The recent growth of the Asian American population has been dramatic. In 1960, there were 877,934 Asian Americans living in the United States, making up less than 0.5 percent of the total population (Wu, 2002). In 1985, Asian Americans numbered over 5 million, or 2.1 percent of the total population, which was an increase of 577 percent (Wu, 2002). In 2000, there were over 10 million Asian Americans, making up 4.2 percent of the total U.S. population (U.S. Census Bureau, 2002). The dramatic growth of Asian Americans in the U.S. population is largely related to the influx of immigrants and refugees from mainland Asia and the Pacific Islands during the post-1965 era (U.S. Commission on Civil Rights, 1992). Today, Asian Americans make up a large percentage of all immigrants. This increase has not only drawn more attention to this diverse group of people but will undoubtedly also affect the study of race relations.

In spite of the fact that Asian Americans are a vastly diverse community with important intragroup differences in language, religion, politics, culture, class, and color, Asian ethnics share a common bond based upon their historical treatment as racial minorities in the United States. They have long been acutely aware of their potential as targets due to the offenders' focus on their racial distinctiveness (Fong, 1998). Asian immigrants, like other racial minorities, have endured strong resistance to their incorporation as full citizens. At different times and places, they have faced discriminatory immigration and naturalization policies; discriminatory federal, state, and local laws; discriminatory treatment by the government; hostility from the general public; and racial violence (see Okihiro, 2001; Takaki, 1998).

This chapter has presented the thoughts and reflections of Asian Americans. These narratives demonstrate how bias affects the way Asian Americans perceive themselves and how they think they are perceived in the context of the larger community. Asian Americans are reminded of their "inferior" racial identity and expend much energy thinking about how others in their community perceive them (see Tuan, 1998, p. 104). This chapter also illustrates the importance of narrative research, particularly in demonstrating the psychic and emotional injury racial bigotry and hate crimes cause on targeted communities.

I have also articulated the importance of difference and the stigmatization of difference. Ancheta (1998) argues that "differences set Asian Americans apart from whites; differences set Asian Americans apart from blacks; and differences frequently set Asian Americans apart from each other" (p. 171). The stigmatization of Asian Americans has undoubtedly shaped their immigration status, the perception of them as foreigners and model minorities, and their treatment in the United States. As with Asian Americans, images of people in different groups can be shaped to fit the purpose for which they are needed regardless of the way people actually behave (Levin, 2002, pp. 8–9). Furthermore, as Levin points out, during difficult times, such as periods of intense competition and scarce jobs, even though the underlying cause of conflict may be economic, dehumanizing stereotypes may be used to justify mayhem and bloodshed against a group.

NOTES

1. Despite their high levels of education, Asian American men receive lower salaries when compared to their white male counterparts. In 1990, highly educated Asian American males received 10 percent less than white males even when they were more likely to hold advanced degrees. Asian American men were also less likely to hold a job as executives, administrators, or managers when compared to white men (23% versus 31%;

Espiritu, 1996). The use of "family income" by politicians has also obscured this disparity, given that Asian American families have more workers per family than white families (Takaki, 1998).

2. See *United States v. Ebens*, 800 F.2d 1422,1427 (6th Cir. 1986).

3. Having an entire racial population blamed for the action of one individual is also a common phenomenon for African Americans (Mann, 1993).

REFERENCES

Abelmann, N., & Lie, J. (1995). *Blue dreams: Korean Americans and the Los Angeles riots.* Cambridge, MA: Harvard University Press.

Adler, P. A., & Adler, P. (2001). *Sociological odyssey: Contemporary readings in sociology.* Belmont, CA: Wadsworth Thomson Learning.

Ancheta, N. N. (1998). *Race, rights, and the Asian American experience.* New Brunswick, NJ: Rutgers University Press

Anti-Defamation League. (2004). Retrieved November 10, 2004, from http://www.adl.org/combating:hate/

Asante, M. K., & Min, E. (Eds.). (2000). *Socio-cultural conflict between African American and Korean American.* Lanham, MD: University Press of America.

Bell, J. (2002). *Policing hatred: Law enforcement, civil rights, and hate crime.* New York: New York University Press.

Bowling, B. (1993). Racial harassment and the process of victimization. *British Journal of Criminology, 33*(2), 231–250.

Champion, D. J. (1993). *Research methods for criminal justice and criminology.* Englewood Cliffs, NJ: Regents/Prentice Hall.

Chow, R. (2001). Fire at my face: Growing up immigrant. In P. W. Hall & V. M. Hwang (Eds.), *Anti-Asian violence in North America: Asian American and Asian Canadian reflections on hate, healing, and resistance* (pp. 105–119). New York: Alta Mira Press.

Delgado, R. (2001). Storytelling, counterstorytelling, and "naming one's own reality." In R. Delgado & J. Stefancic (Eds.), *Critical race theory: An introduction.* New York: New York University Press.

Delgado, R., & Stefancic, J. (2001). *Critical race theory: An introduction.* New York: New York University Press.

Dillof, A. M. (1997) Punishing bias: An examination of the theoretical foundations of bias crime statute. *Northwestern University Law Review, 91*(3): 3.

Espiritu, Y. L. (1997). *Asian American women and men.* Thousand Oaks, CA: Sage.

Fong, T. P. (1998). *The contemporary Asian American experience.* Upper Saddle River, NJ: Prentice Hall.

Fong, T. P. (2002). *The contemporary Asian American experience: Beyond the model minority* (2nd ed.). Upper Saddle River, NJ: Prentice Hall.

Garofalo, J., & Martin, S. E. (1993). The law enforcement response to bias-motivated crime. In R. J. Kelly (Ed.), *Bias crime: American law enforcement and legal responses* (pp. 64–80). Chicago: Office of International Criminal Justice, University of Illinois at Chicago.

Gerstenfeld, P. B. (2003). *Hate crimes, causes, controls and controversies.* Thousand Oaks, CA: Sage.

Gotanda, N. (1995). Reproducing the model minority stereotype: Judge Joyce Kar-
lin's sentencing colloquy in People v. Soon Ja Du. In W. L. Ng, S.-Y. Chin, J. S.
Moy, & G Y. Okihiro (Eds.), *Reviewing Asian America, locating diversity*. Pullman:
Washington State University Press.

Hagan, F. E. (1997). *Research methods in criminal justice and criminology* (4th ed.). Boston: Allyn & Bacon.

Hamm, M. S. (1993). *American skinheads: The criminology and control of hate crime*.
Westport, CT: Praeger.

Harvard Law Review. (1993). Racial violence against Asian Americans. In B. Perry
(Ed.), (2003) *Hate and bias crime: A reader* (pp. 223–234). New York: Routledge.

Herek, G. M., & Berril, K. T. (1992). *Hate crimes: Confronting violence against lesbians
and gay men*. Newbury Park, CA: Sage.

Hwang, Victor (2001). "The Interrelationship Between Anti-Asian Violence and
Asian America." In Hall, Patricia Wong and Victor M. Hwang (Eds.), *Anti-Asian
Violence in North America: Asian American and Asian Canadian Reflections on Hate,
Healing, and Resistance* (pp. 43–66). Walnut Creek, AltaMira Press.

Iganski, P. (2001). Hate crimes hurt more. *American Behavioral Scientist*, 45(4),
627–638.

Iganski, Paul. (2002). Introduction: The problem of hate crimes and hate crime laws.
In P. Iganski (Ed.), *The hate debate: Should hate be punished as a crime?* (pp. 1–14).
London: Profile Books Ltd., in association with the Institute for Jewish Policy
Research.

Jacobs, J. B., & K. Potter. (1998). *Hate crimes: Criminal law and identity politics*. New
York: Oxford University Press.

Jacoby, J. (2002). Punish crime, not thought crime. In P. Iganski (Ed.), *The hate debate:
Should hate be punished as a crime?* (pp. 114–122). London: Profile Books Ltd., in
association with the Institute for Jewish Policy Research.

Lawrence, F. (1999). *Punishing hate: Bias crimes under American law*. Cambridge, MA:
Harvard University Press.

Lawrence, F. (2002). *Punishing hate: Bias crimes under American law* (2nd ed.).
Cambridge, MA: Harvard University Press.

Kim, C. J. (2000). *Bitter fruit: The politics of Black-Korean conflict in New York City*. New
Haven, CT: Yale University Press.

Lee, J. F. (Ed.). (1992). *Asian Americans: Oral histories of first to fourth generation Americans form China, the Philippines, Japan, India, the Pacific Islands, Vietnam and Cambodia*. New York: The New Press.

Levin, J. (2002). *The violence of hate: Confronting racism, anti-Semitism, and other forms
of bigotry*. Boston: Allyn & Bacon.

Levin, J., & McDevitt, J. (2002). *Hate crimes revisited: America's war on those who are
different*. Cambridge, MA: Westview Press.

Levin, J., & Rabrenovic, G. (2004). *Why we hate*. New York: Prometheus Books.

Lopez, H. (1997). Racial restrictions in the law of citizenship. In N. Gates (Ed.), *Critical race theory: Racial classification and history* (pp. 109–125). New York: Garland
Publishing.

Mann, C. R. (1993). *Unequal justice: A question of color*. Bloomington: Indiana University Press.

Mathur, A. (2001). Some substitute stories, out of school. In P. W. Hall & V. M. Hwang (Eds.), *Anti-Asian violence in North America: Asian American and Asian Canadian reflections on hate, healing, and resistance* (pp. 93–104). Walnut Creek, CA: AltaMira Press.

Matsuda, M., Lawrence, C. R. III, Delgado, R., & Crenshaw, K. W. (1993). *Words that wound: Critical race theory, assaultive speech, and the First Amendment*. Boulder, CO: Westview Press.

National Asian Pacific Legal Consortium (NAPALC). (1999). *Audit of violence against Asian Pacific Americans*. Washington, DC: Author.

O, C. (1992). To be more American. In J. F. Lee, (Ed.), *Asian Americans: Oral histories of first to fourth generation Americans form China, the Philippines, Japan, India, the Pacific Islands, Vietnam and Cambodia* (pp. 104–106). New York: The New Press.

Ogawa, B. (1999). *Color of justice* (2nd ed.). Boston: Allyn & Bacon.

Okihiro, G. Y. (1994). *Margins and mainstreams: Asians in American history and culture*. Seattle: University of Washington Press.

Okihiro, L. (2001). *The Columbia guide to Asian American history*. New York: Columbia University Press.

Omi, M., & Winant, H. (1994). *Racial formation in the United States: From the 1960s to the 1990s* (2nd ed.). New York Routledge.

Perry, B. (2001). *In the name of hate: Understanding hate crimes*. New York: Routledge.

Perry, B. (2003a). *Hate and bias crime: A reader*. New York: Routledge.

Perry, B. (2003b). Where do we go from here?: Researching hate crime. *Internet Journal of Criminology (IJC)*. Retrieved December 21, 2008 from http://www.internet journalofcriminology.com/

Pincus, F. L., & Ehrlich, H. (Eds.). (1999). *Race and ethnic conflict: Contending views on prejudice, discrimination, and ethnoviolence* (2nd ed.). Boulder, CO: Westview Press.

Smedley, A. (1998). 'Race' and the construction of human identity. *American Anthropologist, 100*(3), 690–702.

Takaki, R. (1998). *A history of Asian Americans: Strangers from a different shore* (Rev. ed.). New York: Back Bay Books.

Tuan, M. (1998). *Forever foreigners or honorary whites?* New Brunswick, NJ: Rutgers University Press.

United States v. Ebens, 800 F.2d 1422, 1427 (6th Cir. 1986).

U.S. Census Bureau. (2000). U.S. Census 2000. Retrieved December 21, 2008 from http://quickfacts.census.gov/qfd/states/34/34035.html

U.S. Census Bureau. (2002). United States Census 2000. Washington DC: U.S. Department of Commerce Economics and Statistics Administration, U.S. Census Bureau.

U.S. Commission on Civil Rights. (1992). *Civil rights issues facing Asian Americans in the 1990s*. Washington, DC: Author.

Wang, L.-i. (1999). The complexities of hate. *Ohio State Law Journal, 60*(3), 799–900.

Wang, L.-i. (2000). *Hate crimes law*. St. Paul, MN: West Group.

Wu, F. (2002). *Yellow: Race in America beyond black and white*. New York: Basic Books.

Yamamoto, E. K. (1999). *Interracial justice: Conflict and reconciliation in post-civil rights America*. New York: New York University.

Zia, H. (2000). *Asian American dreams: The emergence of an American people*. New York: Farrar, Straus and Giroux.

CHAPTER 5

ISLAMOPHOBIA AND HATE CRIME

Scott Poynting

According to the Runnymede Trust's (1997) report, *Islamophobia: A Challenge for Us All*, the term *Islamophobia* was originally "coined in the late 1980s, its first known use in print being in February 1991, in a periodical in the United States. The word is not ideal, but is recognizably similar to *xenophobia* and *Europhobia* and is a useful shorthand way of referring to dread or hatred of Islam—and, therefore, to fear or dislike of all or most Muslims" (p. 1). The Runnymede report enumerated eight ideological elements of Islamophobia.

1. Islam as monolithic, static, and unresponsive to new realities;
2. Islam as separate and other—not having any aims or values in common with other cultures, not affected by them and not influencing them;
3. Islam as inferior to the West—barbaric, irrational primitive, sexist;
4. Islam as violent, threatening, aggressive, supportive of terrorism, engaged in "a clash of civilizations";
5. Islam as a political ideology, used for political or military advantage;
6. That criticisms made by Islam of the West are rejected out of hand;
7. That hostility toward Islam is used to justify discriminatory practices towards Muslims and exclusion of Muslims from mainstream society; and
8. That anti-Muslim hostility is accepted as natural and normal.

To this list could be added the sexualizing of the supposed deviance of the "Muslim Other" (Dagistanli, 2007).

This demonization of the Muslim Other as a racialized folk devil involves the dynamics of moral panic. Poynting, Noble, Tabar, and Collins (2004) have described the ideological assemblage outlined above as "the pre-eminent folk devil of our time" (p. 3). Arun Kundnani (2007) has argued that, "Ultimately, the impact of this stigmatising discourse is to be measured in the numbers of racially motivated attacks" (p. 128).

THE IMPACT

The state is not widely disposed to recognize and record such numbers of racially motivated attacks (Poynting & Perry, 2007, pp. 155–156), but the trend is undeniable. For example, in the United States, the number of civil rights complaints reported to the Council on American-Islamic Relations (CAIR) increased from 322 in 1999–2000 to 2,467 in 2006, an increase over the period of 766 percent (CAIR, 2007, p. 8). During 2005–2006, the increase was from 1,972 to 2,467, or an increase of 25 percent on the 2005 figure (CAIR, 2007, p. 8).

In Canada, the Canadian Islamic Congress (CIC; 2003) reported a 16-fold increase in anti-Muslim hate crime from the year up to 9/11 to the year following: a rise from 11 to 173 incidents. The figures in Canada also continue to rise. Pending the effecting of a federal antidiscrimination plan in which nationwide hate crime statistics will be compiled, the trends can be gleaned from the records of the Toronto Police Service: a rise from 132 incidents in 2005 to 162 in 2006, or an increase of 23 percent in one year (McClintock & LeGendre, 2007).

In the United Kingdom, religious hate crime attacks, mostly against Muslims, increased in the capital by a factor of six in the weeks of 2005 following the July 7 London transport bombings, according to the records of the London Metropolitan Police (BBC News, 2005; Kundnani, 2007, p. 128;).

In Australia, a Human Rights and Equal Opportunities Commission survey of 186 Arab-background and Muslim residents in Sydney and Melbourne (Poynting & Noble, 2004) registered that 87 percent of the Muslim respondents had been victims of racism, abuse, or racist violence since 9/11, with three-quarters of them having experienced increased racism since that date. A report on complaints to the telephone hotline of the Community Relations Commission for a Multicultural New South Wales (CRC) set up on September 12, 2001, to monitor the anticipated anti-Muslim reaction (Dreher, 2005), showed 248 incidents of reported racial hatred in New South Wales in the two months following 9/11. In about half the cases where the victim's religion could be discerned, over two-thirds were Muslim; and nearly all others (except 3) were Sikh, most of these probably misidentified as Muslim, as recorded during the 1991 Gulf War and also as in other countries after 9/11.

These few figures give a clear indication of a tendency that stretches across the global West, but they don't tell much either about the experience and the processes of hate crime, or about its causes. The following sections present snapshots of some serious anti-Muslim hate crimes since 9/11, then consider questions of motivation.

INSTANCES OF ISLAMOPHOBIA

On October 4, 2001, less than a month after the 9/11 attacks, Indian immigrant Vasudev Patel was shot dead in a racist murder at the gas station where he was working in Mesquite, Texas. "God bless America!" exclaimed the assassin, as he discharged a large caliber pistol, firing at close range into Patel's upper body (Pierre, 2002). Because many of the critics of the figures quoted above argue that the figures exaggerate anti-Muslim hate crime, by counting crimes with other motivations or hate crimes motivated by race or nationality but not religion, it may be instructive to listen to the perpetrators in cases where they speak of their motives. In this case the killer, Mark Anthony Stroman, said he wanted to "retaliate on local Arab Americans, or whatever you want to call them" (p. A1). Stroman boasted that his crime was "what every American wanted to do" but "didn't have the nerve." What do we want to call them, the victims of such crimes? Stroman, a white supremacist, called them "Arab Americans, or whatever." In the days before he murdered Vasudev Patel, he had shot dead a Pakistani-background shop assistant and shot and blinded a Bangladeshi immigrant clerk. On the day he was arrested, he said he was planning to shoot people in a Dallas mosque (Pierre, 2002, p. A1). Even if Stroman and those like him, in their conflation of the objects of their hatred, think that Indians, Pakistanis, Bangladeshis, and all attendees of mosques are "Arabs," these were Islamophobic hate crimes.

On July 10, 2005, three days after Britain's notorious two-figure date, 7/7, Pakistani visitor Kamal Raza Butt was beaten to death by a gang of youths in Nottingham, England, as he emerged from a corner store. They abused him as "Taliban." The young man who delivered the killer blow was never convicted, for want of witnesses prepared to testify (Athwal, 2006; Booth, 2005; Dodd, 2005a; Kundnani, 2007, p. 128). One member of his cohort was subsequently convicted of manslaughter by common purpose and sentenced to 18 months' imprisonment. Nottinghamshire Police labeled the crime as "racially aggravated," but not Islamophobic. They asserted that it was not linked to an anti-Muslim backlash to the London bombings. Meanwhile, their superintendent deemed it "inappropriate to comment on the possible motive," and claimed that it was a "localised" and "isolated" incident (Dodd, 2005a). The figures, as shown above, tell a different story. Azad Ali, the chair of the Muslim Safety Forum, stressed that the shouted abuse and the crime were Islamophobic. He declared that it would spread fear among Muslim Britons. This spread of fear, of course, is a key purpose of hate crime. "This has sent shivers down the community," said Ali. "People are very worried, if this is the start of an escalation" (Dodd, 2005a). The statistics show that they were right.

In Australia on December 11, 2005, a racist riot by a mob of some five thousand on Sydney's Cronulla beach violently targeted Muslims and those of "Middle Eastern appearance" (Poynting, 2006). According to police, paramedics, and press who were present, it was a minor miracle that no one was killed in the mayhem. One young Arab-background man was bashed, and bottles were smashed over his back. Another was found by police, beaten and lying in a pool of blood. Residents watched a group of men jump on a further victim's head (Overington & Warne-Smith, 2005, p. 20). By that night, at least 13 people were reported injured and 12 had been arrested (Kennedy, Murphy, Brown, & Colquhoun, 2005, p. 1). Many of the crowd had waved or even worn Australian flags, and had chanted "Aussie! Aussie! Aussie!" along with "Fuck off, Lebs [Lebanese]!" and "Fuck off, wogs!" (Four Corners, 2006). Prime Minister John Howard infamously denied that racism lay behind the riots. They took place in the context of a racist moral panic about the failure of Muslim immigrants to integrate to Australian society, a discourse to which the prime minister and his conservative coalition government had opportunistically contributed over the previous decade, especially since 9/11 and 7/7.

On what basis were the Cronulla victims selected? The campaign of mobile phone text messages, repeated in the press and on commercial talk-back radio, had urged Aussies to "get down to North Cronulla to help support Leb- and wog-bashing day." A Russian-born Afghan immigrant, Ali, found himself surrounded in the melee; two Bangladeshi students were chased and had their fleeing car pelted with bottles; a teenage girl wearing the *hijab* was pursued over a sand hill, and had her head-cover ripped off and waved around like a trophy. Riot participants explained to ABC TV reporter Liz Jackson that they were motivated by outrage at the imagined asserting of *sharia* law in Australia and at supposed Muslim disrespect for women (Four Corners, 2006).

INSTIGATION

There is a powerful argument that this sort of event can be instigated by pronouncements of populist politicians that are at best opportunistic and irresponsible. In recent years, these have often involved attacks on multiculturalism and have been concerned with the purported failure of Muslim immigrants to "integrate" to what is seen as the "mainstream" society. The more extreme versions of this ideology cast Muslim communities as inherently disrespectful of Western law and even criminally inclined. Thus, these versions implicate the "war on terror" with a "war on (ethnic minority) crime" or gangs (Poynting et al., 2004). In the months before the Cronulla rioters shouted "Fuck off, Lebs," Australia's Education Minister Brendan Nelson had threatened government surveillance of mosques and Muslim schools to ensure they were promoting "Australian values," and announced that those who would not integrate could "clear off" (PM, 2005). At the same time, Treasurer Peter Costello was telling Muslims that if they did not respect Australian values and law, if they preferred *sharia* law, then they could leave the country (Lateline, 2005).

In October 2006, British Member of Parliament for Blackburn—a northern English town with a large Muslim immigrant population—Jack Straw, a former and subsequent government minister, decried the wearing by Muslim women of the face-covering veil, or *niqab*, saying that it was a "visible statement of separation and of difference" (McClintock & LeGendre, 2007, p. 6). He said that he asked his constituents to remove it during consultations and suggested that it was detrimental to community relations. His statement was publicly supported by British Prime Minister Tony Blair and other leading Labour politicians. Ironically, it led to a defiant increase in the wearing of the *niqab* by British Muslim women, especially the young (Suleaman, 2006). It also led, according to British Muslim organizations, to "increased levels of hostility and harassment against Muslim women" (Bennetto, Herbert, & Clarke, 2006; McClintock & LeGendre, 2007, p. 6).

In April 2006, a young man was stabbed to death in a Brussels railway station after two youths had accosted him to steal his MP3 player. The perpetrators were immediately (and falsely) reported to be North African immigrants. The *Brussels Journal* Web site, for example, which calls itself "The Voice of Conservatism in Europe," stated baldly that Joe Van Holsbeeck "was stabbed five times in the heart by North African youths" (as it turned out, they were Polish) and referred to "the fact that the killers are Muslim youths" (Belien, 2006). This incident and its aftermath took place amid strong anti-immigrant campaigning and popular feeling: the anti-immigrant Flemish Bloc, which espoused repatriation of North African immigrants, had gained 24 percent of the regional elections in 2004. In October 2005, their leader, Filip Dewinter, had told a media interviewer, "'Xenophobia' is not the word I would use. If it absolutely must be a 'phobia' let it be 'islamophobia'. Yes, we're afraid of Islam. The islamisation of Europe is a frightening thing" ("Complaint Against . . . ," 2005). By the end of 2005, some 20 Belgian municipalities had banned women from being fully veiled in the streets (Bureau of Democracy, Human Rights, and Labor, 2006). A racialized witch hunt followed the murder of Van Holsbeeck; journalist Luc van Balberghe, for example, expostulated that "society is thoroughly fed up with the dominance of murdering, thieving and raping Vikings from North Africa" (cited by Belien, 2006). For example, even the Moroccan-background Brussels MP Fouad Ahidar said that Van Holsbeeck's murder "stinks of racism," and claimed that there was a "growing group of criminal Moroccan and Turkish youths" attacking "victims who look like infidels" (Bond, 2006a).

Later that month, 23-year-old Moroccan immigrant Mohamed Bouazza was drowned in a river in Antwerp after being reportedly chased by "racist white youths" following an altercation outside a nightclub (McClintock & LeGendre, 2007, p. 5). Then, the following month, a deranged right-wing racist student, Hans van Themsche, purchased a rifle and told fellow students he was going to kill "macaques" (a racist term for foreigners). He first shot and badly wounded Songul Koç, a young Turkish woman wearing a headscarf, then Oulemata Oudibo, a pregnant Malian nanny, and the two-year-old Belgian child who was in her care, Luna Drowart, before being shot by a policeman (Bond, 2006b; McClintock & LeGendre, 2007, p. 5).

MEDIA

A 2002 report by the European Monitoring Centre on Racism and Xenophobia cited negative stereotypes of Muslims within the British media and the representing of asylum seekers as terrorists and the "enemy within" after 9/11 for the increase in violent assault, abuse, and property damage against Muslims (Allen & Neilsen, 2002, pp. 40–41). Certain sectors of the media had aggravated Islamophobia by claims of terrorists coming into Britain as asylum seekers. "Such instances were used to justify hostility in order to stop them from eradicating British values and exploiting its social welfare system at the same time. As a result, the distance between issues relating to asylum seekers and those of 9/11 began to be gradually narrowed, until the two had almost become identifiable as one" (Black, 2002). Inayat Bunglawala, of the Muslim Council of Britain, affirmed that the report corroborated the Council's media watch. "Under the cover of the war on terrorism, safeguards have been lowered for reporting on Muslims." He observed that terms like "fifth columnists" and "Muslim scroungers" had become common currency (Black, 2002).

Poynting and Mason (2006) argue that the notion from before 9/11 of these communities constituting a fifth column, coupled with media coverage of individuals such as militant cleric Abu Hamza, "have led to an amplification spiral in Britain demonising Muslims as the dangerous Other," and that "the immediate consequence of this was a range of attacks against Arab and Islamic people and communities within Britain" (p. 373). Kundnani (2007) gives a detailed and perceptive account of these processes, especially in relation to political rhetoric and governmental policies.

In Canada,[1] similar anti-Muslim racism has been identified in the media, and the implications for hate crime have been seen as comparable. A 2002 survey across Canada of some 300 Muslims of South Asian, Arab, African, and European background found that over half those surveyed believed the Canadian media were more biased since 9/11. Significantly, the report observed a "startling similarity between media myths on Islam and Muslims and the hate-text of many documented anti-Muslim incidents" (Khan, Saloojee, & Al-Shalchi, 2004). Ismael and Measor (2003) observe that, after 9/11, the blend of the xenophobic fears of the 'other', and that of terrorism, provided media consumers in Canada with a clear path to the conclusion that Islam was a faith in which acts of unspeakable violence were acceptable and that terrorism was endemic to Muslim and Arab culture. This framed Arab and Muslim societies and individuals as somehow fundamentally different from the average Canadian. By refusing to represent the diversity of Islam as a faith, the obfuscation of its tenets, and through their lack of coverage of the articulated ideas of Muslims the world over endorsing peace and supportive of human rights, the media conducted reductive exercises of the highest order.

This media framing of Muslims did not begin with 9/11, but the "war on terror" did see the intensification of existing media Islamophobia. Indeed, the CIC's *Anti-Islam in the Media* report (2005) observed that

From 1998 (the year Anti-Islam in the Media was launched) until September 11, 2001, CIC media research showed a modest average annual reduction of 17% in the use of anti-Islam language and terminology. Following that watershed date, however, and continuing during 2002, the data gathered revealed a substantial reversal of this trend. By 2003, the level of anti-Islam occurring in the Canadian media had returned to pre-9/11 levels.

The CIC (2005) has identified a number of key terms commonly used to denigrate Muslims, including the following:

- Armed Islamic group
- Canadian-based Islamic extremist
- Extreme: branches of Islam
- Extremist: Islamic group, Islamic regime
- Hard-line: Islamic regime, Muslims, Muslim regime
- Global Islamic militancy
- Fanatic: Islamic
- Fundamentalist: Islamic terror, Islamic terrorist, strain of Sunni Islam
- International: Islamic extremist, Islamic movement militancy
- Islamic: dictatorship, extremist, extremist group, extremism, fighters, fundamentalist, fundamentalism, fundamentalist terrorist groups, hard-liner, -inspired terrorist attacks, insurgency, insurgent, Jihad, Jihad militant, guerrillas, militia, hard-liners, hijacker, forces militancy, militant, militant group, purists, radical, radicalism, rebel, resistance, separatists, suicide bomber, terrorist, terrorist cells, terrorist group, terrorism, violence
- Islamist: cell, terrorism, group, militancy
- Militant: Islamic, Islamic government, Islamic group, Islamic organization, Islamic mullahs, Islamist group, Muslim
- Murderous: Islamic militant
- Muslim: activist, dictator, extremist, fundamentalist, fundamentalist militant, guerrillas, militia, militant, mercenaries, mob, vigilante group, rebel

- Puritanical Islamic militia
- Radical: armed Islamic group, Islam, Islamic fighters, Islamic group, Islamic militia, Islamist, Islamist group, Muslim, Muslim faction, Muslim organization, Islamic militant
- Violent Islamic group. (CIC, 2005)

Likewise, in Australia, Peter Manning's (2004) content analysis of the two major Sydney daily newspapers in relation to Muslims and Arabs for a year before and a year after 9/11 gives an indication of the extent and nature of the anti-Arab and anti-Muslim bias of the press. The study of the liberal broadsheet *Sydney Morning Herald* and the more right-wing Murdoch tabloid *Daily Telegraph*, as well as their Sunday stablemates, found that 30 percent of articles in these newspapers over the period concerned, dealing with the chosen categories of Arabs, Muslims, and refugees/asylum seekers, referred to "Lebanese rapists" and 45 percent to asylum seekers (Manning, 2004, p. 11). These references reflected two racialized moral panics about Middle Easterners and Muslims, which, in combination with the panic over "Muslim" terrorism, had exercised the Australian media over the period (Poynting et al., 2004). The proportion of items mentioning the words *Muslim/Islam* as well as the words *extremist, fundamentalist,* or *terrorist* increased by a factor of about 10 in the *Telegraph* and 6 in the *Herald* for the year following 9/11 (Manning, 2004). "Of those articles in the international news, [the] proportion of the total [that] mention the words 'violent', 'death', 'attack', 'kill', 'bomb', 'gun', 'terror', 'suicide' or 'gunmen' whenever the words 'Arab', 'Palestinian', 'Muslim' or 'Islam' are used is 58%" (Manning, p. 13).

In its study of bias against Arabs and Muslims in the Australian media since 9/11, the Anti-Discrimination Board of New South Wales (ADB) found that

> over the past 18 months, debates in the media about September 11, the international 'war on terror', the prospect of US-led attacks on Iraq, the Tampa dispute, Australia's policies regarding asylum seekers, and the ongoing debates about law and order in Sydney, have had the cumulative effect of generating a 'moral panic' in Australia. The central feature linking, simplifying and blurring these debates is race, encompassing concepts of ethnicity, culture, religion and nationality. Print, radio and television news media representations have increasingly drawn on race as the explanation for or cause of conflict, deviant behaviour or social problems. (ADB, 2003, p. 40)

Thus, "[w]hen heard in the media, the voices of Arabic and Muslim community leaders were perceived as less credible sources in shaping media stories, and were called on to defend their communities rather than to identify the agenda for addressing the impact of the criminalisation of their communities" (ADB, 2003, p. 78).

In the Human Rights and Equal Opportunity Commission (HREOC) survey of Arab and Muslim Australians, some 47 percent of respondents believed their communities had been vilified in the media (Poynting & Noble, 2004). In HREOC's national consultation, Arab and Muslim community interviewees argued that a lot of media coverage produces a climate conducive to the vilification and discrimination against them, and can lead to racial hatred and discrimination. Said one participant: "I reckon that the media and the propaganda that the media has caused is a big cause of discrimination against Arabic and Muslim people" (HREOC, 2004, p. 65). Another remarked, "If I wasn't Muslim myself I wouldn't like them either the way the media portrays them" (HREOC, 2004, p. 64).

Poynting and colleagues (2004, pp. 168–169) have argued that this sort of media vilification, besides inducing vigilante-type violence and individual acts of racist hatred, also calls for the forces of the state to be deployed against the "enemy within." Conversely, the state's targeted repressive measures are rationalized by "where there's smoke there's fire" logic: why should people object to covert surveillance, ongoing harassment, secret police, heavily armed dawn raids, and the like, for "our" protection, if they have nothing to hide? Moreover, state terror of this sort seems to be interpreted by outraged citizens of the dominant culture as some sort of moral license for their own violent racial attacks. This phenomenon is consonant with Barbara Perry's (2001) thesis that the media (along with the state) convey "permission to hate," which is instrumental in inculcating a feeling of entitlement to engage in vigilante, retributive, or message-sending racist violence against subordinated and/or minority groups.

Let us now consider some cases where the state has acted symbiotically with the media in ways that promote Islamophobia.

TERROR PLOTS, TRAVESTIES, AND TRAGEDIES

Outlined here are four examples of the damaging triangular dynamic between police or security forces and their spokespeople, the media, and political leaders engaged in the politics of Islamophobia. The first case is the shooting by police in London of the innocent Jean Charles de Menezes on July 22, 2005. The day after the failed London backpack bombings, and two weeks after the devastating 7/7 suicide attacks, a sevenfold leaden "tragedy" was lodged in the head of the young Brazilian-born electrician on the London Tube, as he went to work. Five specially trained officers were piled on top of him: the close range could not have been closer. You could not call it an accident.

Prime Minister Tony Blair called it a "regrettable tragedy." He did not regret the state's policy of "shoot to kill." Newspapers on the following Monday proclaimed de Menezes an "innocent man"; on Saturday they had condemned him as a "train bomber." They reported wild inventions of wires protruding from his reported heavy coat, suspicious in summer. The coat turned out to be as fictitious as the wires; he wore a light denim jacket. De Menezes was executed, without the benefit of judge, jury, or any decent prior investigation. Further evidence of guilt and imminent murderous intent as far as the media were concerned was that he was reported to look afraid of police and to flee them. Flee he did not. While a purported eyewitness account said he jumped the ticket barrier, and the police story at one stage was that he did not stop when challenged by armed plainclothes police, the official record now shows he entered the station with his electronic travel card, calmly mounted the train and sat in the first available seat (Independent Police Complaints Commission, 2006). He did have good reason to be terrified. A plainclothes officer grabbed him without warning, pinning his arms and throwing him to the floor. Just before the seven "tragic" dum-dum bullets were discharged into his brain, he was described by media sources as looking like a frightened rabbit (Calvert & Leppard, 2005). Suicide bombers are cowards, we are repeatedly told in the media. The police, however, were bravely doing their dangerous job.

The final piece of damning evidence reported at the time in the media was the Brazilian's reported "Asian" appearance: a mistaken identity and an erroneous inference, two mistakes in one (Burleigh & Fenton, 2005). The Metropolitan Police Commissioner, Sir Ian Blair, announced falsely some hours after the killing that de Menezes was "directly linked" to the antiterrorist investigation that had included surveillance of the block of flats where the Brazilian lived, and the media repeated this. By the time they were reporting the terrible mistake, they were assiduous in exculpating the police; and even the liberal *Guardian* was justifying the "shoot to kill" policy (Ali, 2005, p. 59). Tariq Ali (2005) surmises that "a premeditated execution was ordered." He asks rhetorically whether such "taking out" is employed "[a]s a deterrent in a country where capital punishment is forbidden." He reasons that such "public execution" cannot possibly deter suicide bombers; it can only put off dark-skinned people from taking the Tube (p. 64).

Since the shooting, the media have been careful to confine their criticism to the police bungling of the operation, rather than the practice of what the Israelis call *targeted assassination*. (The hollow-point projectiles to the head are only intended to stop the suspect; the killing is a mere tragic side effect.) Even two and a half years later, the yellow press was leaking details about traces of cocaine in de Menezes' blood and repeating police spin speculating that these traces would have made him jumpy and suspicious-looking. The Brazilian's real "crime" was looking too much like the targeted "Asian" 7/7 suspect for whom he was mistaken—though looking at the photos of the two men (even the police photos specially doctored for the public inquiry and the media), one would have to wonder who was taking the cocaine. There has since been little media questioning of the policy of targeting the communities concerned, not even when another innocent man, Mohammed Abdul Kahar, in a further case of mistaken identity by police, was without warning shot in the shoulder during an armed police raid on his home in East London in June 2006, and he and his brother Abul Koyair were mishandled and wrongfully arrested and interrogated (Walker & Fickling, 2006).

The second case examined here is the alleged plot to blow up the famous Old Trafford football stadium, home of the Manchester United team.[2] In April 2004, more than 400 police raided houses and businesses around Manchester, arresting 10 people who were interrogated for several days and subsequently released without charge (Panja & Bright, 2004). During the time in which the suspects were detained, the *Sun* ran the front-page headline "Man U Suicide Bomb." The inside story, "Exclusive: Man United Suicide Blasts Foiled," said that two bombers had planned to sit in separate parts of the football ground to detonate their bombs in order to maximize casualties. Greater Manchester Police called a press conference in which it stated: "We are confident that the steps that we have taken to date have significantly reduced any potential threat in the Greater Manchester area . . . Greater Manchester Police and Manchester United Football Club have put in place extra security measures to reassure the public of the safety of . . . matches" (Oborne, 2006). It later transpired that the Old Trafford bomb plot was a total fabrication leaked by police sources to the press. Police had found two used ticket stubs for different parts of the football ground kept by one of the Kurdish suspects detained—himself a Manchester United fan—as a souvenir. This find ballooned into the supposed major terrorist conspiracy. The government refused to confirm or deny the accuracy of intelligence that suggested the stadium was the subject of a terrorist plot. The consequence was that more rumors spread; local media speculated Manchester Airport and the Trafford Centre may also be terrorist targets (Oborne, 2006).

The third case presented here is the so-called "ricin plot" in London in 2002. The plot story unraveled in the Old Bailey in April 2005, when one failed Algerian asylum seeker, Kemal Bourgass, was convicted of "conspiracy to cause a public nuisance by the use of poisons and/or explosives to cause disruption, fear or injury" in an unfeasible plan to make and use poison with ricin, and all his eight co-accused were acquitted or had charges dropped (Carrell & Whitaker, 2005, p. 6). Bourgass, an "obsessive loner," was sentenced to 17 years' imprisonment for the public nuisance conspiracy, though no conspirators were convicted (Cowan & Campbell, 2005).

The ricin plot story began after September 2002, when an Algerian illegal entrant, Mohammed Meguerba, had been arrested in Britain for identity fraud, and he absconded after being released on bail, having suffered an epileptic attack (Carrell & Whitaker, 2005, p. 6). He was captured in Algeria in December 2002 by security police and almost certainly was tortured. Under interrogation, he gave an inconsistent and factually inaccurate account of a terrorist conspiracy, naming Kemal Bourgass and a number of others as fellow conspirators (Dodd, 2005b, p. 7). In early January 2003, a flat in North London was raided by police, who found a home chemistry kit and various common seeds, which were said to be ingredients for ricin and other poisons, along with (here and in later raids) written instructions, available on the Internet, for making poisons and bombs. Several young men were arrested, but Bourgass remained at large until caught by chance in an immigration raid. Authorities quickly announced that ricin had been found; although that report was soon found to be untrue, and at best a mistake, it was not publicly retracted.

In stories emanating, significantly, not from London but from Washington, the *Sydney Morning Herald* bore headlines like "Bases the target in ricin plot theory" (Risen & Van Natta, 2003) and "CIA looks into possible al-Qaeda link to ricin plot" ("CIA Looks into . . . ," 2003), as the ricin story went around the world. The following month, arguing for war against Iraq, Tony Blair addressed the British public on television, and Colin Powell addressed the world at the United Nations, claiming there were established links between Iraq and the ricin plot in England. This claim was no more true than the inventions about Iraqi weapons of mass destruction. Some days before, 150 police had invaded Finsbury Park Mosque in London, breaking down the doors with a battering ram. Not one of those arrested who frequented the mosque was found guilty of terror offences, apart from Kamel Bourgass, who by then had been arrested for stabbing a policeman to death during the immigration raid in Manchester. Four of his innocent codefendants spent over two years in Belmarsh prison awaiting trial, and some do not even know Bourgass.

As a failed asylum seeker, Bourgass was undoubtedly a desperate and disturbed man. He claimed to fear torture and death for him and for his family had he been arrested and returned to Algeria. Carrell and Whitaker (2005) described him as inhabiting a marginal world:

> Far from being an al-Qa'ida mastermind dispatched by Osama bin Laden and his lieutenants . . . Bourgass emerges as an embittered loner . . . [an] illegal immigrant . . . whose petty criminality was constrained by . . . poverty and poor English. (p. 6)

This description does not bespeak membership of a well-funded and highly organized terrorist network. It is surely unlikely that a cadre of such would call attention to himself or endanger his mission by being arrested, as was Bourgass in 2002, for shoplifting (Carrell & Whitaker, 2005, p. 7).

Yet Bourgass indeed had castor beans, cherry pips, and apple seeds stored in plastic cups in his closet, along with the solvent acetone and photocopied recipes, available on the Internet, for ricin and other toxins. Despite the premature, unretracted, and extremely convenient media releases, scientific tests did not find a single trace of any ricin ever actually made. The prosecution case involved a plot to smear ricin on door handles of cars; scientists have said such a measure would be highly unlikely to kill anyone, since ricin is not absorbed through the skin (Campbell, 2005). The poison, had it actually been produced, would not have been suitable for mass killings and has only ever been used for single assassinations. This must have been well comprehended, as part of the trade, by the ubiquitous "US government source," although from the "source's" point of view it would not do for such information to be widely known. In the end we are left with a "ricin plot" with no ricin, and a ringleader with no ring.

The fourth and final example offered here is one of the few cases so far taken to court in Australia under the antiterror laws: that of the Sydney medical student Izhar ul-Haque. In December 2007, Justice Michael Adams of the New South Wales Supreme Court ruled inadmissible the evidence from security agents whom he adjudged had kidnapped and falsely imprisoned ul-Haque. The student had admitted training with a Kashmir-centered guerrilla group, Lashkar e Taiba, which was not proscribed as a terrorist organization at the time. The agents had apprehended ul-Haque at a railway station in 2003 and taken him by car to a park where he was offered "the easy way or the hard way." He was taken back to his house, which was then being searched by more than 20 officers, and interrogated until dawn. The agents had only a search warrant and no lawful basis to detain or interrogate him. Ul-Haque was taken into custody four months later after refusing to be an informer for antiterrorism investigators, one of a number charged on weak grounds to demonstrate and to test new antiterror laws. There was much media fanfare over the case, with headlines like, "He wants to die a martyr—Sydney terror suspect accused of plotting holy war" (Miranda, 2004, p. 3) and many prosecution leaks and briefings damaging to his reputation and his defense. Despite the flimsy case against him and private admissions by federal police that he was no danger to Australian society, ul-Haque was refused bail and kept for a month and a half in a super-maximum security isolation cell. After he had been persecuted for three years with a nonexistent case, the prosecution show trial collapsed.

In each of these cases, police sources briefed the media with incorrect information about supposed terrorists or terrorist plots, which the media obligingly sensationalized. In each of the cases, it was either with the complicity of political leaders engaged in the politics of fear, or at best with the leaders declining to set the record straight, although they had knowledge of the falsity of the reports.

The triangle between police, media, and political fear-mongers works in a similar way to the dynamics of fear of ("ethnic") crime gangs (Poynting et al., 2004). The police feed the media stories about folk devils, often racialized ones. The media run with the stories, emphasizing the racial or ethnic aspects as risk factors. The media demand that strong action be taken in the face of such risk, and that the police and security forces be given appropriate support by government and communities in the war against crime or war on terror. Politicians attempt to outbid each other to demonstrate their toughness on crime or terrorism, and publicize their bids in the media. They are careful to eschew political correctness, and to "call a spade a spade," even when it means casting blame on marginalized communities. Poynting et al. (2004) found that the tabloid media especially tend to blame racialized communities, accusing them of undermining the war on crime or terror and possibly even supporting crime and terrorism. These accusations lead to further racial profiling or ethnic targeting by police and security forces, which leads to more suspects and more stories to feed to the media.

ETHNIC TARGETING, RACIAL PROFILING, AND STATE TERROR

State surveillance, harassment, and intimidation of Muslim communities have been practiced in nations allied with the United States in the "war on terror." Britain responded in a rush to the events of 9/11 with the most draconian legislation in Europe—invoking a State of Emergency in order to pass the controversial Anti-Terrorism, Crime and Security Act two months after 9/11. Home Secretary David Blunkett admitted that he invoked this measure as a way of derogating from the European Human Rights Convention (Young, 2001). This extreme reaction may in part have been in answer to the UK being labeled as a so-called haven for "terrorists," as a result of media coverage given to radical Islamic leaders and organizations in Britain who publicly expressed sympathy for al-Qaeda and who have been accused of recruiting for its network (Poynting & Mason, 2006). One such, Abu Hamza, has since been imprisoned for seven years for propagating these views after a conviction for incitement to murder.

The notion that a danger is posed to Britain by groups supporting al-Qaeda stemmed from the belief that 9/11 constituted an attack on the ideals of the "West" as a whole, rather than a single attack on the United States specifically. This belief was consistent with Samuel Huntington's (1997) "Clash of Civilisations" thesis, a picture of the new post–Cold War enemy of the West that predated 9/11 but became extremely popular in the media and on the political right after that date.

Will Hutton (2004), for instance, propounded this thesis in the *Observer*:

Radical Islam represents the biggest challenge to Western civilisation since the demise of fascism and communism. Rooted in a pre-Enlightenment worldview in which religious text has the force of law and the Islamic community is innately superior to all others, the belief that there is redemption for martyrs in the afterlife fuels extraordinary acts of terrorism.

The racially targeted and draconian "antiterrorism" measures pursued by the British government, and the populist xenophobia manipulated by the opposition (for example in the 2005 election campaign) both contribute to fifth-column fears of the clashing "other." The minister responsible for counterterrorism, Hazel Blears, said during the 2005 election campaign that Muslims in Britain faced disproportionate police "stop and search" measures and targeting under antiterrorism powers, since the terrorist threat came from people "falsely hiding behind Islam" (Dodd & Travis, 2005).

Such targeting takes place not only in the streets but in the supposed corridors of learning. The university where I work has been visited, along with other higher-education institutions in the north of England, by special antiterrorism police requesting that academic staff monitor the written assignments of Muslim students for signs of "radicalization," and report any cases found.

According to Massoud Shadjareh, chair of the Islamic Human Rights Commission:

> The war on terror has had a devastating effect [on British Muslims] . . .
> We have become targets of the security apparatus and are seen as an enemy
> within unjustifiably. This has resulted in a backlash against the Muslim com-
> munity. We have become the hidden victims. People are having to live, being
> terrorised, in the name of the war on terror. (Campbell, Norton-Taylor, &
> Dodd, 2005, p. 12)

In Canada, Muslims and Arab organizations as well as civil liberties groups identified the danger that the new antiterrorist measures posed for their constituents, not only of state harassment, but by propagating stereotypes of criminality and terrorist sympathies. The president of the Canadian Islamic Congress, Professor Mohamed Elmasry, asserted that the measures would make Muslim Canadians "the most targeted group in the country" (Poynting & Perry, 2007). Indeed, the 2005 Canadian Council on American-Islamic Relations report documents extensive experiences in which law enforcement agents (security agents, federal and provincial police) "approached" or "contacted" Arabs and Muslims, often with no explanation for doing so. In fact, of the 467 respondents, 8 percent had been contacted—the vast majority (84%) of whom were Canadian citizens; among those who were not directly contacted, nearly half (43%) knew at least one other Canadian Muslim who had been (Canadian Council on American-Islamic Relations, 2005). Furthermore, 19 percent of respondents who had been thus contacted reported that this was not a single event, but consisted of multiple contacts. The effect that these contacts had on those "visited" is precisely the same as that of hate crime:

> 46 percent said they felt fearful, anxious, "freaked out," paranoid, confused
> and/or nervous when contacted by security officials. 24 percent indicated

feeling harassed and pressured, violated and/or discriminated against. 5 percent indicated feeling outraged, furious or angry. 14 percent felt indifferent. (Canadian Council on American-Islamic Relations, 2005, p. 13)

The menace and intimidation of the contacts was surely amplified by many of them taking place in the respondents' places of employment, casting public suspicion on them and threatening their livelihood (Poynting & Perry, 1997, p. 164). One respondent reported that he actually lost his job soon after the security interview. Thus this ethnic targeting follows and reproduces institutional racism, from policing to the labor market.

Just as menacing were the improper tactics used by law enforcement agents. These tactics included discouraging legal or other third-party assistance; aggressive and threatening behavior; threats of arrest; problematic and suggestive questions (e.g., attitudes toward or knowledge of such things as jihad, al-Qaeda, or loyalty to Canada as opposed to loyalty to their religious faith); improper identification; attempts to recruit participants as informants; and interrogation of minors. Some respondents were subject to many of these tactics; many were aware of others who shared similar experiences. The ultimate result of these patterns, in addition to increasing the alienation and mutual distrust between Muslims and law enforcement agents, is to intimidate the targeted communities. It also adds credence to widespread beliefs that Muslims *are* of dubious loyalty to Canada, and suspect in their acquiescence of, if not support of, terrorism; where there's smoke, there's fire. Unfounded or unjustified though the police surveillance and ethnic targeting may be in reality, it nevertheless casts a shadow of doubt (Poynting & Perry, 2007, p. 164). The state harassment of Muslims thus "makes people feel comfortable with their prejudices and grants those who hold pre-existing racist attitudes permission to express those attitudes and expect them to be taken seriously. It empowers individual prejudices and fuels popular fears" (Bahdi, 2003, p. 314).

In Australia, the "visits" to Muslims by security forces and police began by the end of September 2001. The Australian Security Intelligence Organisation (ASIO), accompanied by the Australian Federal Police (AFP) and local New South Wales police, raided some 30 households and workplaces in Sydney. They brought the media with them and publicized the raids (Kidman, 2001, pp. 4–5; Trad, 2001). All those raided were Muslims, and the Australian tabloid media furnished justification, as well as the desired exposure. Conservative columnist Miranda Devine (2001) thought the targeting quite appropriate:

The perpetrators of the September 11 attacks were young Middle-Eastern Muslim men. Bin Laden's followers are young Middle-Eastern Muslim men. So it is young men of Middle-Eastern Muslim background who will be targeted in Sydney, many of them Australian citizens, who were born here. (p. 28)

The raids were obviously meant as a public show that "something is being done" but were also manifestly intended to intimidate. In one case, "five heavily armed officers stormed the house," forced a man to lie on the floor at gunpoint, and conducted a body search. His wife was escorted downstairs by two federal police officers without being given time to cover herself adequately. The house was penetratingly searched. The man was threatened, "You have small children, you would not like for them to not see you for ten years" (Trad, 2001). That no arrests were made at the time for any terrorism-related offense (although there were some visa infractions, a matter that has also concerned Canadian and British Muslims experiencing such raids) confirms the intimidating rather than investigatory or protective function of the operations.

Again following the Bali bombings in October 2002, ASIO and AFP operatives conducted swoops on suburban homes of Muslim Australians—this time mainly those of Indonesian origin in Sydney, Perth, and Melbourne (Poynting et al., 2004, pp. 171–174). Neighbors of one family raided at dawn in a Perth suburb reported the door being battered in with sledgehammers and windows being smashed by an armed squad wearing helmets, balaclavas, goggles, and flak jackets ("Like Scenes . . . ," 2002, p. 7). In one Perth raid, a 17-year-old girl looking after her three brothers and sisters, one only four years old, told of machine guns being shoved in their faces (Poynting et al., 2004, p. 172).

In both of these series of raids and again in those around July 2005 after the London bombings, the ethnic profiling provoked terror among the communities being targeted. One interviewee, a middle-aged tradesman of Lebanese background from Melbourne, told Poynting and Noble (2004):

> It was increasing, the scare and frightening when they accused me. I felt it was accusation. Maybe not officially, but the way they talked to me, three, two from Federal Police and one from ASIO, to come and talk to me like this . . . At home I'm scared that one day they'd come in the same way they did to some people in Sydney and other places, we heard, break things and scare children, scared women. (p. 12)

Muslim leaders said the raids had "caused hysteria and fear that anyone in the community could be targeted" ("Muslims Condemn . . . ," 2002). Such operations send a concerted message of intimidation to whole communities to which those being raided belong. For that very reason, the media were taken along in the raids of 2001, 2002, and 2005. On several occasions the media identified the families concerned, and they were consequently subjected to vigilante-style harassment. As the operations were probably counterproductive for intelligence-gathering purposes (scarcely inspiring community collaboration and sharing of information), and no one raided was actually charged with terrorist offenses, this cannot have been the raids' raison d'etre unless they were badly botched. They did, however, serve to reassure the white, non-Muslim "mainstream" that indeed something was being done about these supposed terrorists or terrorist sympathizers in their midst, and to intimidate the targeted communities into maintaining a low profile. The mainstream media literally went along with this state terrorizing of Muslim communities.

If we accept the definition of "state crime" by Green and Ward (2004) as "state organisational deviance involving violation of human rights" (p. 2), then it is clear that many of the instances adduced above constitute state crime. This is so whether one follows Green and Ward's argument about human rights as the moral claim to the satisfaction of basic human needs, or the harder definition of human rights, which has to do with international legal codification.

A range of international human rights instruments mandates the right to religious freedom and the right not to be discriminated against on the basis of religious affiliation. These instruments include the United Nations Charter; the Universal Declaration of Human Rights; the International Covenant on Civil and Political Rights (1976); the International Covenant on Economic, Social and Cultural Rights (1976); the Declaration on the Elimination of All Forms of Intolerance and of Discrimination Based on Religion or Belief (The Religion Declaration; 1981); The International Convention on the Elimination of All Forms of Racial Discrimination (1963); the Declaration on the Rights of Persons belonging to National or Ethnic, Religious and Linguistic Minorities (1992) and the UNESCO Declaration on Cultural Diversity (2001) (Poynting & Mason, 2008). The states concerned are practicing ethnic targeting and racial profiling in the application of antiterrorism measures and doing so with religious, cultural, political, and racial discrimination, and they are thus engaged in state crime, which is at the same time "bias crime."

Thus it can be argued that, in addition to engendering hate crime through modeling anti-Muslim discrimination and violence and thus legitimating the targeting of Muslims for acts of vengeance and Islamophobic hatred, the state itself is in many such cases perpetrating hate crime. This chapter has outlined the rise in the level of Islamophobic hate crime in Western nations since 9/11. It has shown how such hate crime can be promoted, whether wittingly or not, by populist political figures, abetted by mass media. It has sketched some cases of ethnic targeting or racial profiling of Muslim communities in Britain, Canada, the United States, and Australia by way of example. It has argued, finally, that these can be tantamount to perpetrating "state hate crime," as well as demonstrably stimulating the committing of hate crime by individuals and groups.

NOTES

1. Material from the following sections on the media in Canada and Australia has been published in Poynting and Perry (2007).

2. I am grateful to Gabe Mythen for drawing my attention to this case.

REFERENCES

Ali, T. (2005). *Rough music: Blair/Bombs/Baghdad/London/Terror*. London: Verso.

Allen, C., & Nielsen, J. S. (2002). Summary report on Islamophobia in the EU after 11 September 2001. Vienna, Austria: European Monitoring Centre on Racism and Xenophobia.

Anti-Discrimination Board of New South Wales. (2003). Race for the headlines: Racism and media discourse. Sydney: Author. Retrieved October 12, 2008, from http://nla.gov.au/nla.arc-39681

Athwal, H. (2006, May 18). 18-month sentence for manslaughter of Pakistani man. *IRR News*. Retrieved October 13, 2008, from http://www.irr.org.uk/2006/may/ha000022.html

Bahdi, R. (2003). No exit: Racial profiling and Canada's war against terrorism. *Osgoode Hall Law Journal, 41*(1–2), 293–316.

BBC News. (2005). Hate crimes soar after bombings. Retrieved October 13, 2008, from http://news.bbc.co.uk/1/hi/england/london/4740015.stm

Belien, P. (2006, April 19). Murder shocks Brussels while PM and Cardinal blame victims. *The Brussels Journal*. Retrieved October 12, 2008, from http://www.brusselsjournal.com/node/995

Bennetto, J., Herbert, I., & Clarke, J. (2006, October 14). Attacks on Muslims rise after veils row. *The Independent*. Retrieved October 13, 2008, from http://www.independent.co.uk/news/uk/crime/attacks-on-muslims-rise-after-veils-row-420002.html

Black I. (2002, May 24). End growing anti-Muslim prejudice, EU report urges. *Guardian*. Retrieved October 12, 2008, from http://www.guardian.co.uk/media/2002/may/24/broadcasting.terrorismandthemedia

Bond, P. (2006a, May 8). Belgium: Teenager's murder exploited for right-wing agenda. *World Socialist Website*. Retrieved October 13, 2008, from http://www.wsws.org/articles/2006/may2006/belg-m08.shtml

Bond, P. (2006b, June 21). Belgium: Racist murderer linked to Flemish nationalists. *World Socialist Website*. Retrieved October 13, 2008, from http://www.wsws.org/articles/2006/jun2006/belg-j21.shtml

Booth, J. (2005, July 12). Asian man dies in suspected racist attack in Nottingham. *Times Online*. Retrieved October 13, 2008, from http://www.timesonline.co.uk/tol/news/uk/article543198.ece

Bureau of Democracy, Human Rights, and Labor. (2006). *International Religious Freedom Report 2006*. U.S. Department of State. Retrieved October 13, 2008, from http://www.state.gov/g/drl/rls/irf/2006/71371.htm

Burleigh, J., & Fenton, B. (2005, July 23). Bomb suspect gunned down on Tube after frantic chase with armed police. *Daily Telegraph* (London), p. 3.

Calvert, J., & Leppard, D. (2005). Police shot wrong man: Suspect was innocent Brazilian electrician. Timesonline. Retrieved October 13, 2008, from http://www.timesonline.co.uk/tol/news/uk/article547590.ece

Campbell, D. (2005, April 14). The ricin ring that never was. *Guardian*, p. 25.

Campbell, D., Norton-Taylor, R., & Dodd, V. (2005, April 23). Words of warning backed by little clear evidence. *Guardian*, p.12.

Canadian Council on American-Islamic Relations. (2005). *Presumption of guilt: A national survey on security visitations of Canadian Muslims*. Retrieved October 13, 2008, from http://www.caircan.ca/downloads/POG-08062005.pdf

Canadian Islamic Congress. (2003). *Islamic Congress finds most police departments have incomplete data on rising tide of hate-motivated crimes.* Retrieved October 13, 2008, from www.canadianislamiccongress.com/mc/media_communique.php?id=305

Canadian Islamic Congress. (2005). *Anti-Islam in the media 2003.* Retrieved October 12, 2008, from http://canadianislamiccongress.com/rr/rr_2003.php

Carrell, S., & Whitaker, R. (2005, April 17). Ricin: The plot that never was. *Independent on Sunday*, pp. 6–7.

CIA looks into possible al Qaeda link to ricin plot. (2003, January 29). *Sydney Morning Herald.* Retrieved October 12, 2008, from http://www.smh.com.au/articles/2003/01/28/1043534056145.html

Complaint against extreme-right leader for "islamophobia." (2005, November 24). *European Jewish Press.* Retrieved October 13, 2008, from http://www.ejpress.org/article/4336

Council on American-Islamic Relations. (2007). *The status of Muslim civil rights in the United States 2007: Presumption of guilt.* Author. Retrieved October 13, 2008, from http://www.cair.com/pdf/2007-Civil-Rights-Report.pdf

Cowan, R., & Campbell, D. (2005, April 14). Detective murdered by an obsessive loner. *Guardian*, p. 9.

Dagistanli, S. (2007). "Like a pack of wild animals": Moral panics around "ethnic" gang rape in Sydney. In S. Poynting & G. Morgan (Eds.), *Outrageous! Moral panics in Australia* (pp. 180–195). Hobart, Tasmania, Australia: ACYS Press.

Devine, M. (2001, November 11). Where security counts, tolerance goes two ways. *Sun Herald*, p. 27.

Dodd, V. (2005a, July 13). Islamophobia blamed for attack. *The Guardian.* Retrieved October 11, 2008, from http://www.guardian.co.uk/uk/2005/jul/13/race.july7/print

Dodd, V. (2005b, April 16). Doubts grow over al-Qaida link in ricin plot. *Guardian.* Retrieved October 13, 2008, from http://www.guardian.co.uk/uk/2005/apr/16/terrorism.alqaida

Dodd, V., & Travis, A. (2005, March 2). Muslims face increased stop and search. *Guardian.* Retrieved October 12, 2008, from http://www.guardian.co.uk/politics/2005/mar/02/terrorism.immigrationpolicy1

Dreher, T. (2005). "Targeted": Experiences of racism in NSW after September 11, 2001. *UTS Shopfront Series*, Monograph No 2. Retrieved October 13, 2008, from http://epress.lib.uts.edu.au/dspace/bitstream/2100/46/6/Targeted%20WEB%20April%2007.pdf

Four Corners. (2006, March 13). *Riot and revenge.* Australian Broadcasting Corporation. Reporter: Liz Jackson. Retrieved October 13, 2008, from http://www.abc.net.au/4corners/content/2006/s1590953.htm

Green, P., & Ward, T. (2004). *State crime: Governments, violence and corruption.* London: Pluto Press.

Human Rights and Equal Opportunity Commission. (2004). *Isma—listen: National consultations on eliminating prejudice against Arab and Muslim Australians.* Retrieved October 13, 2008, from http://www.hreoc.gov.au/racial_discrimination/isma/report/index.html

Huntington, S. P. (1997.) *The clash of civilizations and the remaking of World Order.* New York: Touchstone.

Hutton, W. (2004, January 11). Why the West is wary of Muslims. *Observer*. http://www.guardian.co.uk/world/2004/jan/11/religion.uk

Independent Police Complaints Commission. (2006). *Stockwell One: Investigation into the shooting of Jean Charles de Menezes at Stockwell underground station on 22 July 2005*. Retrieved October 13, 2008, from http://news.bbc.co.uk/1/shared/bsp/hi/pdfs/08_11_07_stockwell1.pdf

Ismael, T. Y., & Measor, J. (2003). Racism and the North American media following 11 September: The Canadian setting. *Arab Studies Quarterly*, 25(1/2), 101–136.

Kennedy, L., Murphy, D., Brown, M., & Colquhoun, T. (2005, December 12). Race riots explode. *Sydney Morning Herald*, pp. 1–4.

Khan, S., Saloojee, R., & Al-Shalchi, H. (2004). *Today's media: Covering Islam and Canadian Muslims*. Ottawa, Canada: Canadian Council on American-Islamic Relations.

Kidman, J. (2001, September 30). ASIO swoop in hunt for bin Laden link: Muslim woman claims gunpoint interrogation. *Sun-Herald*, pp. 4–5.

Kundnani, A. (2007). *The end of tolerance: Racism in 21st century Britain*. London: Pluto Press.

Lateline. (2005, August 23). *Respect Australian values or leave: Costello*. Australian Broadcasting Corporation (Reporter: Tony Jones). Retrieved October 13, 2008, from http://www.abc.net.au/lateline/content/2005/s1444603.htm

Like scenes from a movie. (2002, October 31). *Daily Telegraph* (Sydney), p. 7.

Manning, P. (2004). *Dog whistle politics and journalism: Reporting Arabic and Muslim people in Sydney newspapers*. Sydney, Australia: Australian Centre for Independent Journalism, University of Technology.

McClintock, M., & LeGendre, P. (2007). *Islamophobia: 2007 hate crime survey*. Human Rights First. Retrieved October 13, 2008, from http://www.humanrightsfirst.info/pdf/07601-discrim-hc-islamophobia-web.pdf

Miranda, C. (2004, April 30). He wants to die a martyr—Sydney terror suspect accused of plotting holy war. *Daily Telegraph* (Sydney), p. 3.

Muslims condemn "heavy-handed" tactics. (2002, November 1). *Age*. Retrieved October 13, 2008, from http://www.theage.com.au/articles/2002/10/31/1036026979308.html

Oborne, P. (2006, February 15). *The use and abuse of terror: The construction of a false narrative on the domestic terror threat*. London: Centre for Policy Studies.

Overington, C., & Warne-Smith, D. (2005, December 17–18). Countdown to conflict. *Weekend Australian*, pp. 17, 20.

Panja, T., & Bright, M. (2004, May 2). Man U bomb plot probe ends in farce. *The Observer*. Retrieved October 13, 2008, from http://www.guardian.co.uk/news/2004/may/02/uknews

Perry, B. (2001). *In the name of hate: Understanding hate crimes*. New York: Routledge.

Pierre, R. E. (2002, September 14). Victims of hate, now feeling forgotten. *Washington Post*, p. A1.

PM. (2005, August 24). Teach Australian values or "clear off", says Nelson. *PM program, ABC Radio* (Reporter: Samantha Hawley). Retrieved October 13, 2008, from http://www.abc.net.au/pm/content/2005/s1445262.htm

Poynting, S. (2006). What caused the Cronulla Riot? *Race and Class*, 48(1), 85–92.

Poynting, S., & Mason, V. (2006). "Tolerance, freedom, justice and peace"?: Britain, Australia and anti-Muslim racism since 11th September 2001. *Journal of Intercultural Studies, 27*(4), 365–392.

Poynting, S., & Mason, V. (2008). The new integrationism, the state and Islamophobia: Retreat from multiculturalism in Australia. *International Journal of Law, Crime and Justice.*

Poynting, S., Noble, G., Tabar, P., & Collins, J. (2004). *Bin Laden in the suburbs: Criminalising the Arab Other.* Sydney, Australia: Institute of Criminology.

Poynting, S., & Noble, G. (2004). *Living with racism: The experience and reporting by Arab and Muslim Australians of discrimination, abuse and violence since 11 September 2001.* Report to the Human Rights and Equal Opportunity Commission. Retrieved October 12, 2008, from http://www.hreoc.gov.au/racial_discrimination/isma/research/index.html

Poynting, S., & Perry, B. (2007). Climates of hate: Media and state inspired victimisation of Muslims in Canada and Australia since 9/11. *Current Issues in Criminal Justice, 19*(2), 151–171.

Risen, J., & Van Natta, D. (2003, January 25). Bases the target in ricin plot theory. *Sydney Morning Herald.*

Runnymede Trust. (1997). *Islamophobia: A challenge for us all.* London: Author.

Suleaman, N. (2006, November 5). *How veil remarks reinforced its support.* BBC News. Retrieved October 13, 2008, from http://news.bbc.co.uk/1/hi/uk/6117480.stm

Trad, K. (2001). *The ASIO raids on Muslims: Statements on behalf of victims.* Unpublished transcript of interview. Sydney: Lebanese Muslim Association.

Walker, P., & Fickling, D. (2006, June 13). Police apologise to east London raid family. *The Guardian.* Retrieved October 13, 2008, from http://www.guardian.co.uk/world/2006/jun/13/terrorism.uk

Young, H. (2001, November 15). David Blunkett holds liberty and the judges in contempt. *The Guardian.* Retrieved October 13, 2008, from http://www.guardian.co.uk/world/2001/nov/15/september11.britainand911.

CHAPTER 6

CONCEPTUALIZING ANTI–JEWISH
HATE CRIME

Paul Iganski

ISRAEL, JEWS, AND THE CAUSES
OF ANTISEMITISM ON THE STREETS

Scholarly analyses of the problem of racist violence in Britain and elsewhere in the 1980s and 1990s tended to focus on the national political climate that provided a context for acts of race-hate crime. Perhaps not surprisingly, official analyses of the problem of racist violence confined themselves to statements about the role of extreme right-wing groups in creating a climate for, and being implicated in, racist attacks, rather than examining the culpability of the state itself when focusing on the politics of hate crime. Such statements peppered the policy literature on racist violence across the 1980s and 1990s. This chapter is concerned with a different, and more contemporary, political context for hate crime: the evident backlash on London's streets, and elsewhere, to global political events. Hate crimes against Jews on the streets are often associated with upsurges in the Israel–Palestine conflict and conflicts elsewhere in the Middle East. Given the political contexts of incidents, the chapter considers how individual acts of offending are to be interpreted. Are they acts of political violence on the part of offenders: street-level activists pursuing their politics through violent means? Are they instead outpourings of outrage against the political events in question, by people not normally disposed to violent conduct? Or are they simply manifestations of pre-existing bigotry prompted by the particular political events? And, most importantly for the theme of this chapter, how are incidents to be conceptualized? Can the backlash of incidents against Jews be characterized as antisemitic or alternatively as political protest? These are the questions with which the chapter grapples.

It is perhaps one of the great ironies of contemporary politics that Israel, regarded in the twentieth century as a haven for Jews against persecution and antisemitism in Europe, is now in the twenty-first century the cause of animus toward European Jews—as some commentators allege (see Avnery, 2002). According to this claim, Israel's military policies, and Jews collectively by their identification with Israel, are responsible for many of the anti-Jewish incidents that occur on Europe's streets. Furthermore, such incidents are purportedly not necessarily antisemitic, but an understandable outpouring of anger against the Israeli state. This line of argument has been promoted by critics that are of the notion there is a "new antisemitism" in present-day Europe. Their remedies to the problem of incidents against Jews are attractively simple: a withdrawal by the Israeli military—and by Israeli settlers—from the territories occupied during the 1967 War, and an end to the human rights abuses and oppression of Palestinians in the occupied territories and in Israel itself. Such political goals seem to be shared by the majority—within and outside of Israel—and for some they are an essential step to a permanent settlement in which there is a renunciation of violence and a recognition of two states of Israel and Palestine.

However, political positioning is not the same as scholarly reasoning, and if a more analytical lens is applied to the problem of anti-Jewish incidents, the diagnosis for the causes is seen to be far more complex. This diagnosis also indicates that incidents against Jews will still occur even if there is a settlement to the Israel–Palestine conflict. This chapter offers these perspectives on the problem of anti-Jewish incidents by drawing from an analysis of offender impulses in anti-Jewish hate crime in London first reported in the study *Hate Crimes Against London's Jews* (Iganski, Kielinger, & Paterson, 2005). The chapter unfolds by first discussing data on the patterns and trends in anti-Jewish incidents to provide the context for the analysis that follows. The data indisputably show an association between periods of raised tension in conflicts in the Middle East—and not only the Israel–Palestine conflict—and episodes of increased frequency of incidents against Jews. However, the claim that Israel's military policies and Jews collectively are the cause of such incidents is contested, as is the assertion that the incidents are in any way hardly surprising. In offering these perspectives, the chapter does not aim to defend Israel's military actions and the denial of the civil rights of Palestinians in Israel and the occupied territories. Nor is the aim to condone violence against Jews within and outside of Israel. Instead, the aim is to provide a more nuanced approach to the data on anti-Jewish incidents that are commonly brought into play by both proponents and opponents of the notion of a new antisemitism.

TRENDS IN ANTI-JEWISH INCIDENTS
AND THE ISRAEL–PALESTINE CONFLICT

There are no routinely published official data on anti-Jewish incidents in the United Kingdom. However, the Community Security Trust (CST), which advises and represents Britain's Jewish community on matters of antisemitism, terrorism, and security, has been systematically compiling reports of incidents since 1984, with information gathered from victims, press reports, and the police (Whine, 2003). While there have been evident fluctuations in the annual number of incidents recorded, the overall trend over time has been upward. In 2006 the CST recorded its highest yearly number of incidents—594 in total (CST, 2007, p. 4). As with all such recorded crime data, caution must be exercised in interpreting apparent trends because they may well reflect a greater propensity for victims to report incidents for a variety of reasons just as much as representing a real rise in victimization. However, there have been no crime victimization surveys focusing on anti-Jewish incidents in Britain, and the annual British Crime Survey provides data of little value given the small number of identifiable Jews included in the survey sample (as Britain's Jews constitute only approximately 0.5 percent of the population). In the absence of survey data, the recorded incidents are currently the best data available, and the apparent rise in incidents does appear to concur with dominant perceptions in some quarters of Britain's Jewish communities about the growing problem of contemporary antisemitism.

The numbers of recorded incidents rise and fall in relation to tensions in the Israel–Palestine conflict and conflicts elsewhere. A peak in the number of incidents between September and November 2001 is associated with the terrorist attacks against the World Trade Center and the Pentagon, attacks which, according to Whine (2003), "many in the Arab world blamed on Israel" (p. 31). A peak from April and May 2002 is associated with the violent conflict involving the Israel Defence Force in Jenin in April 2002. A peak in April 2003 coincided with the Iraq war, and a peak in July and August 2006 with the Israel–Hezbollah conflict in Lebanon. Two observations can be made about these episodes. First, from the world events with which they are associated, it is obvious that the Israel–Palestine conflict is not the only trigger for incidents. As there is an association between rises in incidents and other conflicts for which there have been conspiracy theories about Jews being implicated—such as the 9/11 terror attacks and the invasions of Iraq—the peaks in incidents are not likely to disappear entirely with a settlement of the Israel–Palestine conflict. Second, there is nothing "new" in the overspill effect of tensions in the Middle East upon anti-Jewish incidents on the streets. Whine has argued that the trend started to become apparent in Britain in the 1990s following the deportation by Israel of Hamas activists to Lebanon in

December 2002 and was more marked after the attack by the Israeli army on the Lebanese village of Qana in March 1996.

ANTI-JEWISH INCIDENTS AS AN OUTPOURING OF ANGER AGAINST ISRAEL'S MILITARY POLICIES

Some scholars and other commentators, while making it explicit that they don't condone the targeting of Jews in the overspill of Middle East tensions onto Europe's streets, have argued that it is not surprising that such incidents occur because of the identification of Jews with Israel. One such scholar, Brian Klug (2003), has argued that

> when the state of Israel claims Jews as its own, and when Jews en masse proclaim Israel to be theirs, it is not surprising if others fail to make the distinction between Jewish state and Jewish people.
> If Jews as Jews align themselves with Israel, publicly and predominantly, then hostility towards Israel is liable to spill over into hostility towards Jews as such. Not that this is justifiable; it is never justifiable to lump all members of a religious or ethnic group together, dissolving the individual into the collective. (p. 137)

In the same vein, Norman Finkelstein (2005) has asked, "Should it really surprise us if the cruel occupation by a self-declared *Jewish* state engenders a generalized antipathy to Jews?" and he argues that "In some quarters anger at Israel's brutal occupation has undoubtedly spilled over to an animus toward Jews generally. But however lamentable, it's hardly cause for wonder" (p. 81). While Klug (2003) rejects the label of antisemitism for the incidents in question, Finkelstein continues to use it (although he rejects notions of a new antisemitism), and given that in his view Israel is culpable for the upsurges of anti-Jewish incidents, then Israel, and Jews, are causing antisemitism. Because this allegation understandably strikes a sensitive nerve for many Jews and non-Jews alike, it is important to quote Finkelstein's words so as to be careful not to misrepresent them:

> The causal relationship would seem to be that Israel's brutal repression of Palestinians evoked hostility toward the "Jewish state" and its vocal Jewish supporters abroad . . . Yet, it is precisely this causal relationship that Israel's apologists emphatically deny: if Israeli policies, and widespread Jewish support for them, evoke hostility toward Jews, it means that Israel and its Jewish supporters themselves might be causing antisemitism. (pp. 77–78)

Finkelstein (2005) has not been alone in this assertion. Israeli peace activist Uri Avnery, writing in the Israeli newspaper *Haaretz* in 2002, argued that the government of the then Israeli Prime Minister Ariel Sharon was

[a] giant laboratory for the growing of the antisemitsm virus. It exports it to the whole world. Antisemitic organizations, which for many years vegetated on the margins of society, rejected and despised, are suddenly growing and flowering. Antisemitsm, which had hidden itself in shame since World War II, is now riding on a great wave of opposition to Sharon's policy of oppression. (Avnery, 2002)

If Israel's military policies are solely held culpable for upsurges in anti-Jewish incidents, then the solutions are attractively simple, as proposed by Finkelstein (2005). First,

If, as all the important studies agree, current resentment against Jews has coincided with Israel's brutal repression of the Palestinians, then a patent remedy and quick solution would plainly be to end the occupation. A full Israeli withdrawal from the territories occupied in 1967 would also deprive those real antisemites exploiting Israel's repression as a pretext to demonize Jews—and who can doubt they exist?—of a dangerous weapon, as well as expose their real agenda. (p. 85)

Second, "the more vocally Jews dissent from Israel's occupation, the fewer will be those non-Jews who mistake Israel's criminal policies and the uncritical support (indeed encouragement) of mainline Jewish organizations for the popular Jewish mood" (Finkelstein, 2005, p. 85). However, time will tell if Finkelstein's remedy works, as Jews in Britain have indeed been speaking out publicly against Israel's military activities. Most vocally of late, a number of prominent Jewish academics and public figures in the arts, and other Jews, signed up to the launch of *Independent Jewish Voices* with an advertisement in *The Times* newspaper and the *Jewish Chronicle* with coverage elsewhere in the British press (see Klug, 2007).

ANTISEMITIC INCIDENTS: A QUESTION OF DEFINITION

In the observations made above about the association between tensions in the Middle East and episodes of increased incidents against Jews, it was noted that such an association is not "new." The question to which this chapter now turns is whether the incidents are actually antisemitic. This question is not just a matter of semantics, for the matter of definition has become highly politicized. The issue for one scholar, Brian Klug, concerns what he alleges is the political misuse of the concept of antisemitism. The chief problem, according to Klug—who has been a prominent critic of notions of a new antisemitism—boils down to the smearing of the charge of antisemitism by some partisan supporters of Israel and Zionism, against their opponents, to suppress and delegitimize criticism of Israeli military policy and the Zionist political project in general. This charge echoes sentiments that have been prevalent in some elements of the British press about alleged slurs being made against critics of Israel. Famously in 2002, one contributor to the *Observer* newspaper complained: "Criticize Israel and you are an antisemite just as surely as if you were throwing paint at a synagogue in Paris" (Beaumont, 2002). Elsewhere, the seal of authority was given to such claims by Archbishop Desmond Tutu, no less, who argued that "the Israeli government is placed on a pedestal [in the U.S.], and to criticize it is to be immediately dubbed antisemitic" (Tutu, 2002). More recently, Finkelstein (2005) has alleged that "the hysteria over a new antisemitism hasn't anything to do with fighting bigotry—and everything to do with stifling criticism of Israel" (p. 76).

One response adopted by Klug to the supposed misappropriation of the concept of antisemitism has been, in his words, to "reclaim the word 'antisemitism' from the political misuses to which it is being put" (Remba & Klug, 2004). In a number of essays Klug conceptualizes antisemitism as a doctrine, an ideology, a discourse, and particular sentiments about Jews. It is instructive to unfold the key dimensions of his conceptualization as it can be used as one measure to determine, as Klug himself does, which incidents against Jews might be labeled antisemitic and which might be labeled otherwise. As a means of faithfully reflecting the reasoning employed, it is helpful to quote Klug (2003). He defines antisemitism as

> [a] form of hostility towards Jews as Jews, in which Jews are perceived as something other than what they are. Or more succinctly: hostility towards Jews as *not* Jews. For the "Jew" towards whom the antisemite feels hostile is not a *real* Jew at all. Thinking that Jews are really "Jews" is precisely the core of antisemitism. (pp. 123–124)

Accordingly, Klug (2003) argues that "Antisemitism is best defined not by an attitude to Jews but by a definition of 'Jew'" (p. 124). This "Jew" is characterized as belonging to

> [a] sinister people set apart from all others not merely by its customs but by a collective character: arrogant, secretive, cunning, grasping, always looking to turn a profit. Wherever they go, the Jews form a state within a state, preying on the societies in whose midst they dwell. Mysteriously powerful, their hidden hand controls the banks and the media, dragging governments into war if this suits their Jewish agenda. (Klug, 2006)

In advocating this very exact conceptualization of antisemitism as an ideology that has at its core a precise characterization of the "Jew," Klug (Remba & Klug, 2004) inevitably concludes that many of the incidents against Jews on the streets characterized by some commentators as manifestations of the "new

antisemitism" are not in fact motivated by antisemitism. Consequently, referring to the upsurge of anti-Jewish incidents in France, for instance, Klug
(Remba & Klug, 2004) reduces them to "ethno-religious conflict":

> [W]hen alienated Moroccan and Algerian youths in the banlieues of Paris,
> outraged by conditions in the occupied territories, attack Jewish individu-
> als and institutions, the situation is essentially different. This is not, as
> some say, a new "mutation" of an old "virus." Fundamentally, it is an ethno-
> religious conflict between two communities with opposed identifications:
> roughly, French Muslims with Palestinian Arabs versus French Jews with
> Israeli Jews. Certainly . . . antisemitism is part of the "mix." But it is not the
> driving force. For this reason, while such incidents should be condemned,
> it is misleading to classify them as antisemitic.

Seemingly persuaded by Klug's 2003, (2004) conceptualization, the European Monitoring Centre on Racism and Xenophobia (EUMC; 2004) (now
the European Union Agency for Fundamental Rights [FRA]) in its report,
Manifestations of Antisemitism in the EU 2002–2003, concluded that

> anti-Israeli or anti-Zionist attitudes and expression are antisemitic in those
> cases where Israel is seen as being a representative of "the Jew", i.e. as a
> representative of the traits attributed to the antisemitic construction of
> "the Jew" . . . strictly speaking, we would have to qualify hostility towards
> Jews as "Israelis" only then as antisemitic, if it is based on an underlying
> perception of Israel as "the Jew". If this is not the case, then we would
> have to consider hostility towards Jews as "Israelis" as not antisemitic,
> because this hostility is not based on the antisemitic stereotyping of Jews.
> (pp. 13–14)

INTERPRETING POLICE RECORDS
OF ANTISEMITIC INCIDENTS ON THE STREETS

Armed with this conceptualization of antisemitism as a specific ideology about, and characterization of, the "Jew," it is instructive to unpack the
Metropolitan Police Service (MPS) records of antisemitic incidents analyzed for the study *Hate Crimes Against London's Jews*. Part of the research
analyzed in-depth a subsample of 110 incidents recorded as "antisemitic
incidents" by the MPS in April and May 2002. This period represented the
largest peak in incidents—between 2001 and 2004, the period covered by
the research—that directly corresponded to media coverage of the conflict
between the Israel Defence Force and Palestinian nationalists in Jenin. For
comparison, an additional sample of 46 incidents was used in the analysis
covering all recorded incidents in November and December 2002 and August 2003 to represent in the sample months of low and medium, as well as
high, occurrence of incidents. Approximately 20 percent of the incidents in

the subsample showed evidence of anti-Israeli sentiment in the discourse of
the offenders, and in some instances sentiment drawing on the Arab–Israeli
conflict more broadly. The level of such discourse manifest in incidents was
much lower—approximately 5 percent—in months where there were fewer
incidents. While the data arguably show a clear association between the Israel–Palestine conflict and the expression of anti-Israeli sentiment in incidents
against Jews, it is also obvious that these incidents are only a small minority of
all of the incidents recorded by the MPS for the periods in question.

It seems clear that, for some of the incidents, although they were given an
"antisemitic flag" in police records on the crime recording system, the sentiment expressed was manifestly political. For instance, in one incident, a group
of young people forced their way into the offices of the Israeli tourist board
and sprayed the word *terrorists* in large black letters on a wall. The incident obviously involved criminal damage, but there was no evidence to suggest it was
antisemitic—according to the conceptualization being employed—or indeed
even anti-Jewish in sentiment as against anti-Israeli. In a different type of incident, according to police records, anti-Israeli stickers were found on a number of lampposts in Oxford Street, the main shopping hub in central London.
They were clearly anti-Israeli in sentiment: they showed an Israeli flag with a
swastika superimposed at the center along with the caption "fascist state."

Again, while obviously anti-Israeli, given the particular conceptualization
of antisemitism being employed, the stickers were clearly not antisemitic
or even anti-Jewish in content. In addition, they were not targeted at Jews
specifically. Given their location, they were clearly meant for the eyes of the
general public, although the public would of course include Jewish shoppers
and pedestrians in the area. However, arguably, in this particular case the
animus expressed was anti-Israeli, not specifically anti-Jewish, and certainly
not antisemitic as conceptualized by Klug (2003) and the EUMC (2004). The
equation between the Israeli state and Nazism is highly offensive and hurtful
for many Jews and non-Jews, and the police crime report indicated that the
person who reported the stickers perceived them as racist and was distressed
by them. The equation is certainly slanderous: there are no gas chambers in
Israel, no master-race eugenics program, no final solution, or any other such
resemblances of the Nazis (Jacobson, 2003). Yet the U.S. State Department in
its Report on Global Antisemitism (2005) proposed that "the demonization
of Israel, or vilification of Israeli leaders, sometimes through comparisons
with Nazi leaders, and through the use of Nazi symbols to caricature them,
indicates an antisemitic bias rather than valid criticism of policy concerning
a controversial issue." (The EUMC also proposed in its 2005 *Working Definition of Antisemitism* that "'antisemitism' *can be* [emphasis added] manifest in
'Drawing comparisons of contemporary Israeli policy to that of the Nazis,'"
http://eumc.europa.eu/eumc/material/pub/AS/AS-WorkingDefinition-
draft.pdf, accessed December 19, 2008).

However, while understandably hurtful, such parallels are arguably not intrinsically antisemitic.[1] The context in which the parallels are drawn is critical. For instance, former Israeli Prime Minister Yitzhak Rabin, who was assassinated in 1995, was subjected before his murder to a campaign of vilification by some fellow Jewish Israelis in which he was characterized as cooperating with the Nazis and was pictured in posters wearing an SS uniform (Gavison, 1998, p. 46). More recently, another former Israeli Prime Minister, Benjamin Netanyahu, has drawn parallels between present-day Iran and Nazi Germany (cf. Hirschberg, 2006). It would be inappropriate to characterize either of these incidents as antisemitic rather than highly charged political rhetoric where the label "Nazi" is used to demonize opponents.

Context does matter, and the same sentiments and discourse in a different context arguably become something else. For instance, according to the police records of another reported incident, apparently similar stickers to those in the incident on Oxford Street were found on phone boxes and lampposts close to the Stamford Hill area of north London—a neighborhood populated by a highly visible Hasidic Jewish community. Again, although highly offensive to many Jews and non-Jews, the stickers by themselves might be described as solely anti-Israeli. Yet the indiscriminate targeting of Jews in the neighborhood by the stickers, whether by intent or by accident, clearly crosses a line from anti-Israeli to anti-Jewish animus. They were still not antisemitic, according to the conceptualization being applied, but they were clearly anti-Jewish. In another reported incident, graffiti with the words "Smash Israel" was found on a mailbox and a telephone kiosk. Again, while the sentiment expressed was solely anti-Israeli in substance, it was also anti-Jewish in effect, as the fact that a synagogue was located nearby suggests that Jews attending for worship were being targeted.

Other incidents manifestly, but also with clear intent, have combined anti-Jewish animus with anti-Israeli sentiment. For instance, in one incident, upon arriving in London on a flight from Tel Aviv, some passengers were verbally abused at the arrivals gate by the offenders, who had already been observed being abusive to cabin crew on the flight. The offenders singled out some passengers and shouted, "You're British. How many countries do you need? You're killing Palestinian children. You have no right to be in these countries. You're in England; no one has put a gun to your head. How many countries do you Jews need?" (Iganski et al., 2005, pp. 57–58). In this case, as Jews indiscriminately were being targeted as proxies for the Israeli state, the incident was both patently anti-Israeli and also anti-Jewish. There was no clear evidence, though, to suggest that it was antisemitic, according to the conceptualization of antisemitism adopted to scrutinize these incidents, although the question "How many countries do you Jews need?" perhaps might raise suspicions that it is implying Jewish predation—one of the ideological dimensions of antisemitism. Another reported incident, while manifestly anti-Israeli, was also anti-Jewish in substance and intently anti-Jewish in effect. In this particular case, offensive mail was sent to a care home for Jewish residents; part of the letter stated, "We will avenge Jenin." Drawn next to it was a Star of David with a swastika inside. Although the letter ostensibly manifested political expression, the use of the Star of David, rather than the Israeli flag, and the targeting of a Jewish care home, arguably turned it into an anti-Jewish incident.

In other cases in which Jews were targeted, the anti-Israeli sentiment was accompanied by other abuse and racist bigotry. In one such incident, the victim parked his car outside an Asian restaurant. When he got out of the car to move a board on the sidewalk advertising the restaurant, the offender emerged from the restaurant, began swearing at the victim, and said, "You're not in Israel now. You can't do what you like. Go back to Israel." The offender then continued to swear and, according to the crime report, shouted other racist abuse and kicked the car door, damaging it. This particular incident, judging from the circumstantial evidence, was not premeditated in any way, and it indicates how the Israel–Palestine conflict triggers the venting of bigotry against Jews in general, as well as animus against Jews as Israelis in particular. The fact that the car driver was being abused as a proxy for Israel would not classify this incident as antisemitic according to the conceptualization being employed, and it might be argued that the racist abuse that accompanied the anti-Israeli sentiment was a secondary manifestation. As Klug (2003) has argued, "This is not to say that antisemitism cannot and does not enter into anti-Zionism in the Arab and Muslim world. Clearly it does. Moreover, the longer Israel is at loggerheads with the rest of the region, the more likely it is that antisemitism will take on a life of its own. But equally clearly, this is, as it were, a secondary formation" (p. 134).

As a context for all of the incidents just discussed, it is instructive to recall that only one in five of the subsample of incidents analyzed manifest any anti-Israeli discourse. The majority of the remainder of the incidents manifest other abuse against Jews, and the peak in incidents associated with raised tensions in the Israel–Palestine conflict therefore arguably reveals more the pervasiveness of anti-Jewish bigotry woven into the cultural fabric of society than it indicates an outpouring of anger against the Israeli state. Events in the Israeli–Palestine conflict clearly serve as a catalyst for the venting of that bigotry that simmers beneath the surface for many people.

CONCEPTUALIZING ANTI-JEWISH INCIDENTS

One thing is clear from the analysis of so-called antisemitic incidents recorded by London's Metropolitan Police Service that manifest anti-Israeli animus: we would be hard-pressed to define any of the incidents as manifesting antisemitism conceived as a doctrine or an ideology of the Jew as "the Jew." Most incidents are unequivocally anti-Jewish, but that is not the same thing as antisemitic in the way that antisemitism has been conceived by Klug (2003) and others. But the same observation can be made about the majority of the remainder of antisemitic incidents recorded by the police. In general, the perpetrators of such incidents are not politically inspired zealots or extremists, and the targets generally have no associations with Israel. In many instances the offenses are committed by ordinary people in the course of their everyday lives The majority of incidents do not appear to have been prompted by any political or ideological volition and instead manifest a reflex of bigotry against Jews. The Israel–Palestine conflict serves as a trigger for the venting of such bigotry, but it is not the source of that bigotry. If the conflict is settled, therefore, the frequency of incidents will logically subside, but they will never disappear.

Does it matter how the incidents are conceptualized? Arguably it does. The value of a concept is how it helps us to abstract from, interpret, and comprehend the world around us. Antisemitism is commonly used as a conceptual label to refer to any bigotry, hostility, and discrimination against Jews, and its use is often politically charged: it has metamorphosed into a catch-all concept that in its generality is stripped of any analytic value. At first sight, the very narrowly defined conceptualization of antisemitism used by Klug (2003) in his attempt to rescue some clarity for the concept appears to bear little relevance to the reality of incidents against Jews on the streets and elsewhere in these early years of the twenty-first century. However, on closer inspection, the majority of incidents provide an indicator of the banality of antisemitism in that the incidents in question are not prompted by an explicit ideological conviction or volition (including those prompted by anti-Israeli sentiment); instead, in their expressive character they display a thoughtless and "common-sense," inarticulate antisemitism that lies beneath the surface of cognition for many individuals, one that has been fed by centuries of stereotypes about Jews. It rises to the surface for some people when the opportunity to vent their simmering bigotry presents itself and it is often triggered by a grievance, an irritation, or conflict: things that are commonplace in everyday life but present a particular reflex opportunity when a Jewish person is involved. Arguably, this is no different from the occurrence of racial incidents more generally.

From one perspective, the examples of incidents reported to the police discussed in this chapter might seem trivial, especially those cases where the incident is confined to the sticking of stickers on street lamps or mailboxes. Finkelstein offers such a perspective in his book *Beyond Chutzpah* (Finkelstein, 2005, p. 76). Nevertheless, each of the London incidents discussed above was serious enough for the victim to take the step of reporting it to the police. Furthermore, support for the establishment in Britain of racially aggravated offenses, and support for similarly conceived hate crime statutes—or bias crime statutes—in the United States is premised on the notion that such crimes hurt more than similar, but otherwise-motivated crimes (Iganski, 2001). They are not only likely to have more damaging emotional and psychological effects upon individual victims, but they also potentially terrorize victimized communities as such victimization, in which persons are targeted because of their identity, constitutes a threat of further victimization for persons of a similar identity. More abstractly, such crimes also strike at one of the core values of liberal democracy: a respect for diversity. They violate the equality principle, a dominant cultural principle enshrined in antidiscrimination law and equality of opportunity provisions in European Union member states and in other countries. That is why attacks against Jews, irrespective of the reasons behind them and even if the victims are singled out because of anti-Israeli animus, constitute in the words of the European Union Monitoring Centre (2004) "a serious threat to basic European values and democracy" (p. 14). Given those core values expressed in the laws of many states, such attacks might indeed be considered surprising. They are even more surprising when it is acknowledged that the victims are commonly ordinary Jews going about their everyday lives, and the perpetrators are acting in an environment in which their human rights are not being routinely abused, or civil rights quashed.

NOTE

1. Although when parallels are drawn between the Israeli state and the practices and atrocities committed by the Nazi regime, many Jews and non-Jews who view Israel and Zionism as central to Jewish identity will regard the discourse as unquestionably antisemitic.

REFERENCES

Avnery, U. (2002, September 28). Manufacturing Antisemites. *Haaretz*. Retrieved December 19, 2008 from http://zope.gush-shalom.org/home/en/channels/avnery/archives_article213/

Beaumont, P. (2002, February 17). The new anti-Semitism? *Observer*. Retrieved December 19, 2008 from http://www.guardian.co.uk/world/2002/feb/17/1

Community Security Trust. (2007). *Antisemitic Incidents Report 2006*. London: Community Security Trust.

European Monitoring Centre (EUMC). (2004). *Manifestations of Antisemitism in the EU 2002–2003*. Vienna, Austria: Author.

Finkelstein, N. G. (2005). *Beyond chutzpah: On the misuse of Antisemitism and the abuse of history*. London: Verso.

Gavison, R. (1998). Incitement and the limits of the law. In R. C. Post (Ed.), *Censorship and silencing: Practices of cultural recognition* (pp. 43–65). Los Angeles: The Getty Research Institute.

Hirschberg, P. (2006, November 14). Netanyahu: It's 1938 and Iran is Germany; Ahmadinejad is preparing another Holocaust. *Haaretz.* Retrieved December 19, 2008 from http://www.haaretz.co.il/hasen/spages/787766.html

Klug, B. (2003). The collective Jew: Israel and the new antisemitism. *Patterns of Prejudice, 37*(2), 117–138.

Klug, B. (2006, March 17). In search of clarity. *Catalyst.* London: Commission for Racial Equality. Retrieved December 19, 2008 from http://www.haaretz.co.il/hasen/spages/787763.html

Klug, B. (2007, February 5). No one has the right to speak for British Jews on Israel and Zionism. *Guardian.* Retrieved December 19, 2008 from http://www.guardian.co.uk/world/2007/feb/05/comment.israelandthepalestinians

Iganski, P. (2001). Hate crimes hurt more. *American Behavioral Scientist, 45*(4), 626–638.

Iganski, P., Kielinger, V., & Paterson, S. (2005). *Hate crimes against London's Jews.* London: Institute for Jewish Policy Research in association with the Metropolitan Police Service.

Jacobson, H. (2003). Wordsmiths and atrocities against language: The incendiary use of the Holocaust and Nazism against Jews. In P. Iganski & B. Kosmin (Eds.), *A new Antisemitism? Debating Judeophobia in 21st century Britain.* London: Profile Books.

Remba, G. D., & Klug, B. (2004, March 24). Anti-Semitism—New or Old? *The Nation.* Retrieved December 19, 2008 from http://www.thenation.com/doc/20040412/exchange

Tutu, D. (2002, April 29). Apartheid in the Holy Land. *Guardian.* Retrieved December 19, 2008 from http://www.guardian.co.uk/world/2002/apr/29/comment

U.S. Department of State. (2005). *Report on global Antisemitism.* Bureau of Democracy Human Rights and Labor, Washington, DC: Author. Retrieved October 13, 2008, from http://www.state.gov/g/drl/rls/40258.htm

Whine, M. (2003). Antisemitism on the streets. In P. Iganski & B. Kosmin (Eds.), *A new Antisemitism? Debating Judeophobia in 21st century Britain.* London: Profile Books.

CHAPTER 7

ANTI-LESBIAN, GAY, BISEXUAL, AND TRANSGENDERED VICTIMIZATION IN CANADA AND THE UNITED STATES: A COMPARATIVE STUDY

Ellen Faulkner

Although victimization against sexual minorities and their supporters is now recognized as a social problem in North America, social science data concerning the prevalence and consequences of such crimes is limited. In the present study, questionnaire data about victimization experiences were collected from six Canadian studies including 1,992 lesbians, gay men, bisexuals, heterosexuals, and queers (781 females, 1,177 males) in five provinces (Nova Scotia, New Brunswick, Ontario, Alberta, and British Columbia). The distribution of bias-related victimization and harassment experiences in the sample resembled patterns reported in U.S. surveys with similar samples. In this chapter the survey and scale of victimization are reviewed. Methodological and substantive issues in empirical research on hate crimes against lesbians, gays, bisexuals, transidentified persons, and heterosexuals who are perceived to be queer are discussed. Rich qualitative data is provided on the experiences of victims, coping mechanisms, reporting experiences, and the impact of fear of potential violence. While prevalence and victim impact have been documented through studies of anti-lesbian, -gay, and -transgendered violence conducted in New Zealand, Scotland, Ireland, and the United Kingdom (Cunneen, Fraser & Tomsen, 1997; Galop, 1998; Gay Men and Lesbians Against Discrimination [GLAD], 1994; Jarmon & Tennant, 2003; Mason, 1993, 1997; Mason & Tomsen, 1997; Moran, Paterson, & Dochetry, 2004; Morgan & Bell, 2003 New South Wales Lesbian and Gay Anti-Violence Project, 2003; Stonewall National Advisory Group, 1996, 1999), and documented by international organizations and human rights groups (Amnesty International, 1997, 2001; Human Rights Watch, 2007; International Lesbian and Gay Association [ILGA], 2007; International Gay and Lesbian Human Rights Commission, 2007), the focus of this chapter will be a comparison of findings from American and Canadian community-based research. This work contributes to the literature on the prevalence and nature of homophobic violence in Canada and the United States.

Based on survey data from a convenience sample of 1,992 persons who self-selected their involvement in community-based studies across Canada, the varieties of victim experiences in hate crimes based on perceived sexual orientation are described. In analyzing the data from six studies, I hope to contribute to knowledge about patterns of victimization. This exploratory research also attempts to assess whether there is a relationship between homophobic violence and gender, socioeconomic status, partnership, age, political involvement, level of outness, and education levels. This study finds that men are more likely to experience victimization than women; however, in some instances, such as sexual harassment, women experienced equal or higher percentages of victimization. Those who are most vulnerable—youth, those from low socioeconomic backgrounds, and those who are single—indicate higher percentages of lifetime experiences of victimization. Those who are more "out" are more likely to experience victimization. Most crimes are perpetrated in public settings by one or more strangers, but victimization also occurred in other locales, and perpetrators included neighbors, co-workers, and relatives. Victims' concerns about police bias and public disclosure of their sexual orientation were important factors in deciding whether to report anti-gay/lesbian crimes. Many participants knew of others who had been victimized. Women were more likely than men to indicate that fear of future heterosexed victimization affects their day-to-day behavior. Participants were more likely to seek help from friends and partners than formal institutions, primarily due to fear of secondary victimization. While these data provide a window into the experiences of queer persons and their supporters who participate in such community-based surveys, such research does not reflect a wide cross section of the "out" community; instead, it may reflect disproportionately a demographic of white, middle- to upper-class, able-bodied gay men. More representative samples are needed in order to determine the experiences of diverse groups not typically involved in such surveys. Gaps in the research and recommendations for future research on this sensitive topic are provided.

Given the similarities across Canadian grassroots studies in terms of the types of survey instruments used, I was able to conduct an analysis of primary and secondary data. I conducted collaborative community-based research in Calgary, Toronto, and Fredericton (Faulkner, 1997, 1999, 2001a, 2004) and used samples collected by other researchers in Vancouver, Halifax, and Fredericton (New Brunswick Coalition of Human Rights Reform,

1990, 1991; Samis, 1995; Smith, 1993). In total, as mentioned above, the studies sampled 1,177 men and 781 women ($N = 1,992$) in five Canadian cities: Toronto, Ontario; Calgary, Alberta; Vancouver, British Columbia; Halifax, Nova Scotia; and Fredericton, New Brunswick. The response rate is not provided in all studies. Some of the data have been published in previous studies. For example, data have been published in reports (Faulkner 1997, 2001a, 2004; New Brunswick Coalition of Human Rights Reform 1990, 1991; Smith 1993) and theses (Faulkner, 1999; Samis, 1995).

In Ontario, a victimization survey was distributed through the 519 Church Street Community Centre with the assistance of the Community Response to Bashing Committee (CRBC) during Toronto's Pride Week in 1995 and 1996 (Faulkner, 1997, 1999). In Alberta in 2000, the survey was distributed with the assistance of Calgary Police Services and the Gay/Lesbian Communities Police Liaison Committee at Calgary Pride events (Faulkner, 2001a). And in 2004, the survey was again distributed in New Brunswick, with the assistance of the Fredericton Pride Committee (Faulkner, 2004). Secondary data were obtained from community-based research previously conducted in Halifax, Nova Scotia; Fredericton, New Brunswick; and Vancouver, British Columbia (New Brunswick Coalition of Human Rights Reform, 1990, 1991; Samis, 1995; Smith, 1993).

THE HISTORICAL CONTEXT

During the years 1993–1997, I volunteered at the 519 Church Street Community Centre ("The 519") in Toronto. As with all victim-assistance models, the face presented to the community and the actual implementation of the model are only as effective as the people who are involved. Without community input and activism, the work that needs to be done to realize the dream behind the model cannot be realized. For this reason, The 519 relies heavily on volunteer committee members who meet on a monthly basis to discuss political issues, conceptualize political activism, and negotiate the work necessary to follow through on these ideas. The 519 facilitates the framework and structure for these meetings.

The community center provides a meeting place for a wide range of groups in downtown Toronto, one of which is the CRBC, of which I was a member from 1993 to 1997. During this five-year period I combined activism with academic research to document two issues: the experience of victims of anti-gay/lesbian violence and the approach taken by the Toronto community to respond to this social problem. Ultimately, the model of victim assistance developed by the CRBC in Toronto offers a unique approach to victim assistance because it operates separately from police services and provides advocacy as well as empowerment to activists who have themselves experienced the effects of heterosexist bias at some point during their lives. This tactic suggests that gays and lesbians are not simply victims of systemic hatred but active agents in seeking social change. It is through the process of organizing to protest anti-gay/lesbian violence that research was conducted, which acted to both enlighten and empower an activist community.

The historical context out of which the CRBC developed set the stage for the revamped victim-assistance approach to advocacy and political activism (see Faulkner, 2001b). Since 1995, attempts have been made to build alliances with Toronto groups working on hate crime issues. However, the work of victim advocates at The 519 is not the first attempt by grassroots groups and supportive volunteers to challenge anti-gay/lesbian violence in Toronto.

In the late 1960s, as the civil rights movement and the sexual revolution made their way across North American university campuses, a gay rights group was organized at the University of Toronto (Gay Archivist, 1991). Toronto's first community gay and lesbian group, called the University of Toronto Homophile Association (UTHA), which later became known as the Community Homophile Association of Toronto (CHAT), was established in the early 1970s. Despite this organizing, the relationship between the lesbian and gay communities and police was rocky. Police targeted sexual minority communities for what they saw as violations of Criminal Code morality laws. Tensions between police and the queer community reached a high point on February 5, 1981, when 200 officers raided four bathhouses and arrested 300 men, charging almost all of them as found-ins of a common bawdy house. The next night, thousands marched down Yonge Street to protest the police action. This was a defining moment for Toronto's diverse queer communities. When the gay bathhouse raids of 1979 and 1981 took place, sexual minorities in Toronto were no longer willing to tolerate interference in their businesses and persecution because of their sexual difference. Lesbians and gay men resisted through public protest and civil prosecution, demanding human rights and change at various social and political levels in Toronto (Berube, 1996; Bruner, 1981; Lesbian and Gay History Group of Toronto, 1981; *The Morand Report*, 1976; The Right to Privacy Committee [RTPC], 1981; Smith, 1990).

In 1979, a group of progressive lawyers organized the RTPC to represent those charged by the Intelligence Bureau of the Metro Toronto Police as keepers or as found-ins of a common bawdy house. Between 1980 and 1984, the RTPC was able to quash the convictions of nearly 90 percent of the 300 persons charged in the 1979 and 1981 Toronto bathhouse raids. The RTPC also organized the largest antipolice demonstrations in recent Toronto history (Smith, 1990, p. 259). A decade of silence and animosity between the lesbian and gay communities and the police followed this serious confrontation.

The political climate changed in the late 1980s, when antiviolence programs sprang up in New York and in San Francisco (Herek & Berrill, 1992, pp. 241–258; Wertheimer, 1992, pp. 227–240). During the 1980s, as a response to increased anti-gay/lesbian violence, efforts had been made to organize queer patrols in Toronto's Church and Wellesley area, forcing communication between police and queer activists (Krawczyk, 1991). In July 1990 lesbians and gays demonstrated in Montreal to protest police brutality (Lesbians and Gays Against Violence, 1990; Wells, 1990). AIDS activism heightened the Toronto queer community's awareness of systemic homophobia. Toronto's Queer Nation formed in 1990 to protest the exclusion of "out" lesbians and gays (Maynard, 1991). Influenced by the political ethos of the times and some high-profile, gay-bashing criminal cases, Torontonians decided to organize against bashing (Shein, 1986). In late 1990 to early 1991, reports of gay bashing began to filter down to The 519. An openly gay executive director, Kyle Rae, and his lesbian assistant, Chris Phibbs Barr, facilitated an environment of compassion and support for victims, and this environment influenced reporting behavior. Based on anecdotal evidence, The 519 began to document and share information with police with the aim of obtaining increased protection and criminal prosecution. In July 1990 the Bashing Reporting Line (BRL) was set up at CRBC was formed. The CRBC decided to focus on education and prevention as well as strengthening ties with local community groups.

THE TORONTO SURVEY

The CRBC obtained funding from the Department of Justice to study anti-gay/lesbian violence, and a victimization survey was distributed in Toronto during Pride Week in 1995 and again in 1996 (Faulkner, 1997, 1999). The survey instrument used in the research was adapted from a survey tool used extensively in the United States (Herek & Berrill, 1992, pp. 281–286). Survey distribution was done through a display table located immediately adjacent to The 519 in the center of Pride Day activities. Umbrella-covered tables and chairs were provided for participants to sit and complete the survey. The table was staffed at all times by the project coordinator, the researcher, or volunteer research assistants. Each person who staffed the table received instruction on how to request that people participate in the survey. Each was instructed to approach a diverse and representative sample of those at the Pride Day event. A cover letter attached to each questionnaire stated The 519's commitment to protecting the anonymity of each respondent. The cover letter also outlined how the survey would be used and whom to contact to ask questions about confidentiality. Respondents choosing to take the questionnaire home with them were asked in the cover letter to return it by August 15, 1995, to The 519.

THE CALGARY SURVEY

In 1999, I joined the Calgary Gay and Lesbian Communities/Police Liaison Committee, a volunteer group that works in partnership with the Calgary Police Service. The Committee comprises community members and police who are concerned about the violence and harassment that gays, lesbians, bisexuals, and transgendered persons experience. After a number of discussions, it was decided that the group would proceed with a research project that would include the distribution of a survey during Pride Week in downtown Calgary. Unlike the Toronto study, the survey distribution in Calgary was initiated by a police and community subcommittee coordinated by Constable Doug Jones, the Gay/Lesbian Liaison/ Hate Bias Crime Coordinator. The Research Subcommittee, which included Richard Gregory, Stephen Lock, Doug Jones, and Ellen Faulkner, met and worked on the survey on numerous occasions during the summer of 2000. Many community and police volunteers took part in the distribution of the survey during the Pride Street Fair in downtown Calgary. Calgary Police Services and the City of Calgary provided funding to print the survey. The Chief of Police, Christine Silverberg, gave her feedback on the survey. As a result, questions about police harassment and abuse were altered. The survey was published in a local newspaper that is broadly circulated throughout the province of Alberta. *Outlooks* provided publicity and printed the survey of anti-gay/lesbian violence in its July 2000 issue ("Calgary Police . . . ," 2000).

THE FREDERICTON SURVEY

In eastern Canada there is no organized community response to anti-gay/lesbian violence. In the summer of 2004, I sent a public inquiry by e-mail to the queer communities in the Maritimes and received feedback that suggested that to date there had been little or no community organizing. However, in 1991 and 1993 there were two community initiatives to study anti-gay/lesbian violence (New Brunswick Coalition of Lesbian and Gay Rights Reform, 1990, 1991; Smith 1993). Since that time, hate crime initiatives have developed within the Halifax and Saint John police departments; however, there has been no organized attempt to link police and queer communities in the Maritimes (Janhevich, 2001, p. 19).

In the summer of 2004, I approached Fredericton, Moncton, and St. John Pride Day organizers to ask for permission to distribute a survey of anti-gay/lesbian violence during Pride Week celebrations. Permission was granted, and I distributed the survey at various Pride Week venues. I advertised the survey in *Wayves* (2004) and on Maritime e-mail lists (*Wayves*, 2004, p. 3). In contrast to Calgary Police Service's involvement in the survey development and distribution, no police personnel were involved in any of the Pride celebrations I attended in New Brunswick.

In Fredericton, where Pride celebrations are fairly new, police were notified about Pride activities, but they did not participate, nor did they choose to attend or show support. There was no police presence at Moncton Pride. During Fredericton Pride Day events, a group of men passed by and yelled, "Faggots!" This incident acted to sour the day's celebratory spirit. On a positive note, Andy Scott, M.P., who had been physically attacked by a man who opposed his support of same-sex marriage, attended our Fredericton celebration. Other candidates running in the upcoming provincial election also attended. In contrast to the Toronto and Calgary studies, the visible queer population in the Maritimes is much smaller and less organized in terms of a response to violence. Despite this lack of community organization, participants shared stories about incidents of anti-gay/lesbian violence they had experienced, which allowed me to assess the community and police response in the Maritimes.

The Toronto, Calgary, and Fredericton survey in its final form is divided into six categories: experiences of anti-gay/lesbian violence; reporting to victim services; reporting to police; seeking medical attention; effect of harassment on behavior; and demographic information. There are 29 questions on the survey instrument, with a total of 153 variables. The questionnaire takes an average of 15 minutes to complete. The survey includes a scale of victimization asking participants how many times they have experienced various forms of harassment in the past year and since the age of 16. Included is also a level-of-outness scale asking participants how out they are to friends, to family, and to colleagues at work. While the scale of victimization and outness scale provide only for close-ended responses, there are many open-ended questions, which allow participants to elaborate on their responses. Participants were asked to provide information on the most recent bias-related incident, locations of attacks, perpetrators, reporting experiences, and institutional responses. A list of local resources and contact persons was made available to participants. The cover page of the survey was given to participants in order to provide them with contact information should they wish to contact the researcher and/or community group for any reason. Participants were given the opportunity of adding contact information in case they wished to participate in an interview or focus group to further discuss their experience.

LIMITATIONS OF CANADIAN STUDIES

There has been no national study focusing exclusively on heterosexist violence in Canada. Purposive sampling has been used to obtain survey and interview respondents in small, localized, community-based Canadian studies to date. This method of sampling has been used in most previous Canadian and American research on anti-gay/lesbian violence (Babbie, 1992,

p. 223). The reason purposive sampling is used by those who study queer populations is that there is difficulty obtaining a random sample of the whole population, due to their invisibility. Because researchers of sexual minorities are likely to choose an approach that allows them to access lesbian and gay populations, purposive sampling tends to result in the overrepresentation of out, middle- to high-income earners, able-bodied individuals, and individuals who are Caucasian and whose first language is English. Purposive sampling does not usually capture transidentified, lesbian women, gay men, and bisexuals who are closeted or older. Generally, the experiences of Caucasian, North American gay men and lesbian women who are out, politically aware, and able-bodied are documented. For example, the majority of participants in the Canadian surveys are Caucasian, and only 18 transgendered persons responded. Approximately 80 percent of Canadian survey participants self-identified as Caucasian. Most surveys overrepresent male experience of anti-gay violence, leaving our understanding of women's experience of heterosexist hate crime understudied. This is therefore a limitation of all anti-gay/lesbian violence studies.

In attempting to measure violence, the scale tends to treat all respondents' experiences of violence in a gender-neutral manner, ignoring power differences between men and women as well as differences in the experience of violence across race and ethnicity, income levels, and sexual orientation. These differences can be measured through simple correlations of the data; nevertheless, differences may get lost as the data are quantified.

Such close-ended scales tend to exclude crucial details about motives, intentions, and consequences. The anti-gay/lesbian violence scale asks whether respondents experienced violence zero, one, or two or more times since the age of 16 or in the past year. While the scale provides information about the incidence of violent attacks, it does not provide information about the damage inflicted or victims' ability to restrain assailants or retaliate. The researchers assume that lesbian and gay respondents are victims of hate-motivated violence, based on self-reports. While such an assumption is appropriate in assessing data, researchers using scales should always qualify the findings in terms of their limitations and should pay attention to context and interpretation.

Given that the research samples in most studies are obtained through accessing a lesbian and gay event, it may be argued that all samples are not random: samples are biased toward those persons who felt comfortable attending lesbian and gay Pride events in urban settings; the self-selected non-random sample may be perceived to be unrepresentative of the whole queer population, and therefore findings are only generalizations of what may be representative of the Pride population's experience of anti-gay/lesbian violence. There are, however, some open-ended questions in the questionnaire; they allow participants to talk about the nature of their experience of anti-gay/lesbian violence, their fears, and their preventative strategies. The qualitative data allow researchers to look for patterns in the responses that are not prompted by the research instrument.

While such samples are arguably not representative of the whole sexual minority population, this criticism needs to be contextualized. There has been much political debate in queer communities that Pride indeed does not reflect a wide cross section of the "out" community; instead, it may reflect dispro- portionately a demographic of white, middle- to upper-class, able-bodied gay men. What is missing from this sample are other gay and lesbian demographic groups who are "out" but show little interest in Pride celebrations that have been criticized as being corporatized and exclusively marketed to a specific gay demographic.

While it is argued that sampling those who attend Pride events skews results toward those who are out and active in queer communities, another argument may be brought forward to support the representativeness of the sample population. Since most participants are randomly chosen from those attending Pride ceremonies in Canada or through gay and lesbian organiza- tions, they provide a probability sample of the overall population in atten- dance at Pride events and those active in queer communities. All those in attendance at queer functions, in particular Pride, have equal opportunity to self-select their involvement or to be approached to participate in the surveys of anti-gay/lesbian violence. The visibility of those attending such queer events represents the segments of the sexual minority communities who are politically active and possibly more likely to experience direct harassment, violence, or discrimination due to such visibleness.

Evidence of a correlation between being "out" and being "victimized" is limited; however, two Canadian studies have explored this correlation. In order to assess it, Calgary and Fredericton participants were asked to pro- vide information about their levels of outness with friends, family, and col- leagues at work. In every victimization category a majority of those who are "completely out" experienced more victimization since the age of 16 com- pared to those who are "not out" and only "somewhat out." This correla- tion was tested in research conducted by Stephen Samis (1995, p. 90), which found that Vancouverites who are more out and visibly queer are more likely to be harassed due to their sexual orientation. Samis found that those who are more visibly out are also more severely hurt in bashing incidents (p. 94). Samis also found a relationship between one's conformity to ("deviant" or "stigmatized") stereotypes and one's proneness to victimization. Herek, Gil- lis, and Cogan's (1999) Sacramento study ($N = 2,259$) found that those who are out of the closet to a larger circle of friends and relatives were more likely to experience bias crime victimization in the five years preceding the study (p. 947). These data are important because they point toward a positive re- lationship suggested in the literature (Berrill, 1990; Comstock, 1991; Harry,

1982, 1990; Herek, 1990, as cited in Samis, p. 94) between being out as a gay, lesbian, or bisexual person and suffering more severe forms of victimization as a result of being out.

Therefore, samples selected from queer communities are drawn from a wide cross section of those most likely to be representative of able-bodied Caucasian queers who are out and supportive of sexual minorities and who are subsequently more likely to be targeted for acts of anti-gay/lesbian violence. This argument fills the gaps in other research on anti-gay/lesbian violence, which presumes the underrepresentativeness of survey samples. The implication for this research and further research is that statistical analyses may be performed on empirical data collected from purposive populations with the intent of providing more in-depth analysis of the experience of out queer populations.

COMPARISON OF SURVEYS

Findings from surveys of anti-gay/lesbian violence and harassment, representing five Canadian regions, are reported in Table 7.1. Although sample characteristics, geographic locations, and sampling strategies varied considerably, all of the surveys found harassment and victimization to be widespread.

Prevalence estimates for anti-gay/lesbian violence vary widely as a result of differing definitions of violence, data collection methods, and time periods used in the studies. Current estimates indicate that the mean proportion of Canadian respondents who were verbally harassed was 68.8 percent; 39.9 percent were threatened with violence; 21.2 percent had had objects thrown at them; 31.6 percent had been chased or followed; 8.2 percent had been spit at; 18.9 percent had been punched, kicked, or beaten; 5.9 percent had been assaulted with a weapon; 22.3 percent had been sexually harassed; 9.5 percent had been sexually assaulted; 14.0 percent had been harassed by police (or subject to police misconduct); 2.5 percent had been beaten or assaulted by police; and 19.2 percent had been harassed/abused at school at least once since the age of 16 because someone presumed them to be gay or lesbian. As Table 7.2 shows, these Canadian findings are somewhat comparable to the findings obtained from American research on anti-gay/lesbian violence (Berrill 1992, p. 20; Herek & Berrill, 1992, p. 270–281; Herek, Gillis, Cogan, & Glunt, 1997, p. 210; Pilkington & D'Augelli, 1995, p. 40).

VARIATIONS IN VICTIMIZATION: GENDER AND SEXUAL ORIENTATION DIFFERENCES

In all Canadian and American studies considered here, gender differences in rates of victimization are evident. As is similar to American trends

Table 7.1 Comparison of Experiences of Harassment since the Age of 16 across Six Canadian Anti-Gay/Lesbian Violence Surveys[a]

Category	Toronto 1995–1996	Nova Scotia 1993	New Brunswick 1990	Vancouver 1995	Calgary 2001	New Brunswick 2004	Totals & averages
Total sample size	439 (22.0%)	294 (14.7%)	176 (8.8%)	420 (21.0%)	554 (27.8%)	109 (5.47%)	$N = 1{,}992$
Response rate	80%	21%	32.0%	—	55.0%	80%	44.6%
Females	215 (41%)	133 (25%)	51 (10%)	122 (23%)	190 (34.7%)	70 (64.2%)	781 (39.2%)
Males	205 (26%)	161 (20%)	125 (16%)	298 (38%)	349 (63.7%)	39 (35.8%)	1,177 (59.0%)
Transgender	18 (66.6%)	—	—	—	9 (33.3%)	—	27 (1.3%)
Verbally assaulted	77.1% ($n = 250$)	72% ($n = 211$)	82% ($n = 144$)	85% ($n = 357$)	62.5% ($n = 346$)	58.7% ($n = 64$)	68.8% ($n = 1{,}372$)
Threatened	51.1% ($n = 157$)	42% ($n = 123$)	35% ($n = 62$)	54% ($n = 226$)	36.1% ($n = 200$)	24.8% ($n = 27$)	39.9% ($n = 795$)
Had property damaged	19.4% ($n = 56$)	12% ($n = 35$)	19% ($n = 33$)	—	21.7% ($n = 120$)	16.5% ($n = 18$)	13.1% ($n = 262$)
Had objects thrown at	27.0% ($n = 78$)	25% ($n = 74$)	17% ($n = 30$)	27% ($n = 113$)	21.3% ($n = 118$)	10% ($n = 11$)	21.2% ($n = 424$)
Chased/ followed	36.8% ($n = 109$)	35% ($n = 97$)	34% ($n = 60$)	41% ($n = 172$)	31.4% ($n = 174$)	18.3% ($n = 19$)	31.6% ($n = 631$)
Spit at	17.5% ($n = 51$)	9% ($n = 26$)	10% ($n = 17$)	—	11.6% ($n = 64$)	6.4% ($n = 7$)	8.2% ($n = 165$)
Punched/ kicked/ beaten	21.8% ($n = 63$)	18% ($n = 53$)	18% ($n = 31$)	33% ($n = 138$)	14.8% ($n = 82$)	10.1% ($n = 11$)	18.9% ($n = 378$)
Assaulted with a weapon	8.1% ($n = 23$)	7.3% ($n = 21$)	—	11% ($n = 46$)	4.7% ($n = 26$)	2.7% ($n = 3$)	5.9% ($n = 119$)
Sexually harassed	38.0% ($n = 112$)	33.3% ($n = 98$)	4.0% ($n = 7$)	9% ($n = 38$)	30.0% ($n = 166$)	22% ($n = 24$)	22.3% ($n = 445$)

(*Continued*)

Table 7.1   **Comparison of Experiences of Harassment since the Age of 16 across Six Canadian Anti-Gay/Lesbian Violence Surveys[a] (*Continued*)**

Category	Toronto 1999	Nova Scotia 1993	New Brunswick 1990	Vancouver 1995	Calgary 2001	New Brunswick 2004	Totals & averages
Harassed by police	21.3% ($n = 62$)	16.5% ($n = 48$)	23.0% ($n = 40$)	18% ($n = 76$)	8.5% ($n = 47$)	6.4% ($n = 7$)	14.0% ($n = 280$)
Beaten or assaulted by police	5.3% ($n = 15$)	2.0% ($n = 6$)	2.0 ($n = 4$)	6% ($n = 25$)	—	—	2.5% ($n = 50$)
Harassed/ abused at school	—	29.0% ($n = 85$)	40.0% ($n = 70$)	24% ($n = 100$)	4.15% ($n = 23$)	—	19.2% ($n = 278$)

[a]Toronto, Ontario, 1995–1996; Halifax, Nova Scotia, 1993; Calgary, Alberta, 2001; Fredericton, New Brunswick, 2004; New Brunswick, 1990; Vancouver, 1995; Victimization experiences collected from 147 lesbians, gay men, and bisexuals (74 females, 73 males; Herek, Gillis, Cogan, & Glunt) Sacramento, CA, 1997; Medians from 24 studies reviewed by Berrill, 1992; Proportions from a sample of 193 lesbian, gay, and bisexual adolescents and young adults from 14 U.S. cities (Pilkington & D'Augelli, 1995). For additional details about this sample, see Hershberger and D'Augelli (1995); Jarmon and Tennant (2003).

(Berrill, 1992, pp. 26–27; Herek et al., 1997; Pilkington & D'Augelli, 1995), males generally experienced greater levels of antigay verbal harassment (by nonfamily members), threats, victimization in school and by police, and most types of physical violence and intimidation (including weapon assaults and being pelted with objects, spat upon, and followed or chased). In studies that overrepresented females (such as the Toronto and Fredericton studies), women generally experienced equal or higher percentages of sexual harassment and attacks by family members and people they know, and women reported greater fear of antilesbian violence. Women in the Toronto sample report more sexual harassment (20% females, 16% males) and sexual assault (9% females, 7% males) than men, which is consistent with the trends from the general population. However, the slightly higher reports from women in the Toronto survey regarding assault with a weapon (4% females, 3% males) are surprising, considering that men in the Toronto sample report being beaten more than women. The Fredericton study also shows a slightly higher experience of sexual harassment among women compared to men (12% women, 10% men). Women in the Fredericton study were also more likely to experience police misconduct (5% females, 2% males), sexual assault (7% females, 1% males), being chased/followed (9% females, 8% males), and verbal assaults (30% females,

Table 7.2 Comparison of the Canadian Data to American and UK Studies of Victimization since Age 16 (in percentages)[1]

Category	1990 CA	1993 CA	1995 CA	1999 CA*	2001 CA*	2004 CA	1992 USA	1995 USA	1997 USA	2003 UK
Total sample size	176	294	420	439	554	109	—	193	147	186
Females	51	133	122	215	190	70	—	42	74	59
Males	125	161	298	205	349	39	—	151	73	127
Verbal assault %	82	72	85	77	63	59	80	80	82	71
Threatened with violence %	35	42	54	51	36	25	41	41	45	50?
Chased/Followed %	34	33	41	37	31	18	33	31	32	56[3]
Objects thrown %	17	25	27	27	21	10	25	33	33	35
Spit At %	10	9	—	18	12	6	13	13	10	18
Punched/beaten %	16	18	37	22	15	10	17	18	14	30
Assault with weapon %	—	7	11	8	5	3	9	9	11	—
Harassed by police %	23	18	18	21	9	7	20	—	—	—
Sexual assault %	—	16	9	17	9	8	5	22	18	10
Property damage %	19	12	—	19	21	17	19	23	17	25[4]

[1] *Canada:* New Brunswick Coalition for Human Rights Reform, 1990, Fredericton, New Brunswick; Smith, 1993, Halifax, Nova Scotia; Samis, 1995, Vancouver, British Columbia; Faulkner, 1999, Toronto, Ontario; Faulkner, 2001, Calgary, Alberta; Faulkner, 2004, Fredericton, New Brunswick. *United States of America:* Medians from 24 studies reviewed by Berrill 1992; Proportions from a sample of 193 lesbian, gay, and bisexual adolescents and young adults from 14 U.S. cities (Pilkington & D'Augelli, 1995). For additional details about this sample, see Hershberger and D'Augelli (1995); Victimization experiences collected from 147 lesbians, gay men and bisexuals (74 females, 73 males) (Herek, Gillis, Cogan & Glunt, Sacramento, CA, 1997). *United Kingdom:* Jarman and Tennant, 2003, Belfast, Ireland. *In some cases the total sample size does not reflect the number of males and females in the sample. This is due to the fact that some participants did not identify their gender.

[2] Lifetime experiences of graffiti 19%, offensive phone calls 18%, hate mail 7% and being blackmailed 6% are combined to represent lifetime percentages of experience of homophobic threats (Jarman and Tennant, 2003, p. 42).

[3] Lifetime experiences of being followed by foot 27%, by car 16%, and stalked 13% are combined to represent lifetime percentages of being chased/followed (Jarman and Tennant, 2003, p. 42).

[4] Lifetime experiences of property vandalised 16% and property stolen 9% are combined to represent lifetime experiences of property damage (Jarman and Tennant 2003, p. 42).

38% males). Women in the Halifax study experienced equal amounts of property damage (8% females, 8% males). American research shows that lesbians report higher rates of harassment by acquaintances and family members (Von Schulthess, 1992). Aurand, Adessa, and Bush (1985) and Larry Gross et al. (1988) reported verbal as well as physical abuse within families of both gay men and lesbians.

In four Canadian studies (Toronto, Halifax, Calgary, and Fredericton), women were more likely to provide qualitative data, suggesting they experienced greater fear of future victimization, and were more likely to modify their behavior than were men; however, several women commented on modifying their behavior because they are women facing sexism as well. As a means to assess levels of fear within the victim population, participants were asked whether the potential for future victimization due to their sexual orientation affected their behavior. While women and men reported equal percentages of being somewhat and greatly affected (73.3% women, 73.5% men, 72% transgender), women were by far more likely to provide qualitative data on how they modify their behavior to prevent attack.

Across American studies, women reported greater fear of anti-gay/lesbian violence (Berrill, 1992, p. 28). One study that focused specifically on the experience of lesbians found that they take precautions to protect themselves from antiwoman and antilesbian remarks, and their safety concerns are compounded by class and race/ethnicity differences (Von Schulthess, 1992). According to Lana Stermac and Peter Sheridan (1993), "It is important to remain aware of the overall high rates of violence against women which may be, at times, difficult to differentiate in terms of motivation (Berrill, 1990)" (Stermac and Sheridan, 1993, p. 35).

In samples in which women were almost equal to men (Halifax and Toronto) or, where women were overrepresented, as in the Fredericton study, women experienced more or equal percentages of sexual harassment. In the Vancouver and Calgary studies, in which men constituted over half to three-quarters of the sample, males experienced higher percentages of sexual harassment. In examining lifetime percentages of sexual harassment across three Canadian studies, it was found that women and men had experienced almost equal percentages of sexual harassment since the age of 16 (women, 25.5%; men, 26.9%) and in the past year (women, 19.3%; men, 19.5%). However, in American and Canadian studies that also ask about sexual assault (rape), the percentage of men having been victimized rises in comparison to women (Berrill, 1992, p. 27; Comstock, 1991, p. 41; Smith, 1993, p. 23). Canadian and American definitions of "sexual assault" differ. A broader definition applies in Canada. "Rape" has a particular and narrower connotation than "sexual assault." The almost equal percentages of women and men experiencing sexual assault and sexual harassment reported in some of the Canadian studies is unusual in comparison to trends in the heterosexual population, which show that women experience higher percentages of this form of victimization.

Men experienced higher percentages of violence in the categories of verbal assault, physical assault, property damage, being spat upon, assault by police, and being chased and followed. Men also reported having experienced a higher percentage of verbal assault than female participants. In the majority of American and Canadian studies of anti-gay/lesbian violence, men consistently experience higher percentages of verbal abuse and threats of physical violence compared to women (Berrill, 1992, pp. 26–27). The exception to this trend is the Fredericton, New Brunswick, study, which found that women experienced more verbal assaults compared to men (30% female, 28% male).

Men report a higher percentage of threats of physical violence than women. This finding corresponds with American studies of anti-gay/lesbian violence, which show that men are more likely than women to be threatened with physical violence (Berrill, 1992, pp. 26–27; Comstock, 1991, p. 41).

Men report a higher percentage of property damage. American research correspondingly shows that a higher percentage of men than women report experiences of vandalism or arson (Berrill, 1992, pp. 26–27; Comstock, 1991, p. 40). However, women in the Fredericton study experienced equal amounts of property damage compared to men (8% female, 8% male).

Men report a higher percentage of being punched, kicked, and beaten. In all North American studies of anti-gay/lesbian violence, men experience higher percentages of physical assault except for the Fredericton study, which found that women experienced equal amounts of physical assault (5.5% women, 5.5% men; Berrill, 1992, p. 27; Comstock, 1991, p. 40; Faulkner, 2004). This trend is consistent with trends in the general population, where men experience more physical assaults than women (Statistics Canada, 1996).

What is unusual in the studies that overrepresent women is that women experience similar or higher occurrences of victimization compared to men. For example, in the Toronto study, men and women report almost similar occurrences of being spat upon, assaulted by police, and chased and followed since the age of 16. The high percentage of Toronto women reporting being spat upon is unusual in North American studies where men tend to report much higher frequency (Berrill, 1992, p. 25; Comstock, 1991, p. 40). Likewise, in the Fredericton study, women experienced slightly more or equal percentages of verbal harassment, being beaten, police misconduct, and being chased and followed since the age of 16 compared to men.

In the Toronto survey of anti-gay/lesbian violence, participants were asked two questions on the victimization scale related to police. Participants were asked whether they had been verbally harassed (name-calling, put-downs, etc.) and physically assaulted (actual physical attack) by police in the past year and since the age of 16. In the Calgary survey, this question was altered to read "police misconduct" due to the feeling on the part of police

that the first question was misleading. This revision was repeated in the
Fredericton survey in order to ensure valid comparison of data.

The six Canadian victimization studies reveal that participants in each
study experienced harassment by police. Caution must be taken when using
the words *harassment* and *bashing* by police, as they could include anything
from police presence in cruising parks to physical and verbal intimidation and
threats. Men generally report a higher percentage of harassment/assault and
police misconduct. In the Toronto study, men reported higher percentages
of police harassment (12.7% men, 7.4% women) and physical assault (2.8%
men, 1.8% women) compared to women. Calgary men experienced more police misconduct compared to women (6% men, 2% women). However, as reported in the Fredericton study, women experienced higher percentages of
police misconduct compared to men (4.5% women, 1.8% men). The trend in
slightly higher percentages of male respondents reporting assault by police
are consistent with findings in other North American anti-gay/lesbian violence surveys (Berrill, 1992, pp. 21, 27, 32; Comstock, 1991, p. 57; National
Coalition of Anti-Violence Programs [NCAVP], 2005, p. 86; National Gay
and Lesbian Task Force [NGLTF], 1984). Reports of harassment by police in the Toronto study were quite high for men in comparison to female
participants (13% men, 7% women); however, women experienced almost
equal percentages of assault by police (2% women, 3% men). As reported
in the Fredericton study, women indicated they experienced slightly more
police misconduct than men (5% female, 2% men). Other Canadian studies
show men with higher or almost equal percentages of harassment by police
compared to women. For example, Calgarian males experienced more police
misconduct than women (6% men, 2% women). American studies tend to
focus on physical assaults rather than harassment by police.

While women and men in the Toronto (male 19.9%, women 16.4%) and
Fredericton (9.1% women, 8.2% men) studies show almost equivalent percentages of being chased or followed, the gaps in percentages are wider in
other Canadian studies. Other Canadian and American studies of anti-gay/
lesbian violence reveal that men consistently report higher percentages of
being chased or followed compared to women (Berrill, 1992, p. 27; Comstock,
1991, p. 40). For example, Calgary men experienced higher percentages of
being chased or followed (22.1% men, 8.5% women).

Gay male respondents consistently reported higher percentages of victimization than lesbians in all categories except for sexual harassment. However, as reported in the Toronto study, lesbian women experience almost
similar lifetime percentages of assault with a weapon (3.5% lesbians, 3.4%
gays) and sexual harassment (17% lesbians, 16% gays). In the studies that
asked bisexuals (Toronto, Calgary, and Fredericton) to report on their experience of victimization, the bisexuals reported they had experienced all types
of victimization. Transgender/transsexual respondents (18 in the Toronto

study, 9 in the Calgary study) experienced some form of anti-gay/lesbian victimization in all victimization categories.

Heterosexual respondents in the Toronto study reported having experienced victimization in every victimization category except assault with a weapon and assault by police. Heterosexuals in the Calgary study reported having experienced victimization in every victimization category. Heterosexuals in the Fredericton study experienced verbal abuse, threats, sexual harassment, and sexual assault because they were presumed to be queer. These findings reveal that lesbian, gay, and bisexual respondents are not the only victims and that some heterosexual respondents who experience attack are presumed to be queer or may be attacked based on the perception that they support queer persons. While the Toronto, Calgary, and Fredericton studies included heterosexual and transgendered/transsexual respondents in its sample population, none of the American surveys of anti-gay/lesbian violence did so, which limits comparison with other studies.

The American NCAVP (2006) notes the consistently growing number of antigay violence victims who identify as heterosexual. The coalition believes there is a two-part cause for this steady increase in part, it is a by-product of a generalized increase in the numbers of victims who have identified as transgender, but heterosexual over the last several years; and in part it is the result of ever larger numbers of heterosexuals mistaken for being lesbian or gay. The NCAVP (2006) thinks "this trend only serves to underscore a central paradox of anti-LGBT violence: its execution is based on offender perception—not fact—of victim identity" (p. 41). In 2005, the number of American antiqueer violence victims who identified as heterosexual remained level for the first time in many years. However, they still represented 11 percent of the victims of anti-gay/lesbian violence (NCAVP, 2006, p. 43). In the same year bisexuals represented 3 percent of the victims of sexual orientation hate crime (NCAVP, 2006, p. 43).

MULTIPLE VICTIMIZATION

In order to assess patterns in the lifetime experiences of victimization, a correlation was made between gender and the experience of homophobic victimization once and more than once since the age of 16 in the Toronto, Calgary, and Fredericton samples. Men indicate they have experienced more victimization since the age of 16 compared to women except for the categories of assault with a weapon (women, 4.6%; men, 4.0%), sexual harassment (women, 25.5%; men 26.9%) and sexual assault (women, 9.3%; men, 9.4%) where the percentages of lifetime experiences of victimization are somewhat similar. Even more surprising are the similarities in percentages of victimization experienced in the past year. For example, women and men report experiencing almost similar percentages of property damage, being spit at, being punched/kicked/beaten, assault with a weapon, sexual harassment, and sexual assault in the past year.

Toronto, Calgary, and Fredericton participants provided information on the multiple victimization (experience of victimization two times and more) that they had experienced since the age of 16. Forty-nine percent of men and 38.1 percent of women had experienced verbal assault two times or more since the age of 16. What is even more disturbing is the numbers who experienced verbal harassment six times or more since the age of 16 (172 men, or 23.9%; 63 women, or 13.1%). Men were more likely to experience multiple incidents of being threatened with physical violence (162 men, or 31.2%; 75 women, or 15.6%) and being chased and followed (122 men, or 25.4%; 67 women, or 13.1%). Men were also more likely than women to report more multiple incidents of sexual harassment (125 men, or 26.4%; 92 women, or 19.2%). It must be noted that in many of the categories, higher percentages of participants responded that they had never experienced any form of victimization than those who did. This finding raises the question of what factors combine to promote homophobic harassment and violence and why it is that some participants experience homophobic hate crime while others do not.

Only one other Canadian study examined multiple experiences of victimization. Samis (1995, pp. 78–79) found that women and men experienced much higher percentages of multiple verbal harassment since the age of 16 (women, 73.9%; men, 73.6%) compared to the Calgary, Toronto, and Fredericton merged sample (49% men, 38% women) but somewhat similar percentages of threats (men, 36.3%; women, 34.5%) being chased and followed (women, 24.1%; men, 23.5%) and sexual harassment (women, 24.1%; men 22.9%). The percentages of multiple victimization experienced by the Vancouver sample more readily reflect the experiences of men in the merged Canadian sample than those of women.

IMPACT OF FEAR OF VICTIMIZATION

The threat of anti-gay/lesbian violence had a major impact on the attitudes and behavior of those surveyed. At least half of the women and half of the men in the Vancouver study think that it is very or somewhat likely they will be bashed in the future due to their sexual orientation (Samis, 1995, p. 85). Half of the men and women in the Vancouver study believed they might be victimized in the future, and more women (80%) than men (75%) said they feared that they would experience some form of institutional discrimination.

In comparison, Berrill (1992) reports: "The median proportion from American studies of anti-gay/lesbian violence reporting that they feared for their safety was sixty-six percent. A median proportion of eighty percent expected to be targeted for anti-gay/lesbian violence and harassment in the future" (p. 24). Also, participants in the Toronto (76%), Calgary (69.7%), Nova Scotia (68%), and Fredericton (58.3%) studies reported having modified their behavior to reduce the risk of attack (Faulkner, 1999, 2001a, 2004; Samis, 1995, pp. 76–77, 85; Smith, 1993, p. 42).

Responses consistently show that the majority are somewhat affected by the potential for anti-gay/lesbian violence (59% men, 56.4% women, 48% transgendered). For example, they took self-defense classes, avoided certain locations, censored their speech and dress, or avoided contact with friends or lovers in public places (Faulkner, 1999, p. 174). Toronto and Calgary and Fredericton respondents used terms such as fearful, hesitant, uncomfortable, worried, anxious, angry, more cautious, careful, nervous, wary, embarrassed, defensive, more covert, conservative, constantly alert, more attentive, and guarded to describe their behavior when they felt they might be at risk because others perceived them to be queer (Faulkner, 1999, p. 174; 2001a, 2004). Transidentified participants are more likely to be greatly affected compared to women and men (24% transidentified, 16.9% women, 14.6% men).

KNOWLEDGE OF ATTACKS ON OTHERS

Many of the lesbian women, gay men, bisexuals, and transidentified respondents, and some heterosexual respondents who were surveyed also reported they fear antiqueer harassment and violence and that they anticipate such victimization in the future. In studies that asked about these concerns, the median proportion reporting that they modified their behavior to prevent future victimization (from the Toronto, Calgary, and Nova Scotia studies) was 71.2 percent; a median proportion of 63.5 percent of Vancouver respondents expected to be the target of anti-gay/lesbian violence or harassment in the future. Berrill's (1992) analysis of findings from nine American victimization studies (excluding those conducted on American campuses) found that "the median proportion of queers reporting that they feared for their safety was 66%; a median proportion of 80% expected to be the target of anti-gay violence or harassment in the future" (p. 24).

A high percentage of Toronto (82%), Calgary (82%) and Fredericton (84.4%) respondents knew of at least one other person who had been attacked (Faulkner, 1999, p. 168; 2001a, 2004). Men in all three studies showed higher percentages of knowing at least one person who had been a victim of gay bashing compared to women (48.5% men, 37.6% women, 2.3% transgendered). The Toronto (Faulkner, 1999, p. 168) study showed that those somewhat affected by fear of anti-gay/lesbian violence were more likely to have been attacked in the past, suggesting that previous experience of victimization increases one's fear of future attack. Over half of Torontonian respondents who were somewhat affected by fear of future victimization had been victimized two times or more since the age of 16 (Faulkner, 1999, p. 168).

The data reveal that based on previous experience of some form of anti-gay/lesbian violence and harassment, respondents are sensitive to future attacks, and also have expectations that such a situation could recur. The expectation of those who have been attacked that they may be harassed or assaulted in the future based on their perceived sexual orientation is not unreasonable in terms of the high lifetime incidence of victimization experienced by the samples overall.

Survey participants identified that their fear of potential antiqueer victimization leads them to alter their behavior in various ways. The qualitative data revealed the following themes: not being openly gay and lesbian; staying in the closet; limiting public displays of affection; modifying dress and behavior; developing street wariness; and political advocacy, resistance, and fighting back.

Toronto, Calgary, and Fredericton participants said that fear sometimes motivates them to remain totally closeted in every area of their lives or closeted in certain situations. Given that this survey was conducted at Toronto, Calgary, and Fredericton Pride Week events, one might expect that most people would be "out" in many areas of their lives. However, many gay men and lesbians make significant efforts to hide their sexual orientation in many parts of their lives. Respondents stated that they feel they are forced to deny many aspects of themselves in order to avoid experiencing antilesbian and antigay harassment or violence.

Participants discussed the covert nature of their sexual orientation. Some stated that while they had previously been out about their sexual orientation, they were now more closeted than openly lesbian or gay. Some feared that being outed would cost them their jobs, families, children, and social status.

Canadian participants reported that they limit public displays of emotion and affection such as kissing, hugging, and hand-holding because of fear of their own victimization and fear for the safety of their lovers or friends.

Canadian participants reported that they modify their dress, appearance, and behavior to look less identifiably gay or lesbian and to look more "mainstream" (heterosexual) because of fear of anti-gay/lesbian harassment or violence. Some respondents stated that they intentionally avoid wearing symbols that could identify themselves as gay or lesbian. Others mentioned that they avoid associating with other lesbians and gays because they fear they will be targeted or outed. Some mentioned that they choose not to help other lesbians and gays who are being discriminated against because they fear that they could be next. Some state that they feel that they must limit their friendships because of fear for their safety.

Some participants indicated their fear of walking on streets. They named a range of precautions they take to protect themselves, including avoiding walking on streets alone at night; changing their route in order to avoid persons who might be watching them; traveling only with friends; having heightened concern and alertness when walking in known lesbian and gay areas; never taking taxis alone, particularly those waiting outside lesbian and gay establishments; and avoiding public transit.

Like their American counterparts, Canadian participants stated that they experience fear in certain neighborhoods that are known to be lesbian and gay, and some said that they experience fear upon leaving or being in lesbian and gay establishments because they sense that they could be a target for violence. Looking at ways that respondents modify their behavior compared to comments about precautions taken on the street, contradictions emerge about individual sense of safety in lesbian- and gay-identified areas. Neighborhoods and establishments that are known to be gay-positive can provide feelings of safety for some lesbians and gay men, while at the same time being places where others feel the most at risk of victimization.

Some respondents stated that they were hesitant to be outspoken about gay and lesbian issues. They stated that they fear a violent reprisal for taking a stand. However, lesbian and gay male survey respondents also reported that they fight back both verbally and physically against anti-gay/lesbian violence and harassment as a means of coping with their awareness of potential violence. Others increased their political will to take a stand. Calgary survey respondents illustrated two polarities in political responses to the threat of violence. One is to avoid and fear involvement, and the other is to fight back. Respondents said they were hesitant to be outspoken about gay and lesbian issues or to become involved in the lesbian and gay community and public battles for human rights. Some stated that they feared a reprisal for taking a stand.

LOCATIONS OF ANTI-GAY/LESBIAN VICTIMIZATION

Respondents (Toronto, Calgary, and Fredericton) were asked to provide information about where the *most recent* incident of anti-gay/lesbian victimization occurred. This question is different from those posed in other surveys of anti-gay/lesbian victimization, which allow respondents to provide information about any incident. (See for example, Samis, 1995, which allowed participants to enter multiple locations of victimization.) The Toronto questionnaire included an open-ended question regarding locations of victimization and perpetrators. Once patterns were established, the Calgary and Fredericton questionnaires provided categories that participants could tick off. Respondents were asked whether they had experienced anti-gay/lesbian victimization in the home, workplace, school or academic setting, gay or lesbian establishment, park, washroom, street, parking lot, institutions, and other locations.

Respondents were given the option to provide qualitative data about other locations where anti-gay/lesbian victimization typically occurs. Violent incidents were reported to occur in all of the above locations with the exception of a washroom. Queers and those assumed to be so were also attacked in restaurants, in Laundromats, at parties, in meetings, at doctor's offices, in heterosexual bars, in gay and lesbian and straight neighborhoods and on public transit, and in theaters. Simply put, lesbians and gay men are targets for anti-gay lesbian victimization in ordinary circumstances of work and life. This trend is also found in American research by Herek, Cogan, and Gillis (2002), who found that "members of sexual minorities face harassment and victimization in schools, in the workplace, and in and around their homes" (p. 336). Herek and colleagues (2002) also found diversity in the perpetrator population. They note that participants were often targeted by strangers, neighbors, schoolmates, co-workers, and relatives (p. 336).

PERPETRATORS

Most of what is known about the perpetrators of anti-gay/lesbian victimization is based on anecdotal information, surveys of victims, and reports by victims to gay community-based victim assistance organizations such as The 519's Bashing Reporting Line (AVP-BRL). Only three Canadian studies (Toronto, Calgary, and Fredericton) asked about the perpetrators of anti-gay/lesbian victimization.

While the New Brunswick, Nova Scotia, and Vancouver studies did not provide information on perpetrators of anti-gay/lesbian violence, the Calgary, Toronto, and Fredericton studies obtained anecdotal information on the perpetrator population that may not come to the attention of police due to the non-Criminal Code definition of the attack or because of the unwillingness of victims to report.

Trends developing across Canadian victimization studies reveal that survey respondents describe perpetrators of anti-gay/lesbian violence as average people who are acting on society's intolerance and hatred of gay, lesbian, bisexual, and transidentitied persons in everyday situations. For example, respondents to Canadian surveys identified perpetrators as strangers, co-workers, students, youth, family members, friends, neighbors, police officers, teachers, landlords, roommates, gang members, customers, doctors, ex-partners/lovers, students, and supervisors. Adult men, male youth, and "strangers" whose gender was not always identified were listed most often as the perpetrators of anti-gay/lesbian violence by Toronto, Calgary, and Fredericton respondents.

Male youth and students were listed as the second- and third-most frequent perpetrators, followed by co-workers, people driving by in vehicles, "others" such as taxicab drivers, ex-partners, house guests, lesbian and gay community groups, sex-trade workers, neighbors, skinheads, police, women, family and relatives, friends, and professionals.

TRENDS IN ANTI-LESBIAN, GAY, BISEXUAL, AND TRANSGENDERED VICTIMIZATION

Although the experience of anti-gay/lesbian violence has been clearly demonstrated, questions remain about whether attacks are on the upswing. For example, over an 11-year period, reports of sexual orientation hate crime documented by the Toronto Police Service fluctuated from 4 percent to 15 percent of the total annual reports (Metropolitan Toronto Police Services, 2003, p. 7). ERL data reveal similar fluctuations (The 519 Church Street Community Centre, 2003). In contrast, data from the NGLTF, New York City Gay and Lesbian Anti-Violence Project, and police department bias units across the United States have all documented victimization over the last decade and a half (Herek & Berrill, 1992; Jenness, 1995). Despite a decrease in reports of victimization to the NCAVP over the last few years, the numbers have begun to rise again. The total number of anti-LGBT incidents reported to the NCAVP increased 4 percent in 2003, from 1,720 incidents in 2002 to 1,792 incidents in 2004. The number of victims tracked by NCAVP member programs rose 4 percent, from 2,042 in 2003 to 2,131 in 2004. The number of offenders (which had remained stable or actually declined in previous years) rose by 7 percent, from 2,467 in 2003 to 2,637 in 2004—a rate almost twice as high as that of either victims or incidents (NACVP, 2005, p. 2). However, as Barbara Perry (2003) notes, "It is not clear whether this reflects a 'real' increase in such violence, or a greater willingness to report victimization" (p. 30). It is difficult to infer from the data whether there have been increases in anti-gay/lesbian victimization. Any such assessment needs to be placed in a historical context with respect to reporting patterns, the emergence of the phenomenon of "hate crime" more generally, and anti-gay victimization that may be associated with the AIDS crisis.

CONCLUSIONS

Over the past 15 years there has been a great deal of response since the first brave gays and lesbians in the early 1980s began openly talking about gay bashing and harassment as a result of the bathhouse raids in Toronto in 1981. Yet as suggested by Kevin Berrill (1992), we need more research to *"better understand the scope and the nature of anti-gay violence and victimization"* (p. 40).

The present study has both substantive and methodological implications for Canadian research on antigay and antilesbian hate crimes. The data indicate that, as in the United States, antigay victimization is a common experience for gay men, lesbians, and bisexuals. In the present sample, roughly 19 percent of the respondents had experienced an antigay assault at some time in their lives, and another 13 percent had experienced an antigay property crime. Verbal harassment and threats were even more prevalent, with approximately 69 percent of the respondents experiencing at least one incident since age 16 (see Table 7.1).

The trends in victimization from Canadian data point to vulnerable groups within this sample. Gay men, those from low socioeconomic backgrounds, those who are active in queer communities, those between 15 and 19 years of age, those who are out, and those who are not in a partnership experience higher percentages of victimization. Women experience victimization in categories which typically characterize female victimization. And women are more likely than men to be attacked by someone they know. As I have noted elsewhere (Faulkner, 2006), "The gender typicality of the victimization patterns suggests gender is the causal variable rather than sexual orientation. More systematic analysis of the data with representative samples needs to be conducted to assess the strength of the gender variable in the data set" (p. 160). These trends in victimization point to policy recommendations focusing on the needs of these vulnerable groups. Outreach needs to be done to ensure that vulnerable groups are able to access information about victim-assistance services, police, and hospitals.

The data reported here corroborate and extend the findings of past research. They also paint a rich portrait of hate crime victimization. As in earlier studies, the hate crimes described by participants most commonly occurred in public locations and were perpetrated by one or more males who were strangers to the victim. Yet as the narratives make clear, it would be inaccurate to conceptualize anti-gay/lesbian violence only in terms of street crimes. Members of sexual minorities face harassment and victimization in schools, in the workplace, and in and around their homes. Whereas queer persons are often targeted by strangers, they are also victimized by neighbors, schoolmates, co-workers, and relatives. Indeed, the respondents' stories dramatically show that people risk victimization whenever they are labeled gay, lesbian, or bisexual. I was struck by the physical and psychological brutality of the hate crimes described in the qualitative data. This brutality has important consequences. For victims, it results in heightened and prolonged psychological distress after the crime. The brutality of hate crimes also has consequences for gay and lesbian communities. Bias-motivated attacks function as a form of terrorism, sending a message to all lesbians, gay men, and bisexuals that they are not safe if they stay visible.

While participants were forthcoming with information about incidents they perceived to be hate-motivated, it is difficult to assess whether all cases were indeed motivated by the hatred of gay and lesbian persons. This highlights one of the difficulties inherent in hate crime research. Directly asking respondents if they are the victim of a hate crime or bias crime is problematic because those terms may have different meanings for different participants. In addition, some victims may avoid explicitly labeling their experience of hate crime out of a need to preserve a sense of personal safety or a feeling of control over events in their life. "Herek, Gillis, and Cogan (1999) found that gay men and lesbians who generally attribute negative events in their lives to sexual prejudice have a lower sense of personal mastery and more psychological distress than those who do not make such attributions. Thus, labelling an incident a hate crime may have a disempowering effect on the victim" (Stermac & Sheridan, 2002).

Hate crime victims were considerably less likely to report the incidents to police than to victim-assistance programs such as The 519. The qualitative data clearly show that concern about secondary victimization is an important reason for nonreporting but not the sole basis for it. The reasons cited by participants suggest a complex calculus in which victims considered the costs and benefits of reporting (e.g., whether or not the perpetrators could be apprehended and punished) and whether the crime could appropriately be considered a police matter.

Because the Canadian questionnaires asked about the most recent incident of anti-gay/lesbian violence, and these may have been incidents that happened in the past, we do not know if they accurately describe current patterns of crime reporting. During the past decade, many police departments in Canada have taken measures to respond to the problem of hate crimes, often with assistance from state and federal government agencies. Police officials increasingly are working with minority communities to improve their response to hate crimes. Undoubtedly, police personnel in many provinces still need clearer policies and better training for dealing effectively with hate crimes based on sexual orientation. But to the extent that nonreporting persists as a problem, effective remedies will have to come from queer communities as well as the criminal justice system. Outreach to gay men, lesbians, bisexuals, and transidentified persons is necessary to overcome their long-standing suspicions of the police. Such efforts will have to originate not only in criminal justice agencies but also in community organizations.

Because the present study was conducted with a convenience sample, generalizations from the findings must be made with caution. I hope that other researchers will attempt to replicate my results with samples from other geographic areas that include lesbians, gay men, bisexuals, and transidentified participants from diverse backgrounds. My hope is that hate crime researchers will conduct more studies using face-to-face interviews and focus groups as an alternative to or in conjunction with self-administered questionnaires. As I have tried to demonstrate here, bringing victims' voices directly into my research yields a more differentiated and nuanced understanding of the nature of hate crimes.

REFERENCES

Amnesty International. (2001). *Crimes of hate, conspiracy of silence: Torture and ill-treatment based on sexual identity.* London: Amnesty International Publications. Retrieved August 23, 2007, from http://www.amnesty.org/

Amnesty International. (1997). *Breaking the silence: Human rights violations based on sexual orientation.* London: Amnesty International UK Section. Retrieved August 23, 2007, from http://www.amnesty.org/

Aurand, S. K., Adessa, R., & Bush, C. (1985). *Violence and discrimination against Philadelphia lesbian and gay people.* Philadelphia: Philadelphia Lesbian and Gay Task Force.

Babbie, E. (1992). *The practice of social research* (6th ed.). Belmont, CA: Wadsworth.

Berrill, K. T. (1990). Anti-Gay Violence and Victimization in the United States. An Overview. *Journal of Interpersonal Violence. 5*(3), 274–294.

Berrill, K. T. (1992). Anti-gay violence and victimization in the United States: An overview. In G. M. Herek & K. T. Berrill (Eds.), *Hate crimes: Confronting violence against lesbians and gay men* (pp. 19–45). Newbury Park, CA: Sage.

Berube, A. (1996). The history of gay bathhouses. In Dangerous Bedfellows, (Ed.), *Policing public sex: Queer politics and the future of AIDS activism* (pp. 187–220). Boston: South End Press.

Bruner, A. (1981). *Out of the closet: Study of relations between the homosexual community and the police.* (Report to Mayor Arthur Eggleton.) Toronto, Ontario, Canada: Toronto City Council.

Calgary Police Service's anti-gay/lesbian violence survey. (2000, July). *Outlooks Magazine.* Calgary, Alberta, Canada, pp. 10–11.

Comstock, G. D. (1991). *Violence against lesbians and gay men.* New York: Columbia University Press.

Cunneen, C., Fraser, D., & Tomsen, S. (Eds.). (1997). *Faces of hate: Hate crime in Australia.* Sydney, Australia: The Hawkins Press.

Faulkner, E. (1997). *Anti-gay/lesbian violence in Toronto: The impact on individuals and communities. A project of the 519 Church Street Community Centre Victim Assistance Programme.* (Department of Justice Canada: Research and Statistics Division/Policy Sector, Report No. TR1997–5e.) Ottawa, Ontario, Canada: Canadian Government Printing Office.

Faulkner, E. (1999). A case study of the institutional response to anti-gay/lesbian violence in Toronto. (Doctoral dissertation, University of Toronto, 1999). *Dissertation Abstracts International,* AAT NQ41150. Retrieved from http://www.lib.umi.com/dissertations/fullcit/NQ41150

Faulkner, E. (2001a). *Anti-gay/lesbian violence in Calgary: The impact on individuals and communities. A project of the Calgary Gay and Lesbian Communities Police Liaison Committee.* Calgary, Alberta, Canada: Calgary Police Services.

Faulkner, E. (2001b). Empowering victim advocates: The community response to anti-gay/lesbian violence in Canada. *Critical Criminology: An International Journal, 10*(2), 123–135.

Faulkner, E. (2004). *Anti-gay/lesbian violence in Fredericton, New Brunswick: The impact on individuals and communities.* Fredericton, New Brunswick, Canada: Fredericton Pride Committee.

Faulkner, E. (2006). Homophobic Sexist Violence in Canada. Trends in the Experiences of Lesbian and Bisexual Women in Canada. *Canadian Woman Studies*, 25(1, 2), 154–161.

Galop, London's Lesbian, Gay and Bisexual Hate Crime Charity. (1998). *Telling it like it is: Lesbian, gay and bisexual youth speak out on homophobic violence.* London: Author.

Gay Archivist. (June 1991). The archivist at work. *Gay Archivist, 9.* Retrieved August 21, 2007, from http://www.clga.ca/Material/Records/docs/chatlga9.htm

Gay Men and Lesbians Against Discrimination. (1994). *Not a day goes by: Report on the GLAD survey into discrimination and violence against lesbians and gay men in Victoria.* Melbourne, Australia: Author.

Gross Larry, Aurand, S. R., & Adessa, R. (1988). Violence and Discrimination Against Lesbian and Gay People In Philadelphia and the Commonwealth of Pennsylvania: A Study by the Philadelphia Lesbian and Gay Task Force. Philadelphia. (June).

Harry, J. (1982). Derivative Deviance: The Cases of Extortion, Fag-Bashing, and Shakedown of Gay Men. *Criminology, 19*(4), 546–564.

Harry, J. (1990). Conceptualizing Anti-Gay Violence. *Journal of Interpersonal Violence, 5*(3), 350–358.

Herek, G. M., & Berrill, K. T. (Eds.). (1992). *Hate crimes: Confronting violence against lesbians and gay men.* Thousand Oaks, CA: Sage.

Herek, G. M., Cogan, J. C., & Gillis, J. R. (2002). Victim experiences in hate crimes based on sexual orientation. *Journal of Social Sciences, 58*(2), 319–339.

Herek, G. M., Gillis, J. R., & Cogan, J. C. (1997). Hate crime victimization among lesbian, gay and bisexual adults: Prevalence, psychological correlates, and methodological issues. *Journal of Interpersonal Violence, 12*(2), 195–215.

Herek, G. M., Gillis, J. R., & Cogan, J. C. (1999). Psychological sequelae of hate-crime victimization among lesbian and gay bisexual adults. *Journal of Consulting and Clinical Psychology, 67*(6), 945–951.

Herek, G. M., Gillis, J. R., Cogan, J. C., & Glunt, E. K. (1997). The impact of victimization among lesbian, gay, and bisexual adults: Prevalence, psychological correlates, and methodological issues. *Journal of Interpersonal Violence, 12*(2), 195–215.

Hershberger, S. L., & D'Augelli, A. R. (1995). The impact of victimization on the mental health and suicidality of lesbian, gay, and bisexual youths. *Developmental Psychology, 31*, 65–74.

Human Rights Watch. (2007). *Lesbian, gay, bisexual, and transgender rights.* Retrieved August 23, 2007, from http://www.hrw.org/doc/?t=lgbt

International Gay and Lesbian Human Rights Commission. (2007). An organization filling the gap between the International Human Rights Movement and the Gay Rights Movement. Retrieved August 23, 2007, from http://www.iglhrc.org/site/iglhrc/

International Lesbian and Gay Association. (2007). Retrieved August 23, 2007, from http://www.ilga.org/index.asp

Janhevich, D. (2001). *Hate crime in Canada: An overview of issues and data sources.* (DOJ Catalogue No. 85–551-XIE.) Ottawa, Ontario, Canada: Statistics Canada.

Jarmon, N., & Tennant, A. (2003). *An acceptable prejudice? Homophobic violence and harassment in Northern Ireland.* Belfast, Ireland: Institute for Conflict Research.

Jenness, V. (1995). Social movement growth, domain expansion, and framing processes: The gay/lesbian movement and violence against gays and lesbians as a social problem. *Social Problems, 42*, 145.

Krawczyk, B. (1991, June). Remembering the RTPC. *Gay Archivist, 9*. Retrieved August 21, 2007, from http://www.clga.ca/Material/Records/docs/remrtpc.htm

Lesbian and Gay History Group of Toronto. (1981). *History of the relationship between the gay community and the Metropolitan Toronto Police: A brief presented to Arnold Bruner for his study of relations between the homosexual community and the police.* Toronto, Ontario, Canada: Author.

Lesbians and Gays Against Violence (Montreal). (1990, July 15). *Stop police brutality* [press release]. Montreal, Quebec, Canada: Author.

Mason, G. (1993). Violence against lesbians and gay men, trends and issues. *Violence Prevention Today, 2*, pp. 3–4. Canberra, Australian Capital Territory, Australia: Australian Institute of Criminology.

Mason, G. (1997). Heterosexed violence: Typicality and ambiguity. In G. Mason & S. Tomsen (Eds.), *Homophobic violence* (pp. 1–14). Annandale, New South Wales, Australia: The Hawkins Press.

Mason, G., & Tomsen, S. (Eds.). (1997). *Homophobic violence.* Annandale, New South Wales, Australia: The Hawkins Press.

Maynard, S. (1991, Fall). When queer is not enough: Identity and politics. *Fuse Magazine*, 14–18.

Metropolitan Toronto Police Service. (2003). 2003 Annual Hate/ Bias Crime Statistical Report. Toronto, Ontario: Hate Crime Unit, Detective Services Intelligence Support. Available at: http://www.torontopolice.on.ca/publications/files/reports/2003hatecrimereport.pdf

Moran, L. J., Paterson, S., & Dochetry, T. (2004, March). *A report on the Bexley and Greenwich Homophobic Crime Survey.* Galop: London's Lesbian, Gay and Bisexual Hate Crime Charity. Retrieved August 20, 2007, from http://www.galop.org.uk/library.html

The Morand Report. (1976). Prepared for the Toronto Metropolitan Police Complaints Bureau by Justice Morand. Toronto, Ontario, Canada: Metropolitan Toronto Police Services.

Morgan, L., & Bell, N. (2003). First Out: Report of the findings of the Beyond Barriers national survey of LGBT people. Glasgow, Scotland: Beyond Barriers. Available Online at http://www.stonewall.org.uk/beyond_barriers/research/851.asp#1. Accessed December 12, 2007.

National Coalition of Anti-Violence Programs. (2005). Anti-Lesbian, Gay, Bisexual and Transgender Violence in 2004. A Report of the National Coalition of Anti-Violence Programs. New York, NY: National Coalition of Anti-Violence Programs. Available at: http://www.ncavp.org/common/document_files/Reports/2004NationalHV%20Report.pdf. Retrieved August 12, 2007.

National Coalition of Anti-Violence Programs. (2006). *Anti-lesbian, gay, bisexual and transgender violence in 2005.* New York: New York Gay and Lesbian Anti-Violence Project. Author. Retrieved August 23, 2007, from http://www.ncavp.org/publications/NationalPubs.aspx

National Coalition of Anti-Violence Programs. (2006). *2006 report on violence against LGBT people.* New York: Author. Retrieved August 23, 2007, from http://www.ncavp.org/

National Gay and Lesbian Task Force. (1984, June). *Anti-gay/lesbian victimization: A study by the National Gay Task Force in cooperation with gay and lesbian organizations in eight U.S. cities.* Washington, DC: Author.

New Brunswick Coalition for Human Rights Reform. (1990). *Discrimination and violence encountered by lesbian, gay and bisexual New Brunswickers.* Fredericton, New Brunswick, Canada: Author.

New Brunswick Coalition for Human Rights Reform. (1991, January). *Human rights for gay New Brunswickers: A brief to the Standing Committee on Law Amendments of the Legislative Assembly of New Brunswick in response to the Report Towards a World Family.* Fredericton, New Brunswick, Canada: Author.

New South Wales Lesbian and Gay Anti-Violence Project. (2003). *You shouldn't have to hide to be safe. A report on homophobic hostilities and violence against gay men and lesbians in New South Wales.* Retrieved August 23, 2007, from http://avp.acon.org. au/research.htm

Perry, B. (2003). Where do we go from here? Researching hate crime. *Internet Journal of Criminology* (pp. 1–30). Retrieved August 20, 2007, from http://www.internet journalofcriminology.com/ijc articles.html

Pilkington, N. W., & D'Augelli, A. R. (1995). Victimization of lesbian, gay, and bisexual youth in community settings. *Journal of Community Psychology, 23,* 33–56.

Samis, S. M. (1995). *An injury to one is an injury to all: Heterosexism, homophobia, and anti-gay/lesbian violence in Greater Vancouver.* Unpublished master's thesis. Simon Fraser University, Vancouver British Columbia, Canada.

Shein, B. (1986). Gay Bashing in High Park: A Tale of Homophobia and Murder. *Toronto Life,* 37–39, 64–69. April.

Smith, C. G. (1993). *"Proud but cautious." Homophobic abuse and discrimination in Nova Scotia.* Halifax, Nova Scotia, Canada: Dalhousie University Nova Scotia Public Research Group.

Smith, G. W. (1990). Policing the gay community. In R. Ng, G. Walker, & J. Muller (Eds.), *Community organizing and the Canadian State* (pp. 259–285). Toronto, Ontario, Canada: Garamond Press.

Statistics Canada. (2004, June 1). Pilot survey of hate crime. *The Daily.* Ottawa, Ontario, Canada: Author. Retrieved August 23, 2007, from http://www.statcan.ca/ Daily/English/040601/d040601a.htm

Statistics Canada. (1996). *A Graphical Overview of Crime and the Administration of Justice in Canada.* Ottawa: Statistics Canada; Canadian Centre for Justice Statistics.

Stermac, L. E., & Sheridan, P. M. (1993). Anti-Gay/Lesbian Violence: Treatment Issues. *The Canadian Journal of Human Sexuality, 2*(1), 33–38. (Spring).

Stonewall National Advisory Group. (1996). *Queer bashing.* Edinburgh, Scotland: Author. Retrieved August 23, 2007, from http://www.stonewall.org.uk/informa tion_bank/violent__hate_crime/resources/191.asp

Stonewall National Advisory Group. (1999). *Breaking the chain of hate. A national survey examining levels of homophobic crime and community confidence towards the Police Service.* Edinburgh, Scotland: Author. Retrieved August 23, 2007, from http://www. stonewall.org.uk/information_bank/violent__hate_crime/resources/192.asp

The Right to Privacy Committee (RTPC). (1981). *The Right to Privacy Committee's brief to the City of Toronto Bruner Study into relations between Metropolitan Toronto Police and Toronto's homosexual community.* Toronto, Ontario, Canada: Author.

The 519 Church Street Community Centre. (2003). *Victim Assistance Program annual reports 1990–2003.* Toronto, Ontario, Canada: Author.

Von Schulthess, B. (1992). Violence in the streets: Anti-lesbian assault and harassment in San Francisco. In G. M. Herek & K. T. Berrill (Eds.), *Hate crimes: Confronting violence against lesbians and gay men* (pp. 65–73). Newbury Park, CA: Sage.

Wayves. (2004, June). Atlantic news: Survey of anti-gay/lesbian violence. *Wayves: For Atlantic Canadians* (p. 3). Halifax, Nova Scotia, Canada: Author.

Wells, P. (1990, July 17). Riot police break up protest by gays: 48 men and women arrested at sit in outside police station. *The Montreal Gazette* (Montreal, Quebec, Canada, p. A3).

Wertheimer, D. M. (1992). Treatment and service interventions for lesbian and gay male crime victims. In G. M. Herek & K. T. Berrill (Eds.), *Hate crimes: Confronting violence against lesbians and gay men* (pp. 227–238). Newbury Park, CA: Sage.

CHAPTER 8

MALE VIOLENCE AGAINST WOMEN IN NORTH AMERICA AS HATE CRIME

Walter S. DeKeseredy

What Elizabeth Pendo (1994) stated 15 years ago still holds true today. There is "tremendous resistance to the recognition of gender-based violence against women as a hate crime and the institutionalized inequality which that resistance reflects" (p. 157). For example, in the United States, neither federal nor state statutes covering hate crime statistics include gender as one of their bases (Gerstenfeld, 2004). Indeed, as Jenness (2004) reminds us, "gender is best envisioned as a 'second-class citizen' in social, political, and legal discourse in the United States that speaks directly to the larger problem of violence motivated by bigotry and manifest as discrimination (i.e., bias-motivated violence)" (pp 182–183). As described in Box 8.1, Canada's position mimics that of the United States. What accounts for this selective inattention? Of course, there are a several explanations, but one of the most widely cited accounts is that hate-motivated violence against women is so common that it is perceived by many people to be a "normal" part of contemporary North American society (Ferber, 2004; Katz, 2006).

Statistically, male violence against women is normal. For example, one out of every four female university/college students in the U.S. and Canada experiences some variation of sexual assault on an annual basis (DeKeseredy & Flack, 2007). Moreover, every year, at least 11 percent of women in North American marital/cohabiting relationships are physically assaulted by their male partners (DeKeseredy, in press). Consider, also, the results of DeKeseredy, Perry, and Schwartz's (2007) representative survey of hate-motivated sexual assaults on female undergraduates at two Ontario institutions of higher learning. These sociologists found that slightly less

---

Box 8.1   Hate Laws: Protection for Females Demanded

A coalition of students, academics and educators is appealing to federal politicians to change the Criminal Code, so females are protected under hate laws.

In an open letter to Prime Minister Stephen Harper and opposition party leaders Stephane Dion, Jack Layton and Gilles Duceppe released yesterday, the Violence in the Media Coalition urges them to "address a vital public safety issue affecting half of the population of Canada that can no longer be ignored."

Currently, the hate law covers individuals by color, race, religion, ethnicity and sexual orientation.

"Omitting girls and women from the list compromises their safety," the letter says. "There is no justification for it. It is a stark piece of unfinished business and one has to seriously wonder why it is taking so long to deal with it."

Peter Jaffe, of the University of Western Ontario and the group's spokesperson, said the coalition has been trying unsuccessfully, to get politicians' attention. "We wrote the open letter to the federal leaders hoping they'd work together on this."

Jaffe said two recent reports on the sexual harassment and assaults that young females encounter in Ontario high schools is a sign of the negative impact hateful images can have in the media.

"Whether you are looking at video games or music videos or if you look at pornography . . . there are more violent images and you begin to think these are acceptable ways to treat women," he said.

Source: Rushowy, K. (2008, March 5). Hate laws: Protection for females demanded. *Toronto Star*, p. A19.

---

than 11 percent of the 384 women in their sample stated that they had experienced one or more of the five variants of hate-motivated sexual assault (see Table 8.1) in the past seven months. Ironically, while Canadian universities and colleges contribute to the advancement of learning and broadening young minds, data presented in Table 8.1 support Ehrlich's (1999) claim that these postsecondary institutions are showing dramatic trends toward intolerance, as evidenced by ongoing, even escalating rates of racial, ethnic, and gender harassment. Some U.S. studies have uncovered similar problems on college campuses (e.g., Van Dyke & Tester, 2008; Southern Poverty Law Center, 2003).

Men who abuse women are not acting in a deviant manner completely opposite to everything they have ever learned about how to treat women. Of course, some abusive men have clinical pathologies (O'Leary, 1993), but most do not (DeKeseredy, 2008; Pagelow 1992, 1993). Fewer than 10 percent of all incidents of intimate violence are caused by mental disorders, and psychological perspectives cannot explain the other 90 percent (DeKeseredy & Schwartz, 1996; Gelles & Straus, 1988). This is one of the key reasons why psychological

Table 8.1   Hate-Motivated Sexual Violence Incidence Rates

Type of Sexual Assault	Number	Percentage
Been threatened with unwanted sexual behaviors	14	3.7
Been sexually harassed	8	2.1
Been verbally sexually harassed	29	7.7
Been touched sexually when you didn't want to be touched (e.g., your breasts, rear end, or genitals)	14	3.7
Had sexual relations when you didn't want to because someone threatened or used some degree of physical force (e.g., twisting your arm, holding you down) to make you	1	0.3

theories of woman abuse are not as popular among criminologists today as they were in the early 1970s (DeKeseredy & Dragiewicz, 2007).

Most men never sexually or physically assault women, but all North American men, including those who live in rural communities, live in a society that can accurately be termed a "rape culture" (Buchwald, Fletcher, & Roth 1993; Katz, 2006), where no man can avoid exposure to patriarchal and pro-rape attitudes. Rare is a man who is not exposed to pornographic media, to mainstream television shows or to movies depicting women as inferior to men, and to rap videos and songs referring to women as "bitches" and "hoes" (Katz, 2006; Schwartz & DeKeseredy, 1997). In fact, pornography plays a major role in woman abuse (Bergen & Bogle, 2000; DeKeseredy & Schwartz, 1998a; DeKeseredy, Schwartz, Fagen, & Hall, 2006).

From the standpoint of many feminist scholars (e.g., Dworkin, 1994), pornography is also a variant of hate-motivated violence against women and it, too, has become "normalized" or "mainstreamed" in North America and elsewhere (Jensen & Dines, 1998), despite becoming increasingly more violent and racist. As Jensen (2007) observes:

> There is no paradox in the steady mainstreaming of an intensely cruel pornography. This is a culture with a well-developed legal regime that generally protects individuals' rights and freedoms, and yet it also is a strikingly cruel culture in the way it accepts brutality and inequality. The pornographers are not a deviation from the norm. Their presence in the mainstream shouldn't be surprising because they represent mainstream values: the logic of domination and subordination that is central to patriarchy, hyper-erotic nationalism, white supremacy, and a predatory corporate capitalism. (p. 17)

Returning to the issue of rap songs, some journalists assert that rap artist Eminem and others who write and sing songs like his are creative. On the other hand, some feminists refer to these "musicians" as promoters of "hate humor" (Katz, 2006). It is hard to disagree with this assessment after hearing Eminem sing, "Put anthrax on your Tampax and slap you till you can't stand" (cited in Katz, p. 159). Nevertheless, despite recognizing the pain caused by such lyrics, a few feminists, such as popular singer and recording artist Tori Amos, oppose the censorship of violent, misogynist rap because they view it as functional for women. According to Amos:

> If you're singing songs that are about cutting women up, usually these guys are tapping into an unconscious male rage that is real, that's exist- ing and they're just able to harness it. So to shut them up isn't the an- swer. They're a gauge; they're showing you what's really happening in the psyche of a lot of people. (cited in MTV.com, 2001, p. 1)

Similarly, other feminists, such as Gronau (1985), contend that feminists should oppose the censorship of pornography, even its most violent forms. She claims that pornography serves to remind women of the rampant sex- ism that victimizes and exploits them. If pornography is censored, then the evidence of sexism is hidden. Gronau further argues that it is more difficult to mobilize women to fight hidden sexism than it is to fight the obvious and extreme form of sexism manifested in pornography. However, this functional conception of pornography as benefiting women represents a minority view among feminists who have written on the topic (Alvi, DeKeseredy, & Ellis, 2000).[1]

Most people would never dare to praise or support musicians, filmmakers, or actors who say hateful things about people's ethnic/cultural backgrounds or spirituality. Still, it seems that our media and society in general do not view hateful songs about women as problematic. Consider Katz's (2006) com- mentary on the marketing of Eminem as a legitimate "rebel" to youth, espe- cially to young white males:

> [I]f you focus on contents of his lyrics, the "rebellion" is empty. If you are a "rebel," it matters who you are and what you are rebelling against. The KKK are rebels, too. They boast about it all the time. They fly the Confed- erate (rebel) flag. But most cultural commentators would never dream of speaking positively about the KKK as models of adolescent rebellion for American youth because the content of what they advocate is so repug- nant. Likewise, Eminem would be dropped from MTV playlists and lose his record contract immediately if he turned his lyrical aggression away from women and gays and started trashing people of color, Jews, Catholics, etc. In that sense, Eminem's continued success makes a statement about how this culture regards women and gays. Sadly, it is a statement that many progressive, feminist, egalitarian, and non-violent people in this era of white male backlash find quite deflating. (p. 169)

Large numbers of Canadian youth listen to Eminem. Nevertheless, in late September 2000, then Ontario Attorney General Jim Flaherty tried to stop him from performing at the Toronto SkyDome, but could not because Canadian hate crime legislation does not include violence against women. Even so, thousands of Ontario residents praised Flaherty for publicly stating that it is possible that "this person would come here and advocate violence against women" ("Ontario Seeks . . . ," 2000, p. 1). At first glance, Flaherty's' efforts make Canada appear to be more progressive and safer for women. As journalist Jeffrey Simpson (2000) notes, "Canadians prefer to think of their country as virtue incarnate, its cup of tolerance running over. They endlessly recycle the cliché about Canada the 'peaceable kingdom' in large part because it makes them feel good about themselves. Canadians are peacekeepers abroad, peaceful citizens at home" (p. 95).

This point is now subject to much debate, given that Canada is now involved in a major war in Afghanistan. Canada is also involved in an invisible war, one that has occurred for at least 2,000 years and that takes the lives of at least 60 women each year (Cross, 2007; DeKeseredy, in press). It is an undeclared war on women (Vallee, 2007), and the bulk of those killed are victims of intimate femicide, which is the "killing of females with whom they have, have had, or want to have, a sexual and/or emotional relationship" (Ellis & DeKeseredy, 1997, p. 592).

Note, too, that every day in the U.S., approximately four women are killed by a male intimate partner (Stout, 2001). Sadly, data presented here and elsewhere support Diana E. H. Russell's (2001) claim that femicide is "some men's 'final solution' for women" (p. 176). Like race-based crimes, it is also intended to maintain a particular socioeconomic group's subordinate status (Gerstenfeld, 2004; Perry, 2003), which has also been normalized (Cross, 2007; DeKeseredy, 2008). Polk (2003) reminds us that, "[T]ime and time again the phrase 'if I can't have you, no one will' echoes through the data on homicide in the context of sexual intimacy" (p. 134). For example, in 16 percent of the cases of intimate femicide that occurred in Ontario, Canada, between 1974 and 1994, the victims were separated from their legal spouses (Gartner, Dawson, & Crawford, 2001). U.S. research also shows that separation is a key risk factor of femicide (Bancroft, 2002; DeKeseredy & Schwartz, in press). In fact, close to 50 percent of men in the U.S. on death row for domestic murder killed their wives or lovers in retaliation for leaving them (Rapaport, 1994; Stark, 2007).

The main objective of this chapter, then, is to join forces with other scholars trying to open the floodgates by making the case for viewing male violence against women in North America as a prime example of a hate crime. The data presented here show that many women and girls belong to "target groups," and their brutal experiences are "part and parcel of a larger hate crime problem" in the U.S., Canada, and in other countries (Jenness, 2004, p. 189).

THE POLITICAL, ECONOMIC, AND SOCIAL CONTEXT OF MALE VIOLENCE AGAINST WOMEN IN NORTH AMERICA

In his commentary on public housing violence research done by Ireland, Thornberry, and Loeber (2003), criminologist Stephen Lab (2003) makes arguments applicable to most types of social scientific research, including the work described in this chapter.[2] For example, he asserts that

> One of the most important things that criminologists often fail to address is the context within which they (their projects or topics) are operating. This is true whether they are proposing a new theory, testing an existing explanation, investigating an emerging phenomenon or evaluating an intervention or program. (p. 39)

What is the broader political, economic, and social context in which male violence against women occurs in North America? According to Canadian psychologist Donald Dutton (2006), "women's rights have finally been acknowledged after centuries of religion-based political oppression" (p. ix). His argument begs the question, "Acknowledged by whom?" Many readers will disagree, but I and many colleagues contend that North America is characterized by a rabid, ongoing, antifeminist backlash (DeKeseredy, 2006; Faludi, 1991), one that routinely involves men from a variety of socioeconomic backgrounds challenging data on the alarming extent of woman abuse presented in a previous section of this chapter and elsewhere (DeKeseredy & Dragiewicz, 2007; Hammer, 2002).

North America is a continent characterized by gross gender inequity. For example, in 30 U.S. states, under law, a man can be awarded conditional exemptions if he raped his wife (Bergen, 2006).[3] Moreover, despite decades of ongoing struggle and activism around the issue of pay equity, women continue to earn about 73.25 percent of what men do in the U.S. (Lips, 2005). Note, too, that on October 3, 2006, Bev Oda, then federal minister for the Status of Women Canada (SWC), announced that women's organizations would no longer be eligible for funding for advocacy, government lobbying, or research projects. Further, SWC was required to delete the word "equality" from its list of goals (Carastathis, 2006).

North America is a patriarchal continent, but every major social institution, such as the family, the workplace, the military, and so on, has been affected by some laws and other means of eliminating sexism (DeKeseredy, Ellis, & Alvi, 2005; Renzetti & Curran, 2002). Nevertheless, as Stanko (1997) observes, "Despite the advantages for some women who have achieved educational and employment recognition, our concern about physical and sexual integrity remains one of our main worries" (p. 630). In addition, "there is little evidence that the general patterns of men's abuse have been interrupted"

(p. 630). Moreover, in millions of North American intimate relationships men use nonviolent means of coercive control that reflect what Evan Stark (2007) refers to as the "deprivation of rights and resources that are critical to personhood and citizenship" (p. 5).

There are also numerous examples of government cuts to progressive efforts aimed at interrupting the patterns of male-to-female violence. One of the most popular pieces of U.S. legislation is the Violence Against Women Act, but most American programs dealing with the results of woman abuse operate on shoestring budgets. Worse, for a long and complicated set of reasons, those who try to provide services for abused women find that to maintain funded facilities, they must conform to strict governmental requirements. To get funds from county mental health budgets, their clients often must have diagnoses and prognoses. Services must be aimed at the individual problems of the client (Schwartz & DeKeseredy, 2008). Also in the United States, Child Protection Services often are required in the first instance to try to maintain the family, even if one member is a batterer or child sexual abuser. Services, money, and programs do not deal with broader social forces in North America. As Miller and Iovanni (2007) put it, "These concessions have shifted the discourse and action away from challenging the root causes of battering—including issues related to power and privilege—and away from prevention efforts" (p. 294).

Some of the responses to former National Football League player Michael Vick constitute another highly problematic example of how contemporary North American society responds to violence against women. He was, and rightfully so, sent to prison for operating an illegal dog-fighting ring, and there was a broad national sense of outrage about his crime. Why do people get so upset by the death of animals, but not by the murder of women? In Pittsburgh, a sports radio personality pointed out that Michael Vick would have never gotten into as much trouble if he had limited himself to raping women. The radio personality was removed from the air, but the fact remains that he was right. Why, in North America, do most athletes accused of battering or rape end up with the charges dismissed and the woman complainant vilified (Benedict, 1997; Katz, 2006)? The outrage and economic pressure (e.g., losing lucrative endorsements) just is not there in North America for people who harm women. Just dogs (Schwartz & DeKeseredy, 2008).

MALE VIOLENCE AGAINST WOMEN IN THE NAME OF HATE: A BRIEF REVIEW OF RECENT RESEARCH

According to McPhail (2003), "Violence against women fits the hate crime paradigm when women are selected as victims due to their gender . . . or due to the perpetrators hatred of women"[4] (p. 270). Hate-motivated male-to-female violence is also used to keep women "in their place" (Perry, 2003). Consider sexual harassment, a problem that a growing number of hate crime scholars (e.g., DeKeseredy, Perry, and Schwartz, 2007; Perry, 2001) and many radical feminists[5] (e.g., Kelly, 1988) deem to be a variant of sexual violence. The sexual harassment of adult women frequently occurs in workplaces, on the streets, in bars, in the military, and in universities (Lenton, Smith, Fox, & Morra, 1999; Sev'er, 1999; Street, Gradus, Stafford, & Kelly, 2007). However, many female elementary and high school students are also victimized by this harm. Following Wolfe and Chiodo (2008), the sexual harassment of such women involves

> acts that are sufficiently severe, persistent, or pervasive to limit a student's ability to participate in or benefit from an education program or activity, or to create a hostile or abusive educational environment. Such harassment can take physical forms (such as a pulling at clothing, rubbing up against another person, or grabbing impinging), as well as verbal forms (such as sexual comments, jeers, rumour spreading, or sexual jokes aimed at an individual). (p. 1)

Young women are targeted by the above behaviors mainly because of their sex and experience frequent victimization. Consider that the Ontario Secondary School Teacher Federation's (1995) provincewide survey found that 80 percent of female students were sexually harassed at school. More recently, Wolfe and Chiodo (2008) gathered survey data from over 1,800 Grade 9 and Grade 11 students from 23 Ontario high schools and found that many young female students are targets of male hate-motivated violence. For example, 46 percent of the female Grade 9 students were victimized by sexual comments, jokes, gestures, or looks.

Sometimes, too, sexual harassment involves violent behavior similar to what happened to one of MacQuarrie, Welch, Carr, and Huntley's (2004) interviewees. Her workplace experiences are described in box 8.2, and she reports that she was abused because she is a woman. The cruel, degrading acts could also be interpreted as attempts to "keep her in her place" (Perry, 2003). Regardless, several factors outlined by McPhail (2003, p. 272) and Webb (1994) make her victimization a hate crime: the use of hate language, the absence of another motive (e.g., robbery), excessive brutality, and lack of provocation. It should also be noted in passing that the woman featured in Box 8.2 is white.

Harassment-related violence sometimes escalates to murder, as it did for Theresa Vince in 1996:

> Theresa Vince was a twenty-five year employee from Sears Canada Inc. At the time of her death she was the Human Resources Training Administrator. On June 2, 1996, Theresa Vince was murdered at her place of work, by her boss, the store manager, who also shot and killed himself. Sixteen

months earlier she had made a complaint of sexual harassment and a poisoned work environment. (Carr et al., 2004, p. 3)

School and workplace harassment are just two of many tactics used to keep women in their place. Perry (2001), among others, contends that separation/divorce assault is another glaring example that can "fit the hate crime model" because it is motivated by a perceived loss of male control and ownership (McPhail, 2003, p. 271). In earlier times, the law—the law of men—helped husbands prevent their wives from leaving them (DeKeseredy & MacLeod, 1997; Dobash & Dobash, 1979). Today, legal provisions are not as sexually symmetrical, and husbands/cohabitors must rely on their own spouse-controlling resources to a great degree. Their violence is a form of informal social control (Black, 1983; Ellis & DeKeseredy, 1997). The use of violence, including sexual assault, as a means of social control escalates when female partners separate, because separation is an extreme public challenge to male partners who believe they won their wives/cohabiting partners and therefore have the right to control them (DeKeseredy & Schwartz, in press).

For example, Tina is one of 43 rural Ohio women who participated in a qualitative separation/divorce sexual assault study conducted by DeKeseredy

---

Box 8.2   Violent Workplace Sexual Harassment in the Name of Hate

One man would throw things at me when he was angry, like a 45-gallon drum, knives, etc. If I bent over the machinery to work, the men would come behind me imitating sexual acts. They would grab my breasts and in between my legs. I was made to do a lot of clean-up jobs in the department because that was woman's work. A supervisor walked into the shower when I was showering to ask if I wanted to work overtime. I wasn't allowed to leave a shift when it was slow like everyone else in the department because the supervisor said I had to stay in case he got horny and if I left I would be disciplined. Sexist jokes were always told to me or about me. The men would show me their penises or bend over and moon me. A few of the men have come from behind me and laid their penises on my shoulder and tried to force oral sex after they taped me to a chair. The men would urinate in the department in the steam holes and at the outside break area. One man defecated in his pants and shook his pant leg and it dropped on the floor. The supervisor told me to finish my work with him . . . I was ducttaped to a chair and hoisted up on a lift truck and left there without being able to use the washroom for the remainder of a shift, with everyone laughing because I am fearful of heights.

Source: MacQuarrie, B., Welsh, S., Carr, J., & Huntely, A. (2004). *Workplace harassment and violence.* London, Ontario, Canada: Centre for Research on Violence Against Women and Children, University of Western Ontario.

and colleagues (2006). Tina wanted to leave her partner but was afraid of losing her children. Asked why her partner sexually assaulted her, she replied:

> Um, to punish me for leaving him. To punish me for getting pregnant, um, to punish me for embarrassing him and um, to control me . . . And then something would happen and he would know it was getting close to the end of our relationship once again and he would start it. And the whole time I would be crying, but I couldn't cry loud enough because if his parents heard us he swore he would take our children away. I know he did this when he thought I was getting ready to leave and he knew that I couldn't live without my children. (p. 236)

Most of DeKeseredy et al.'s (2006) respondents stated that they were raped during or after separation because their partners wanted to show them "who was in charge." Tanya was one of many interviewees who had a partner who was determined not to let her go:

> He did it because I was his and he felt he could. And it was his way of letting me know that, ah, first of all, of letting me know that I was his. And secondly, letting me know that um, that I wasn't safe anywhere. And I, when we were together, when he had forced me to go back together with him, ah, he, ah . . . raped me as another form of, of possession. And I think also as a reminder of what could happen. And ultimately, at one point, I believed he raped me as part of his means of killing my unborn child. (p. 240)

A few of DeKeseredy and colleagues' (2006) respondents were also forced to have sex with their ex-partners' friends as part of a brutal degradation ceremony. This is what happened to Marie:

> Well, him and his friend got me so wasted. They took turns with me and I remembered most of it, but, um, there was also drugs involved. Not as much on my behalf as theirs. I was just drunk. And I did remember most of it and the next morning I woke up feeling so dirty and degraded and then it ended up getting around that I was the slut . . . And in my eyes that was rape due to the fact that I was so drunk. And I definitely didn't deserve that and I was hurting. I was hurting the next day. (p. 239)

Male proprietariness is not limited to male ex-partners. Many men who abuse their female university/college dating partners and current spouses are also especially controlling (Cousins & Gangestad, 2007; DeKeseredy & Schwartz, 1998a; Smith, 1990). Moreover, like many youth who engage in violent gang activities or violent street crimes, many possessive, controlling batterers, rapists, stalkers, and so on are "companions in crime" (Warr, 2002). In other words, their male peers strongly influence them to engage in various types of woman abuse. In fact, a large body of quantitative and qualitative research shows that male peer support is one of the most powerful determinants (DeKeseredy & Schwartz, in press).[6] Male peer support refers to "the attachments to male peers and the resources that these men provide which encourage and legitimate woman abuse" (DeKeseredy, 1990, p. 130).

This form of peer pressure that legitimizes the abuse of women is in all types of culture throughout the world (Bowker, 1983; DeKeseredy et al., 2006). In addition to causing female targets of male hate-motivated violence much pain and suffering (and sometimes death), patriarchal male peer support harms victims' communities, which, according to McPhail (2003, p. 271), is "another hallmark of hate crime." For example, many people assume that rural North American communities have lower crime rates than do metropolitan areas (Weisheit, Falcone, & Wells, 2006), which is commonly explained by asserting that rural communities have higher levels of collective efficacy than do urban ones (Donnermeyer, Jobes, & Barclay, 2006). Put differently, they argue that rural areas are characterized by what Sampson, Raudenbush, and Earls (1998) refer to as "mutual trust among neighbors combined with a willingness to act on behalf of the common good, specifically to supervise children and maintain public order" (p. 1). However, collective efficacy in rural areas takes different shapes and forms, and is not necessarily restricted to deterring or preventing crimes such as woman abuse (DeKeseredy, Donnermeyer, et al., 2007).

What may appear to outsiders as social disorganization is often "simply a different form of social organization if one takes the trouble to look closely" (Wacquant, 1997, p. 346). For example, 67 percent of DeKeseredy et al.'s (2006) respondents reported on a variety of ways in which their ex-partners' male peers perpetuated and legitimated separation/divorce sexual assault. Similarly, Websdale (1998) uncovered evidence of a powerful "ol' boys network" that serves to dominate and oppress rural Kentucky women. Thus, collective efficacy may facilitate some crimes even as it constrains others (Donnermeyer et al., 2006). Donnermeyer and colleagues (2006) found that many rural Ohio men can rely on their male friends and neighbors, including those who are police officers, to support a violent patriarchal status quo while they can count on these same individuals to help prevent public crimes (e.g., vandalism and burglary), which to them is acting on "behalf of the common good." Furthermore, in rural sections of Ohio and other states such as Kentucky, there is widespread acceptance of woman abuse and community norms prohibiting victims from publicly talking about their experiences and from seeking social support (DeKeseredy & Joseph, 2006; Krishnan, Hilbert, & VanLeeuwen, 2001; Navin, Stockum, & Ruggard, 1993).

As is the case in impoverished North American urban areas examined by DeKeseredy, Alvi, Schwartz, and Tomaszewski (2003) and by Miller (2008), DeKeseredy, Donnermeyer, et al. (2007) uncovered that if there are high levels of collective efficacy in their rural Ohio respondents' communities, they do not function to prevent and deter woman abuse. For example, most interviewees (84%) stated that women experiencing unwanted sex in their community is a major problem, and 81 percent reported that rape or sexual assault is also a serious problem. Joan is one of many respondents who perceived sexual assault as "being rampant" in her town:

> It's a big problem. And, a lot of people get by with it. A lot of people! Even these 15-year-old kids that are touching these 7-year-old kids are getting by with it. Yeah and everything is getting way out of hand. Nobody is doing nothing but slapping everybody on the hands and its justified. And it's not justified, what you take from that child or woman, or man is not justified because . . . when you go and take from them that is something you took that will never be given back from nobody. Nobody can refill something that has been taken from you. (p. 300)

Eighty-one percent of the women interviewed by DeKeseredy, Donnermeyer, et al. (2007) stated that they personally know other women who were sexually assaulted, which provides further evidence that such victimization is a major problem in some rural Ohio communities and that little is being done to prevent it. Jayne is one interviewee who knows more than one woman in her community who has either been raped or sexually assaulted in other ways:

> With the girls I know, all of them had had at least one sexual assault experience, if not rape, and mostly it goes unreported because they feel that they're at fault or it's an isolated situation that this person wouldn't do it otherwise. (p. 301)

Given DeKeseredy, Donnermeyer, et al.'s (2007) respondents' own experiences of separation/divorce sexual assault and their knowledge of others with similar experiences, it is not surprising then, that over half (58%) of the interviewees do not feel safe when they are at home, especially since forced sex is strongly related to homicide (Campbell et al., 2003). Not all women are sexually assaulted and not all women feel unsafe at home, but most women, regardless of where they live, fear rape and are scared to venture alone into public places (DeKeseredy & Schwartz, 1991; Gordon & Riger, 1989; McPhail, 2003), which contributes to an absence of collective efficacy in their communities (DeKeseredy et al., 2003).

The behavior inducing a fearful state in wide numbers of women is often not rape itself, but leers, suggestive comments, being followed for blocks down the street, being yelled at from cars, obscene phone calls, being "hit on" in restaurants and bars, and other forms of harassment (Radford, 1987; Schwartz & DeKeseredy, 1991). These behaviors are either not against the law or else deemed to be so "minor" that virtually any police force will ignore them. Yet, as Kelly and Radford (1987) point out, "at the time women are being followed/flashed at/harassed they do not know how the event will end. It is only in retrospect that such events can be defined as 'minor'" (p. 243).

The large numbers of women who report to survey researchers (e.g., De-Keseredy et al., 2003) that they had been the objects of discomfiting sexual remarks reaffirms women's vulnerability in public parts of their communities. Such remarks are constant reminders of "the relevance of their gender" (Gardner, 1995, p. 9). Contrary to popular mythology, public space is not "democratic" (DeKeseredy, Alvi, Schwartz, & Perry, 1999). It is decidedly gendered to the extent that women's social behavior in public places is closely regulated (Green, Hebron, & Woodward, 1987). Harassment is one such mechanism of social control (Perry, 2003).

Public space is simultaneously racialized for many women. For example, 21 percent of the women who participated in DeKeseredy et al.'s (1999) public housing survey ($N = 216$) experienced sexual harassment, and 10 percent of them experienced racial harassment. These results speak to the intersectionality of race and gender whereby female hate crime victims are doubly burdened. Just as sexual harassment is a reminder of gender, so too is racial harassment a reminder of racial difference. These women's location at the margins of both gendered and racialized structures of oppression leave women of color at a heightened risk of harassment in public spaces. Gendered imagery plays a supporting role in constructing people of color—men and women—as the "other" (Mullings, 1994; Perry, 2003). Women of color, then, tread both gendered and racialized boundaries.

What McPhail (2003) stated five years ago is still relevant today: "Currently, much of the literature on gender-bias violence consists of conceptual arguments within legal circles and little empirical research" (p. 275). Still, we are witnessing a slow growth in empirical work on male hate-motivated violence against women, and federal government agencies such as the Social Sciences and Humanities Research Council of Canada are starting to fund surveys on this issue, including one administered on two Canadian postsecondary school campuses by DeKeseredy, Perry, and Schwartz (2007). More theoretical work is also necessary, and it is to one recent example of an attempt to explain male-to-female gender bias violence that I now turn to.

TOWARD A SOCIAL THEORY OF GENDER-BIAS VIOLENCE

To the best of my knowledge, few social scientists have applied a hate crime perspective to the problem of male violence against women. DeKeseredy, Perry, and Schwartz (2007) are members of this small cohort and they draw upon Perry's (2003) application of Messerschmidt's (1993, 1997) structured action theory to explain hate-motivated sexual assaults on Canadian female undergraduate students. Perry and masculinities theorists, such as Messerschmidt (1993) and DeKeseredy and Schwartz (2005), contend that for many men, crime or deviance is the only perceived available technique of expressing and validating their masculinity. Certainly, hate crime is a behavior that seriously threatens many communities and is committed primarily by groups of young white men (Perry, 2001). Still, most young white men do not belong to hate groups and do not commit hate crimes against female undergraduates. However, according to DeKeseredy, Perry, and Schwartz, those who do, view "others" (e.g., gays, lesbians, feminists, people of color) as unfair and under-serving competitors and takers of "white" seats in university/college classrooms (Perry, 2003). They also experience a "sense of confusion over the meanings of both masculinity and whiteness, triggered by the perceived loss of white male privilege" (Ferber, 2000, p. 31). Thus, much of the violence uncovered by DeKeseredy, Perry, and Schwartz's campus survey is traced to the desire of white male students to assert their perceived superiority and dominance, as well as to their desire to prove the very essence of their masculinity: white heterosexuality. Many men do not view such violence as breaking a cultural norm (on violence) as much as affirming "a culturally approved hegemonic masculinity: aggression, domination, and heterosexually" (Perry, 2003, p. 155).

DeKeseredy, Perry, and Schwartz (2007) also recognize that not only white men sexually assault women who threaten their masculine power and privilege. Men from other racial/ethnic backgrounds also attack females deemed to be creating a "new world they don't like" (Ezekiel, 1995, p. xxv). For example, Muslim women with more education make some Muslim men feel insecure and challenge their sense of entitlement (Gerami, 2005), which, in turn, could result in sexual assaults as means of repairing damaged masculinity and/or of keeping women in their "proper place." In sum, then, doing hate-motivated sexual violence on the college campus is way of reestablishing or maintaining a particular type of masculinity (Messerschmidt, 1993).

The above theory has yet to be tested using self-report survey data elicited from men. Nevertheless, it constitutes a recent attempt to address one of the "missing pieces" problems in hate crime scholarship identified by Perry (2006). Similarly, Stark's (2007) work on the coercive control of women is a novel means of making woman abuse "fit the hate crime paradigm" (McPhail, 2003, p. 272).

CONCLUSIONS

This chapter is not the first attempt to declare male violence against women a hate crime or a violation of human rights. In fact, the assertion that woman abuse violates women's civil liberties was most fully developed at the international level (Stark, 2007), and international policies and statements have portrayed woman abuse as more than individual acts of violence against individual women. Furthermore, international reports have emphasized multifaceted, preventive measures that go beyond a focus on abuse to a broader emphasis on improving the position of women in society (DeKeseredy & MacLeod, 1997). For example, a manual prepared for the United Nations (1993) by an international group of experts included the following measures that might be included in a prevention strategy:

- reforming the law to foster equality;
- reforming the law to prohibit corporal punishment;
- promoting equal opportunities and human rights;
- combating stereotypes in the media;
- offering economic opportunities to ensure economic independence;
- providing affordable housing;
- providing child support; and
- improving social policies (p. 85)

International documents do not treat male-to-female violence as a unique social problem, but, rather, link it to other forms of violence and structural violations against women (DeKeseredy & MacLeod, 1997). This perspective is clearly stated in the paragraph quoted below from the *Report of the Fourth World Conference on Women*, held in Beijing, China, in 1995:

> Violence against women both violates and impairs or nullifies the enjoyment by women of human rights and fundamental freedoms. Taking into account the Declaration on the Elimination of Violence against Women and the work of the Special Rapporteurs, gender-based violence, such as battering and other domestic violence, sexual abuse, sexual slavery and exploitation, and international trafficking in women and children, forced prostitution and sexual harassment, as well as violence against women, resulting from cultural prejudice, racism and racial discrimination, xenophobia, pornography, ethnic cleansing, armed conflict, foreign occupation, religious and anti-religious extremism and terrorism are incompatible with the dignity and the worth of the human person and must be combated and eliminated. (United Nations, 1995, p. 95)

There may be a strong international emphasis on gender violence as hate crime and as a violation of women's human rights, but as McPhail (2003) puts it, in North America, "Gender as a status category has taken a detour on the road to hate crime policy acceptance but is traveling the road nonetheless" (p. 275). Still, the journey is never-ending and constantly evolving (DeKeseredy & Perry, 2006). For example, it may seem painfully obvious, but worth stating again nonetheless: More empirical, theoretical, and political work on gender-bias hate crime is needed. Of course, the same can be easily said about any given type of hate crime throughout the twentieth century (Perry, 2006).

Nevertheless, as is the case with all types of social scientific inquiry, regardless of how much attention is devoted to hate crime, the study of any variant of this social problem will always be incomplete. As we progress through this new millennium and witness a major growth in the extant literature, Barbara Perry (2006) and others will probably continue to give us "a synopsis of what we don't know about hate crime" (p. 128).

NOTES

1. See Vance (1984) for a nonfunctional, anticensorship, feminist approach to pornography.

2. This section includes modified sections of work published previously Schwartz and DeKeseredy (2008).

3. A husband is exempt in these states if his wife is mentally or physically impaired, unconscious, asleep, or unable to consent (Bergen, 2006).

4. This section includes modified sections of work published previously by DeKeseredy, Donnermeyer, Schwartz, Tunnell, and Hall (2007).

5. Many scholars (e.g., Simpson, 1989) believe that radical feminism has had the greatest impact on woman abuse research. Radical feminists contend that the most important set of social relations in any society are found in patriarchy. All other social relations, such as class, are secondary and originate from male–female relations (Maidment, 2006). Applied to woman abuse, radical feminist theory asserts that men engage in this behavior because they need or desire to control women (Daly & Chesney-Lind, 1988). This statement made by Jill Radford (1987) exemplifies this perspective: "It is clear that men's violence is used to control women, not just in their own individual interests, but also in the interests of men as a sex class in the reproduction of heterosexuality and male supremacy" (p. 43).

6. See DeKeseredy (1990), DeKeseredy and Schwartz (1998b, 20002, 2005), and Schwartz and DeKeseredy (1997) for in-depth reviews of the sociological literature on the relationship between male peer support and woman abuse.

REFERENCES

Alvi, S., DeKeseredy, W. S., & Ellis, D. (2000). *Contemporary social problems in North American society.* Toronto, Ontario, Canada: Addison-Wesley.

Bancroft, L. (2002). *Why does he do that?: Inside the minds of angry and controlling men.* New York: Berkley.

Benedict, J. (1997). *Public heroes, private felons: Athletes and crimes against women.* Boston: Northeastern University Press.

Bergen, R. K. (2006). Marital rape: New research and directions. *VAWnet,* February, 1–13.

Bergen, R. K., & Bogle, K. A. (2000). Exploring the connection between pornography and sexual violence. *Violence and Victims, 15,* 227–234.

Black, D. (1983). Crime as social control. *American Sociological Review, 48,* 34–45.

Bowker, L. H. (1983). *Beating wife-beating.* Lexington, MA: Lexington Books.

Buchwald, E., Fletcher, P. R., & Roth, M. (Eds.) (1993). *Transforming a rape culture.* Minneapolis, MN: Milkweed Editions.

Campbell, J. C., Webster, D., Koziol-McLain, J., Block, C., Campbell, D., Curry, M. A., et al. (2003). Risk factors for femicide in abusive relationships: Results from a multisite case control study. *American Journal of Public Health, 93,* 1089–1097.

Carastathis, A. (2006, October 11). New cuts and conditions for Status of Women Canada. *Toronto Star.* Retrieved October 11, 2006, from www.dominionpaper.ca/canadian_news/2006/10/11new_cuts_a.html

Cousins, A. J., & Gangestad, S. W. (2007). Perceived threats of female infidelity, male proprietariness, and violence in college dating couples. *Violence and Victims, 22,* 651–668.

Cross, P. (2007, July 6). Femicide: Violent partners create war zone for women. *Toronto Star,* p. AA8.

Daly, K., & Chesney-Lind, M. (1988). Feminism and criminology. *Justice Quarterly, 5,* 497–538.

DeKeseredy, W. S. (1990). Male peer support and woman abuse: The current stake of knowledge. *Sociological Focus, 23,* 129–139.

DeKeseredy, W. S. (2006). Future directions. *Violence Against Women, 12,* 1078–1085.

DeKeseredy, W. S. (2008, March 5). Violent men, victimized women. *National Post.* Retrieved March 5, 2008, from http://www.nationalpost.com/opinion/story.html?id=357742

DeKeseredy, W. S. (in press). Girls and women as victims of crime. In J. Barker (Ed.), *Women and the criminal justice system: A Canadian perspective.* Toronto, Ontario, Canada: Emond Montgomery Publications.

DeKeseredy, W. S., Alvi, S., Schwartz, M. D., & Perry, B. (1999). Violence against and the harassment of women in Canadian public housing. *Canadian Review of Sociology and Anthropology, 36,* 499–516.

DeKeseredy, W. S., Alvi, S. Schwartz, M. D., & Tomaszewski, E. A. (2003). *Under siege: Poverty and crime in a public housing community.* Lanham, MD: Lexington Books.

DeKeseredy, W. S., Donnermeyer, J. F., Schwartz, M. D., Tunnell, K. D., & Hall, M. (2007). Thinking critically about rural gender relations: Toward a rural masculinity crisis/male peer support model of separation/divorce sexual assault. *Critical Criminology, 15,* 295–311.

DeKeseredy, W. S., & Dragiewicz, M. (2007). Understanding the complexities of feminist perspectives on woman abuse: A commentary on Donald G. Dutton's *Rethinking domestic violence. Violence Against Women, 13,* 874–884.

DeKeseredy, W. S., Ellis, D., & Alvi, S. (2005). *Deviance and crime: Theory, research and policy.* Cincinnati, OH: LexisNexis.

DeKeseredy, W. S., & Flack, W. F., Jr. (2007). Sexual assault in colleges and universities. In G. Barak (Ed.), *Battleground criminal justice* (pp. 693–696). Westport, CT: Greenwood.

DeKeseredy, W. S., & Joseph, C. (2006). Separation/divorce sexual assault in rural Ohio: Preliminary results of an exploratory study. *Violence Against Women, 12,* 301–311.

DeKeseredy, W. S., & MacLeod, L. (1997). *Woman abuse: A sociological story.* Toronto, Ontario, Canada: Harcourt Brace.

DeKeseredy, W. S., & Perry, B. (2006). Introduction: The never-ending and constantly evolving journey. In W. S. DeKeseredy & B. Perry (Eds.), *Advancing critical criminology: Theory and application* (pp. 1–8). Lanham, MD: Lexington Books.

DeKeseredy, W. S., Perry, B., & Schwartz, M. D. (2007, November). *Hate-motivated sexual assault on the college campus: Results from a Canadian representative sample.* Paper presented at the annual meetings of the American Society of Criminology, Atlanta, GA.

DeKeseredy, W. S., & Schwartz, M. D. (1991). British left realism on the abuse of women: A critical appraisal. In R. Quinney & H. Pepinsky (Eds.), *Criminology as peacemaking* (pp. 154–171). Bloomington: Indiana University Press.

DeKeseredy, W. S., & Schwartz, M. D. (1996). *Contemporary criminology.* Belmont, CA: Wadsworth.

DeKeseredy, W. S., & Schwartz, M. D. (1998a). *Woman abuse on campus: Results from the Canadian national survey.* Thousand Oaks, CA: Sage.

DeKeseredy, W. S., & Schwartz, M. D. (1998b). Male peer support and woman abuse in postsecondary school courtship: Suggestions for new directions in sociological research. In R. K. Bergen (Ed.), *Issues in intimate violence* (pp. 83–96). Thousand Oaks, CA: Sage.

DeKeseredy, W. S., & Schwartz, M. D. (2002). Theorizing public housing woman abuse as a function of economic exclusion and male peer support. *Women's Health and Urban Life, 1,* 26–45.

DeKeseredy, W. S., & Schwartz, M. D. (2005). Masculinities and interpersonal violence. In M. S. Kimmel, J. Hearn, & R. W. Connell (Eds.), *Handbook of studies on men and masculinities* (pp. 353–363). Thousand Oaks, CA: Sage.

DeKeseredy, W. S., & Schwartz, M. D. (in press). *Dangerous exits: Escaping abusive relationships in rural America.* New Brunswick, NJ: Rutgers University Press.

DeKeseredy, W. S., Schwartz, M. D., Fagen, D., & Hall, M. (2006). Separation/divorce sexual assault: The contribution of male peer support. *Feminist Criminology, 1,* 228–250.

Dobash, R. E., & Dobash, R. (1979). *Violence against wives: A case against the patriarchy.* New York: Free Press.

Donnermeyer, J. F., Jobes, P., & Barclay, E. (2006). Rural crime, poverty, and community. In W. S. DeKeseredy & B. Perry (Eds.), *Advancing critical criminology: Theory and application* (pp. 199–218). Lanham, MD: Lexington Books.

Dutton, D. G. (2006). *Rethinking domestic violence.* Vancouver, Canada: University of British Columbia Press.

Dworkin, A. (1994). Pornography happens to women [Electronic version]. Retrieved May 1, 2008, from http://www.nostatusquo.com/ACLU/dworkin/PornHappens.html

Ehrlich, H. J. (1999). Campus ethnoviolence. In F. Pincus & H. J. Ehrlich (Eds.), *Ethnic conflict* (pp. 277–290). Boulder, CO: Westview.

Ellis, D., & DeKeseredy, W. S. (1997). Rethinking estrangement, interventions and intimate femicide. *Violence Against Women, 3,* 590–609.

Ezekiel, R. S. (1995). *The racist mind: Portraits of American Neo-Nazis and Klansmen.* New York: Viking.

Faludi, S. (1991). *Backlash: The undeclared war against American women.* New York: Crown.

Ferber, A. L. (2000). Racial warriors and weekend warriors: The construction of masculinity in mythopoetic and white supremacist discourse. *Men and Masculinities, 3,* 30–56.

Ferber, A. L. (2004). Introduction. In A. L. Ferber (Ed.), *Home-grown hate: gender and organized racism* (pp. 1–18). New York: Routledge.

Gardner, C. B. (1995). *Passing by: Gender and public harassment.* Berkeley, CA: University of California Press.

Gartner, R., Dawson, M., & Crawford, M. (2001). Women killing: Intimate femicide in Ontario, 1874–1994. In D.E.H. Russell & R. A. Harmes (Eds), *Femicide in global perspective* (pp. 147–165). New York: Teachers Press.

Gelles, R. J., & Straus, M. A. (1988). *Intimate violence: The causes and consequences of abuse in the American family.* New York: Simon & Schuster.

Gerami, S. (2005). Islamist masculinity and Muslim masculinities. In M. S. Kimmel, J. Hearn, & R. W. Connell (Eds.), *Handbook of studies on men & masculinities* (pp. 448–454). Thousand Oaks, CA: Sage.

Gerstenfeld, P. B. (2004). *Hate crimes: Causes, controls, and controversies.* Thousand Oaks, CA: Sage.

Gordon, M., & Riger, S. (1989). *The female fear.* New York: Free Press.

Green, E., Hebron, S., & Woodward, D. (1987). Women, leisure and social control. In J. Hanmer & M. Maynard (Eds.), *Women, violence and social control* (pp. 75–92). Atlantic Heights, NJ: Humanities Press.

Gronau, A. (1985). Women and images: Feminist analysis of pornography. In C. Vance & V. Burstyn (Eds.), *Women against censorship* (pp. 127–155). Toronto, Ontario, Canada: Douglas and McIntyre.

Hammer, R. (2002). *Antifeminism and family terrorism: A critical feminist perspective.* Lanham, MD: Roman & Littlefield.

Ireland, T. O., Thornberry, T. P., & Loeber, R. (2003). Violence among adolescents living in public housing: A two site analysis. *Criminology & Public Policy, 3,* 3–38.

Jenness, V. (2004). The dilemma of difference: Gender and hate crime policy. In A. L. Ferber (Ed.), *Home-grown hate: Gender and organized racism* (pp. 181–204). New York: Routledge.

Jensen, R. (2007). *Getting off: Pornography and the end of masculinity.* Cambridge, MA: South End Press.

Jensen, R., & Dines, G. (1998). The content of mass-marketed pornography. In G. Dines, R. Jensen, & A. Russo (Eds.), *Pornography: The production and consumption of inequality* (pp. 65–100). New York: Routledge.

Katz, J. (2006). *The macho paradox: Why some men hurt women and how all men can help.* Naperville, IL: Sourcebooks.

Kelly, L. (1988). *Surviving sexual violence.* Minneapolis: University of Minnesota Press.

Kelly, L., & Radford, J. (1987). The problem of men: Feminist perspectives on sexual violence. In P. Scraton (Ed.), *Law, order and the authoritarian state* (pp. 237–253). Philadelphia: Open University Press.

Krishnan, S. P., Hilbert, J. C., & VanLeeuwen, D. (2001). Domestic violence and help-seeking behaviors among rural women. Results from a shelter-based study. *Family Community Health, 24,* 28–38.

Lab, S. P. (2003). Let's put it into context. *Criminology & Public Policy, 3,* 39–44.

Lenton, R., Smith, M. D., Fox, J., & Morra, N. (1999). Sexual harassment in public places: Experiences of Canadian women. *Canadian Review of Sociology and Anthropology, 36,* 517–540.

Lips, H. M. (2005). *Sex and gender: An introduction.* New York: McGraw-Hill.

MacQuarrie, B., Welsh, S., Carr, J., & Huntely, A. (2004). *Workplace harassment and violence*. London, Ontario, Canada: Centre for Research on Violence Against Women and Children, University of Western Ontario.

Maidment, M. R. (2006). Transgressing boundaries: Feminist perspectives in criminology. In W. S. DeKeseredy & B. Perry (Eds.), *Advancing critical criminology: Theory and application* (pp. 43–62). Lanham, MD: Lexington Books.

McPhail, B. (2003). Gender-bias hate crimes: A review. In B. Perry (Ed.), *Hate and bias crime: A reader* (pp. 261–280). New York: Routledge.

Messerschmidt, J. W. (1993). *Masculinities and crime: Critique and reconceptualization*. Lanham, MD: Roman & Littlefield.

Messerschmidt, J. W. (1997). *Crime as structured action: Gender, race, class, and crime in the making*. Thousand Oaks, CA: Sage.

Miller, J. (2008). *Getting played: African American girls, urban inequality and gendered violence*. New York: New York University Press.

Miller, S., & Iovanni, L. (2007). Domestic violence policy in the United States. In L. L. O'Toole, H. R. Schiffman, & M. L. Kiter Edwards (Eds.), *Gender violence: Interdisciplinary perspectives* (pp. 287–296). New York: New York University Press.

MTV.com. (2001, September 28). Tori Amos says Eminem's fictional dead wife spoke to her [Electronic version]. Retrieved May 1, 2008, from http://www.thedent.com/mtvart0901.html

Mullings, L. (1994). Images, ideology and women of color. In M. Baca-Zinn & B. T. Dill (Eds.), *Women of color in U.S. society* (pp. 265–290). Philadelphia: Temple University Press.

Navin, S., Stockum, R., & Ruggaard, J. (1993). Battered women in rural America. *Journal of Human Educational Development, 32*, 9–16.

O'Leary, D. (1993). Through a psychological lens: Personality traits, personality disorders, and levels of violence. In R. J. Gelles & D. R. Loseke (Eds.), *Current controversies on family violence* (pp. 7–30). Thousand Oaks, CA: Sage.

Ontario Secondary School Teacher Federation. (1995). *The joke's over: Student to student sexual harassment in secondary schools*. Toronto, Ontario, Canada: Author.

Ontario seeks to stop Eminem concert. (2000, October 26). *Daily Texan* [Electronic version]. Retrieved May 1, 2008, from http://www.dailytexanonline.com/home/index.cfm?event=displayArticleprinterfriendly&u . . .

Pagelow, M. D. (1992). Adult victims of domestic violence: Battered women. *Journal of Interpersonal Violence, 7*, 87–120.

Pagelow, M. D. (1993). Response to Hamberger's comments. *Journal of Interpersonal Violence, 8*, 137–139.

Pendo, E. A. (1994). Recognizing violence against women: Gender and the hate crime statistics act. *Harvard Women's Law Journal, 17*, 157–183.

Perry, B. (2001). *In the name of hate: Understanding hate crimes*. New York: Routledge.

Perry, B. (2003). Accounting for hate crime. In M. D. Schwartz & S. E. Hatty (Eds.), *Controversies in critical criminology* (pp. 147–160). Cincinnati, OH: Anderson.

Perry, B. (2006). Missing pieces: The paucity of hate crime scholarship. In W. S. DeKeseredy & B. Perry (Eds.), *Advancing critical criminology: Theory and application* (pp. 155–178). Lanham, MD: Lexington Books.

Polk, K. (2003). Masculinities, femininities and homicide: Competing explanations for male violence. In M. D. Schwartz and S. E. Hatty (Eds.), *Controversies in critical criminology* (pp. 133–146). Cincinnati, OH: Anderson.

Radford, J. (1987). Policing male violence—policing women. In J. Hanmer & M. Maynard (Eds.), *Women, violence and social control* (pp. 30–45). Atlantic Highlands, NJ: Humanities Press International.

Rapaport, E. (1994). The death penalty and the domestic discount. In M. Fineman & R. Mykitiuk (Eds.), *The public nature of private violence* (pp. 224–254). New York: Routledge.

Renzetti, C. M., & Curran, D. J. (2002). *Women, men, and society.* Boston: Allyn & Bacon.

Rushowy, K. (2008, March 5). Protection for females demanded. *Toronto Star*, p. A19.

Russell, D. E. H. (2001). Defining femicide and related concepts. In D.E.H. Russell & R. A. Harmes (Eds.), *Femicide in global perspective* (pp. 12–28). New York: Teachers College Press.

Sampson, R. J., Raudenbush, S. W., & Earls, F. (1998). *Neighborhood collective efficacy: Does it help reduce violence?* Washington, DC: U.S. Department of Justice.

Schwartz, M. D., & DeKeseredy, W. S. (1991). Left realist criminology: Strengths, weaknesses and the feminist critique. *Crime, Law and Social Change, 15,* 51–72.

Schwartz, M. D., & DeKeseredy, W. S. (1997). *Sexual assault on the college campus: The role of male peer support.* Thousand Oaks, CA: Sage.

Schwartz, M. D., & DeKeseredy, W. S. (2008). Interpersonal violence against women: The role of men. *Journal of Contemporary Criminal Justice, 24,* pp. 178–185.

Sev'er, A. (1999). Sexual harassment: Where we were, where we are and prospects for the new millennium. *Canadian Review of Sociology and Anthropology, 36,* 469–498.

Simpson, J. (2000). *Star-spangled Canadians: Canadians living the American dream.* Toronto, Ontario, Canada: HarperCollins.

Simpson, S. (1989). Feminist theory, crime and justice. *Criminology, 27,* 605–632.

Smith, M. D. (1990). Patriarchal ideology and wife beating: A test of a feminist hypothesis. *Violence and Victims, 5,* 257–273.

Southern Poverty Law Center. (2003). *10 ways to fight hate on campus: A response guide for college activists.* Montgomery, AL: Author.

Stanko, E. A. (1997). Should I stay or should I go?: Some thoughts on variants of intimate violence. *Violence Against Women, 3,* 629–635.

Stark, E. (2007). *Coercive control: How men entrap women in personal life.* New York: Oxford University Press.

Stout, K. D. (2001). Intimate femicide: A national demographic overview. In D.E.H. Russell & R. A. Harmes (Eds.), *Femicide in global perspective* (pp. 41–49). New York: Teachers College Press.

Street, A. E., Gradus, J. L., Stafford, J., & Kelly, K. (2007). Gender differences in experiences of sexual harassment: Data from a male-dominated environment. *Journal of Consulting and Clinical Psychology, 75,* 464–474.

United Nations. (1993). *Strategies for confronting domestic violence: A resource manual.* New York: Author.

United Nations. (1995). *Focus on women, violence against women.* Report prepared for the Fourth World Conference on Women, Action for Equality, Development and Peace. Beijing, China: Author.

Vallee, B. (2007). *The war on women.* Toronto, Ontario, Canada: Key Porter.

Vance, C. (1984). *Pleasure and danger: Exploring female sexuality.* London: Routledge and Kegan Paul.

Van Dyke, N., & Tester, G. (2008). *The college campus as defended territory: Factors influencing variation in racist hate crime.* Pullman, WA: Department of Sociology, Washington State University.

Wacquant, L.J.D. (1997). Three pernicious premises in the study of the American ghetto. *International Journal of Urban and Regional Research,* July, 341–353.

Warr, M. (2002). *Companions in crime: The social aspects of criminal conduct.* Cambridge, UK: Cambridge University Press.

Webb, D. (1994). Violence against women: Is it a hate crime? *Klanwatch Intelligence Report, 73,* 4–7.

Websdale, N. (1998). *Rural woman battering and the justice system: An ethnography.* Thousand Oaks, CA: Sage.

Weisheit, R. A., Falcone, D. N., & Wells, L. E. (2006). *Crime and policing in rural and small-town America.* Prospect Heights, IL: Waveland Press.

Wolfe, D. A., & Chiodo, D. (2008). *Sexual harassment and related behaviors reported among youth from grade 9 to grade 11.* Toronto, Ontario, Canada: CAMH Centre for Prevention Science.

CHAPTER 9

HATE CRIMES COMMITTED AGAINST
PERSONS WITH DISABILITIES

Frank J. Lane, Linda R. Shaw,
and Martin Kim

On January 30, 1999, eight people were charged with kidnapping, harassment, and conspiracy after torturing Eric Krochmaluk, a 23-year-old man with mental retardation living in Middletown, New Jersey. The perpetrators of the bias crime lured him to a party after work with the promise that a girl at the party wanted to meet him. Once he was there, they stripped him to his underwear, taped him to a plastic lawn chair, shaved his eyebrows, and burned him with cigarettes before they choked him and beat him with a rope knot and beads across his chest, back, and face (Macfarquhar, 1999; Maclay, 2002; Reynolds, 2000; Sherry, 2000). The torture went on for three hours, after which they took him to a wooded area, where he was made to kiss his tormentors' feet and drink urine before he managed to escape and make his way to a security guard (Macfarquhar, 1999; Reynolds, 2000). Seven of the eight perpetrators were convicted of bias assault and sentenced to prison. They were also part of a gang, and each had lengthy arrest records. The prosecuting attorney reported that although Krochmaluk was able to describe the torture, he was unable to comprehend the barbarity of the crime; he didn't appreciate the seriousness of the crime and he simply wanted to make friends with them (Reynolds, 2000). The case is reported to be the first bias crime case against a person with a disability to go to trial in the United States (Maclay, 2002).

Nicholas Steenhout, the former Executive Director of the Progress Center for Independent Living in suburban Cook County, Illinois, was walking to work one day and was verbally assaulted by one of his neighbors. Steenhout ambulated with a wheelchair and used a service dog. The neighbor told

Steenhout to "get your f*cking dog off (his) property" (Steenhout, 2002, p. 1). Steenhout tried to explain that the dog was not urinating or defecating on his property, but the neighbor continued, calling him a "f*cking cripple" and "God punished you and I hope he punishes you some more" (p. 1). Moreover, he was told that people like him should be in nursing homes.

After multiple attempts, Steenhout reached the local police department and indicated that he wished to file a complaint on the basis of bias speech. He was told by the officer that no such crime existed in Illinois. Moreover, he was told that if he let his dog on his neighbor's property again, he would be brought to the police station in handcuffs.

The victim, perpetrator, and law enforcement officer characteristics in the cases of Eric Krochmaluk and Nicholas Steenhout illustrate situations where persons with disabilities have been victims of a bias-motivated crime. In addition, they will be used throughout this chapter to describe circumstances that are specific to disability-motivated crimes and the experience of persons with disabilities.

INTRODUCTION

The discussion about persons with disabilities as potential victims of bias-motivated crimes is relatively new to the hate crime literature. Disability was the last protected class to be included in the reauthorization of the Hate Crime Statistics Act (HCSA) in 1996. At the time, several other groups of citizens also lobbied for inclusion as protected classes (such as gender and the aged), but disability was the only new class that was included.

Persons with disabilities represent roughly 20 percent of the United States population, or approximately 54 million people (McNeil, 2001). Moreover, the proportion of American citizens with disabilities is expected to increase as the population ages over the next 10 years. Any issue that affects a portion of the population as large as those with disabilities should be regarded as an important issue. A large body of research exists that documents the widespread discrimination against persons with disabilities, or what some refer to as the "disability experience" (Vash, 1994).

It has been suggested that persons with disabilities have been discriminated against because of their disability status to a greater extent than any other minority group in history (Smart, 2001). Research shows that compared to the general population, persons with disabilities are victims of crime at a rate 2 to 10 times higher; live at or below the poverty line at a rate 2 to 3 times greater; and experience the highest rate of unemployment (69%) compared to any other minority group. These data are consistent with historical accounts of abuse toward persons with disabilities (Burgdorf, 2000).

The disability experience, however, seems inconsistent with data on bias crime incidents. Since the inclusion of disability in the HCSA, data collected by the Federal Bureau of Investigation (FBI) suggest that persons with disabilities are 350 times less likely to be the victim of a bias crime than a victim chosen because of race (McMahon, West, Lewis, Armstrong, & Conway, 2004). In addition, reports of disability-motivated bias crimes rank the lowest of all protected categories. McMahon et al. theorized that there is error in the data collected and suggested several possible explanations for the low numbers, including the possibility that disability-motivated bias crimes are underreported.

The idea that crimes committed against persons with disabilities is the lowest of all protected classes is counterintuitive, considering research data and historical accounts of prejudice and discrimination. The disparity between the two phenomena supports the theory that bias crimes committed against persons with disabilities may go underreported. When considered differently, it also seems to be a moral imperative to first determine whether a sizable number of disability-motivated bias crimes go unreported before concluding that the crimes occur less often.

Within the bias crime literature, the specific area of bias crimes committed against persons with disabilities is in critical need of attention. A small body of literature has emerged on the subject to generate hypotheses about why the numbers of crimes reported have been low.

DEFINITION OF DISABILITY

Establishing a standard definition of disability is problematic because governmental agencies use different definitions to define it (Zola, 1993). As a result, definitions are inconsistent and vary from narrow to broad. Governmental agencies are responsible, in part, for ensuring there are adequate resources available for persons with disabilities; consequently, definitions are, in large part, influenced by economics. For example, the Social Security Administration (SSA) defines disability narrowly in terms of limitations in *major life activities* and *work*. Children under the age of 16 and adults over the age of 65 are not considered to be disabled by SSA because they are typically "excluded" from work (Smart, 2001). The World Health Organization (WHO) defined disability more broadly in an attempt to establish a transagency or transcultural definition of disability. In the International Classification of Functioning, Disability, and Health (ICF) model, disability is conceptualized as a biopsychosocial model (WHO, 2001). This model incorporates the societal and individual factors that prevent an individual from fully participating in *life* activities. Although work is included in the ICF definition, the definition is certainly not limited to work.

According to Smart (2001), disabilities fall within four general categories: physical disabilities (see below), intellectual disabilities (e.g., mental retardation), cognitive disabilities (e.g., traumatic brain injury and learning disability), and psychiatric disabilities (e.g., schizophrenia). Physical disabilities include visual impairments, hearing impairments, mobility impairments, and health disorders (Smart, 2001). The HCSA recognizes only two broad categories of disability, physical and mental. The physical disability category includes those physical and cognitive disability categories discussed above, whereas the mental disability category includes intellectual and psychiatric disabilities.

The term *hate crime* is a crime that is committed in whole, or in part, by the offender's bias toward the victim. Although the term *bias crime* is the most accurate term for the offense, the terms bias crime and hate crime will be used interchangeably throughout this chapter.

INCLUSION OF DISABILITY IN FEDERAL HATE CRIME LEGISLATION

In 1990, President George H. W. Bush signed into law the HCSA, which requires the attorney general to collect data on crimes committed where the victim is chosen based on his/her membership in a protected category; the original categories included race, religion, ethnicity, and sexual orientation (Perry, 2001). In 1996, disability was included as a protected category in the act (McMahon et al., 2004), although data collection did not begin until 1997. Disability was the only group added, even though other groups such as gender, children, police officers, union members, and the elderly also lobbied for inclusion under the act. There were four primary reasons that disability was included. The first and most persuasive was the enactment of the Americans with Disabilities Act (ADA) only a few years prior, in 1990; the ADA included disability as a standard in civil rights legislation and discrimination law within the federal government (McMahon et al., 2004). By the time the ADA was passed, Congress had heard testimony from hundreds of people with disabilities concerning discrimination in their everyday lives. Therefore, it appears that the foundation had already been laid to introduce disability into the act. The other reasons include (1) the large number (54 million) of United States citizens living with a disability, (2) the existence of a degree of collective identity among people with disabilities in American society (National Council on Disability, 2000; Shapiro, 1994), and (3) the historical evidence of discrimination.

U.S. Citizens with Disabilities

Persons with disabilities represent the largest single minority group in the United States. As mentioned above, approximately 54 million Americans, or 20 percent of the U.S. population, have a disability (National Council on

Disability, 2000), and it is anticipated that the proportion of persons with disabilities will increase as the population ages (National Council on Disability). U.S. Census projected population data show an increasing trend in the proportion of individuals of retirement age, age 65 and up. Specifically, it is anticipated that by the year 2030, approximately 20 percent of the U.S. population will be retirees, compared to 12.5 percent currently (U.S. Census Bureau, 2004). Considering that approximately 50 percent of persons over the age of 65 report various health impairments, the proportion of people with disabilities in the United States is anticipated to increase dramatically. Therefore, problems faced by people with disabilities will be augmented on a national level as the population ages.

Collective Identity

Collective identity is important to the discussion of disability-motivated hate crimes because it not only provides another explanation for why disability was included in the legislation (National Organization on Disability, 2000; Shapiro, 1994), but it serves as a foundation for a later discussion on advocacy. The theoretical underpinnings of the idea of collective identity can be found in various sociological concepts. Durkheim's theory of collective consciousness is one such example (Cerulo, 1997). Collective consciousness stresses the importance of shared attributes or similarities around which any group coalesces (Cerulo, 1997). A group's belief system is one example of a shared attribute that is part of collective identity. Group beliefs are important because they function to assist others to understand how a group interprets events and collective action is taken (Albert & Whetten, 1985).

Although each disability type may have a unique collective identity (e.g., Lighthouses for the Blind having a collective identity for individuals who are legally blind), the Independent Living (IL) movement espouses the collective identity of all persons with disabilities to a greater extent than does any other organizational movement. The civil rights movement contributed much the development of the IL philosophy, which focuses heavily on equal access, entitlement, and benefit rights. The IL philosophy is applied as an action-oriented model throughout all Centers for Independent Living (CILs). The CILs receive funding from the federal government through the Rehabilitation Act of 1973. The centers are required to provide four core services for receiving federal dollars: information and referral, advocacy, independent living skills training, and peer counseling (Rubin & Roessler, 2001). Although each center receiving federal monies is required to provide these services, many provide additional services based on local needs, and some agencies have begun providing criminal justice advocacy to help persons with disabilities who have been the victim of crime navigate the criminal justice system.

History of Discrimination

The history of discrimination against persons with disabilities has been put succinctly by Smart (2001), who concluded that "no other racial, cultural, ethnic, linguistic, religious, political, national, sexual orientation, or gender group has experienced (such a) pervasive degree of generalized prejudice and discrimination" (p. 72), including the killing of babies with disabilities, forced sterilization of persons with disabilities, institutionalization, mass murder, sexual abuse in families, assisted suicides, physical abuse in institutions, aversive conditioning, electroconvulsive therapy, psychosurgery, experimentation, and excessive medication (Goffman, 1963; Lifton, 1986; Smart, 2001).

Although history is replete with examples of prejudice and discrimination toward people with disabilities, no example is as extreme in its behavior or as explicit in its goal as the medical killings in Nazi Germany. Although many associate the genocide during Nazi Germany with the killing of Jews, the first citizens targeted for extinction were people with disabilities (Lifton, 1986; Smart, 2001).

The term *life unworthy of life* had been introduced in Germany as early as the 1920s. Hitler was preparing the country for war, and any citizen who couldn't work was regarded a liability on the state (Lifton, 1986). This philosophy was used to argue the point that individuals who were "mentally ill, feeble minded, and retarded and deformed" (p. 46) were a tremendous economic burden on the country. Consequently, a physician-assisted death or "euthanasia" was not to be compared to the criminal act of killing; rather, the physician had performed a useful act for people regarded as *already dead* (Lifton, 1986).

Revisiting the events of Nazi Germany serves two purposes. First, it brings to the forefront the historical evidence of the targeting and killing of individuals because of their membership in a disability group. Second, it brings to light a way of thinking that not only supported mass killing in Germany in the early 1940s but also served as the foundation for the involuntary sterilization of United States citizens with disabilities from the 1930s to as recently as the 1970s.

DATA ON BIAS CRIMES COMMITTED AGAINST PEOPLE WITH DISABILITIES

McMahon et al. (2004) obtained data from the Summary Reporting System (SRS) and the National Incident Based Reporting System (NIBRS) on bias crimes committed against people with disabilities. These reporting systems make up the Uniform Crime Reporting (UCR) program that is used to generate the Hate Crime Statistics (HCS) reports published by the FBI. McMahon et al.'s analysis was of data collected from the period between 1997 and 2001, a total of five years. Not all law enforcement agencies participated in the UCR system, preventing a complete universe, but McMahon et al. estimated that the 12,000 law enforcement agencies that participated across 49 states represented jurisdictions covering approximately 85 percent of the U.S. population.

A total of 41,442 bias crimes were reported for the five-year period (McMahon et al., 2004). The majority of the bias crimes were committed because of the victim's race (22,030), followed by religion (7,846), sexual orientation (6,371), ethnicity (5,428), and disability (127). McMahon et al. calculated that the relative risk of being the victim of a racially motivated bias crime (1.19) was 350 times that of disability (.002).

The most common types of hate crimes committed against persons with disabilities were simple assault, intimidation, and property damage, a pattern which was consistent across all protected categories. However, the risk for simple assault was greater for people with disabilities than for any other group. The top three locations for bias crimes that were committed because of the victim's membership in race, ethnicity, or disability group were personal residence, street, and other. Residence was the location with the greatest risk for all five protected categories, but it represented the location with "the greatest degree of risk" for persons with disabilities, as did college campuses and government buildings (p. 70). McMahon et al. (2004) also compared hate crimes by physical- and mental-disability groups. Consistent with the previous analysis, the top three types of crimes for both groups were simple assault, intimidation, and property damage. However, intimidation was the most likely hate crime for persons with physical disability, whereas simple assault was the most common for persons with a mental illness disability.

McMahon et al. (2004) asserted that it is unlikely that people with disabilities experience bias crimes at a rate lower than other protected categories because of the relatively large size of the group compared to the other protected categories. McMahon et al.'s theory can be underscored by research findings from experts in the field of disability studies, who have shown that persons with disabilities experience prejudice and discrimination in almost every aspect of daily life.

THE DISABILITY EXPERIENCE

Employment. Persons with disabilities, as a group, experience a 68 percent unemployment rate (National Organization on Disability, 2001). Only 32 percent of persons with disabilities are employed on a full-time or part-time basis, compared to 81 percent of people without a disability (National Organization on Disability, 2001), and more people with disabilities are working in part-time employment without benefits (National Council on Disability, 2000). Compared to the rest of the U.S. population, persons with disabilities experience the highest unemployment rate of any minority group.

Socioeconomic Status. In addition to the low rate of employment, people with disabilities are 2–3 times more likely to live in poverty (National Organization on Disability, 2003). Individuals with disabilities live with higher levels of poverty, 29 percent versus 10 percent in the general population (National Council on Disability, 2000), and persons with severe disabilities are three times more likely to live at or below the poverty line ($15,000 or less) than a person without a disability (10%;National Organization on Disability, 2003). The 2004 Progress Report on National Disability Policy estimates that approximately 40 percent of persons receiving Temporary Assistance for Needy Families (TANF), also known as "welfare," during 2003–2004 had a disability (National Council on Disability, 2000). The same report projected the current percentage to be much higher. Because persons with disabilities often reside in poverty, they are forced to live in low-income neighborhoods, and low-income neighborhoods are often associated with higher rates of crime (Burger & Youkeles, 2004).

Crime. A review of the literature suggests that the prevalence of violent crimes committed against children and adults with disabilities is higher than against the general population in terms of the rate, frequency, and duration. Further, the offender profile is different when the victim has a disability than for similar crimes where the victim does not have a disability. Moreover, differences exist across age, type of abuse, and disability category.

Rate of crime. Researchers estimate that the incidence of violent crime against adults and children with disabilities is two and a half times greater than in the general population (Baladerian, 2001; Hiday, Swartz, Swanson, Borum, & Wagner, 1999; Sobsey & Doe, 1991; Sullivan & Knutson, 1998). Regarding incidences of sexual abuse in particular, the estimated prevalence is 5 to 10 times higher compared to the general population (Sobsey & Doe, 1991). In an Australian study of individuals with intellectual disabilities, Wilson and Brewer (1992) concluded that rate of sexual assault was 10.7 times higher, robbery was 12.8 times higher, and overall violent crime was 4.2 times higher than the general population.

Frequency. There is a fair amount of consistency in the research concerning the frequency and duration of incidences of abuse sustained by persons with disabilities. In the Sobsey and Doe (1991) study on sexual abuse, they reported that of the participants reporting sexual abuse, approximately 20 percent reported a single incident, 20 percent reported between 5 and 10 incidences, and 49.6 percent reported greater than 10 incidences (Sobsey & Doe, 1991). In addition, 9.7 percent of the participants reported the abuse as "repeated" (Sobsey & Doe, 1991). In a study conducted by Sullivan and Knutson (1998), they found that persons with disabilities experienced abuse more frequently, and the abuse was of increased duration.

Duration. Research on abuse and neglect of women with disabilities identified similar findings. In a study of 946 women with disabilities who participated in the National Study of Women with Physical Disabilities, 62 percent of the women reported they had experienced some form of sexual, emotional, or physical abuse (Nosek, 1996; Nosek, Howland, Rintala, Young, & Chanpong, 1997). The percentage of women experiencing abuse was the same for a group cf nondisabled controls. However, women with disabilities reported experiencing the abuse for longer periods of time (3.9 years) compared to women without a disability (2.5 years; Young, Nosek, Howland, Chanpong, & Rintala, 1997). In addition, women with disabilities experienced forms of abuse that were disability related, including the withholding of such items as medication, transportation, assistance with activities of daily living, and equipment for ambulation (Nosek et al.).

Perpetrator characteristics. Research suggests that the perpetrators of crimes against persons with disabilities are often individuals known to the victim, such as family members, neighbors, and acquaintances the person has because of their disability. The FBI, in its hate crime data reporting guidelines, states that reporting decreases when the victim knows the perpetrator (FBI, 1999a, 1999c). Reporting of crimes where the perpetrator is known to the victim decreases because the victim fears retribution from the perpetrator in the form of further abuse, neglect, or an interruption of services (Sobsey & Doe, 1991). In addition, victims may be reluctant to report crimes because they believe the report lacks value and will not be taken seriously at any level of decision-making in the criminal justice system (Luckasson, 1992).

Sobsey and Doe (1991) found that in 56 percent of the reported cases of abuse, the perpetrator had a relationship with the person with a disability, which is consistent with data from nondisabled victims. However, in the other 44 percent of the cases, the reported abusers had a relationship with the victim that was specific to the disability. In 27.7 percent of the cases, the perpetrator was a personal care attendant, residential care staff, hospital staff, psychiatrist, or individual in another disability-related role. Other roles of perpetrators included transportation providers, therapeutic foster parents, and other persons with disabilities. Although the percentage of cases where the perpetrator is a family member or friend is consistent with the national average, the results of this study suggests the percentage of crimes committed against persons with disabilities where the perpetrator ir *somehow known* to the victim could be as high as 100 percent. This is not an unreasonable supposition when one considers that two-thirds of the respondents to a Harris survey reported that their disability results in social isolation (National Council on Disability, 2000). Social isolation places persons with disabilities almost exclusively in contact with persons known to them, such as family, friends, and caregivers.

In the Sullivar and Knutson (1998) review of abuse of children with disabilities, 98 percent of the perpetrators were family members. In the Sobsey and Doe (1991) study, although 95.6 percent of the victims knew the perpetrator, 65.9 percent of the cases went unreported to law enforcement by the victim. Of the cases that were reported to law enforcement, charges were not filed because of refusal by the police in 19 percent of the cases, refusal by the prosecutors in 5.5 percent of the cases, and court dismissal in 2.2 percent of the cases. Of the cases that were reported, 22 percent were charged and, of the alleged perpetrators who were charged, only 36 percent of those were convicted of the offense.

Disability category. Research has also found disparity in incidences of abuse across disability categories. For example, Sullivan and Knutson (1998) found that 62.1 percent of the children with communicative disorders were abused by someone in the family, compared to 39.4 percent in the nondisabled group. Communication disorders in the Sullivan and Knutson study included children who were deaf. This finding is consistent with that of Sullivan, Vernon, and Scanlan (1987, as cited in Sobsey & Doe, 1991) who reported a review of research suggesting that 54 percent of deaf boys and 50 percent of deaf girls had been sexually abused as children. Muccigrosso (1991), in a review of literature, suggested that 90–99 percent of individuals with developmental disabilities have been sexually abused by the time they turn 18.

A CASE FOR UNDERREPORTING

Many disability theorists are looking to the issue of underreporting as a possible explanation for the relatively low recorded risk of bias crime for people with disabilities (McMahon et al., 2004; "One in a Million," 2002; Sherry, 2003; Sorensen, 2001). McMahon et al. offered the following possible explanations for underreporting of bias crimes:

1. Disability was included as a protected category almost six years after the development of the initial system for hate crime reporting; consequently, only half of the states included disability in their hate crime legislation.
2. The marginal status of people with disabilities results in lack of accessibility to the criminal justice system, so law enforcement has little experience working with people with disabilities, and people with disabilities lack attention from law enforcement.
3. There exists a lack of appellate cases dealing with disability in hate crime legislation.
4. Perpetrators of crimes against persons with disabilities are often known to them, and when the perpetrator is known to the victim, reporting decreases.
5. If reports to law enforcement do not result in convictions, persons with disabilities will lose faith in law enforcement and fail to report the crime.

These reasons, although disability specific, can be conceptualized within a larger criminal justice framework design that results in reporting problems generated from *layers of error.*

PROBLEMS WITH BIAS CRIME REPORTING

Robert Merton used the term "successive layers of error" to describe the problems associated with documenting and collecting crime data (Bureau of Justice Statistics, 2000). These layers of error consist of (1) factors that discourage victims from reporting, (2) factors that affect police decision making, (3) political influences that affect agency crime reporting, and (4) legislative differences in determining the type of offense (Bureau of Justice Statistics, 2000).

Barriers to hate crime reporting can be further compartmentalized into two categories: individual inhibitors and police disincentives (Bureau of Justice Statistics, 2000). Individual inhibitors consist of factors that affect a "person's willingness and likelihood of contacting law enforcement" (Bureau of Justice Statistics, 2000, p. 34). Police disincentives consist of departmental or personal factors, "which interfere with accurate law enforcement identification or recording of a bias crime" (Bureau of Justice Statistics, 2000, p. 34). Individual inhibitors and police disincentives are of particular concern for those exploring possible explanations for why crimes committed against persons with disabilities go unreported. These two categories can affect victim reporting and police decision making and will be examined more closely.

Factors that affect whether a victim reports a crime, or individual inhibitors, include (1) the victim's awareness that a crime has been committed (Block, 1974, p. 2) the victim's belief that the crime is serious enough to warrant law enforcement attention (Gove, Hughes, & Geerken, 1985, p. 3). The victim's belief that law enforcement can do something about the crime, including the victim's confidence in law enforcement (Bureau of Justice Statistics, 2000; Gove et al., 1985); and (4) the victim's relationship to the perpetrator (Bureau of Justice Statistics, 2000). These factors are examined in more detail below.

Awareness that a crime has been committed and belief that the crime is serious enough to warrant law enforcement attention. It has been suggested that the ability of people with disabilities to comprehend the criminal act (McMahon et al., 2004) inhibits individuals with disabilities from reporting a crime. This phenomenon cannot be described more clearly than in the case of Eric Krochmaluk, mentioned at the beginning of this chapter. Clearly, individuals with intellectual and cognitive disabilities are more vulnerable in these circumstances because they may not comprehend the heinousness of the crime in more serious cases, like that of Krochmaluk. In some circumstances, however, the individual may not be aware that a crime has been committed when the offense is subtle and harder to distinguish, such as the bias language in the case of Nicholas Steenhout.

Confidence in law enforcement. Mistrust among persons with disabilities that the criminal justice system will investigate, arrest, and prosecute perpetrators (Mishra, 2001) functions as an individual inhibitor to reporting a crime. Although the rate of crime committed against people with disabilities is estimated to be considerably higher than the rate against the general population, a study of over 400 criminal offenses committed in Boston, Massachusetts, between 1997 and 1999 estimated that approximately 5 percent of the perpetrators of crimes against persons with disabilities are prosecuted, compared to a 70 percent prosecution rate during the same period for the general population (Mishra, 2001). Mishra reported that some of the reasons provided for the alarmingly low prosecution rate include (1) police are concerned about how people with disabilities will "hold up" in court; (2) police believe that people with disabilities have poor memories and do not comprehend the importance of telling the truth; (3) prosecutors are concerned that juries will disregard the testimony of a person with a disability; and (4) victims with disabilities may embellish their accounts to the police. Mishra's contention that people with disabilities are believed to have poor memories and are incapable of comprehending the importance of telling the truth was further supported by Bailey, Barr, and Bunting (2001) and had been previously documented by researchers at the Roeher Institute (1993), a Canadian group that conducts research on crimes against people with disabilities. A low prosecution rate and misinformation about the integrity of a witness with a disability can diminish confidence in law enforcement and, consequently, reduce the likelihood a crime will be reported. If reports to law enforcement do not result in prosecution and conviction, people with disabilities will lose faith in law enforcement, and the benefits will not outweigh the risk associated with reporting a perpetrator who is probably known to the victim.

Relationship to the perpetrator. It has been established that perpetrators of crimes against people with disabilities are often known to them (e.g., family members or caretakers), and victims are less likely to report a crime to law enforcement when the offender is know to the victim (Baladerian, 2001; Sobsey & Doe, 1991). Obviously, the nature of the relationship between the perpetrator and victim is a complex matter when the perpetrator is known to the victim. However, the relationship of the perpetrator to the victim is complicated further if law enforcement officers and politicians believe that a crime cannot be categorized as a bias crime if the perpetrator of a bias crime is known to the victim (Lawrence, 1999). Theorists maintain that the belief that a perpetrator of a hate crime cannot know the victim is misinformed (Bureau of Justice Statistics, 2000; Lawrence, 1999; National Institute of Justice, 1999). In fact, perpetrators of hate crimes can be neighbors or co-workers (Lawrence, 1999; McPhail, 2002).

Even though relationship is not a factor, legislators opposing the inclusion of gender in the HCSA used relationship as the main issue (Lawrence, 1999; McPhail, 2002). The reasons presented were that perpetrators of hate crimes should have no relationship to the victim, and that crimes against women are often perpetrated by individuals known to them, so crimes against women don't fit the hate crime model. Lawrence (1999) indicates that many law enforcement officers are mistaken that the perpetrator cannot be known to the victim. Research conducted by McDevitt (Bureau of Justice Statistics, 2000) suggests that the more experience an officer has with bias crime investigation, the less emphasis he or she places on the relationship of the perpetrator to the victim. Clearly, misinformation suggesting that perpetrators of hate crimes cannot be known to the victim places victims of gender and disability-motivated hate crimes at a disadvantage because the crime-scene dynamics do not conform to accepted beliefs or attitudes about the crime.

The second category of barriers to bias crime reporting consists of police disincentives or those factors that affect police decision making. These factors consist of the following: whether the officer has sufficient evidence to indicate a crime has been committed; whether the victim wishes to formally have the perpetrator charged; the seriousness of the crime; and the level of professionalism of the department (Gove et al., 1985).

Sufficient evidence. Prior to the U.S. Supreme Court Decision on *Apprendi v. New Jersey*, the sentencing enhancement for a crime suspected to be based on animus was presented by the prosecuting attorney and determined by the sentencing judge, which requires a preponderance of evidence (Hoffman, 2003). In *Apprendi v. New Jersey*, Apprendi's sentence was enhanced from a 5- to 10-year minimum to a 10- to 20-year minimum after the sentencing judge determined the preponderance of evidence supported the position that the victims were chosen based on group animus. Apprendi appealed the case to the U.S. Supreme Court, and the sentence was overturned. The majority decision, written by Justice Paul Stevens, stated that due process required by the Fourteenth Amendment requires that any enhancement of sentence beyond that allowed by statute must be submitted to the jury and proved beyond a reasonable doubt (Hoffman, 2003; Oyez, 2000). If prosecutors are required to collect evidence of group animus or bias motivation, which is more difficult to prove beyond a reasonable doubt, then it is possible prosecuting attorneys will scrutinize cases more closely. Although no investigation has been conducted to look at this, anecdotal comments from a Florida LEO investigating hate crimes supported the difficulty in substantiating bias motivation to a prosecuting attorney (M. Endara, personal communication, August 7, 2005).

Professionalism of department. In a 1987 study conducted by McDevitt and his colleagues (Bureau of Justice Statistics, 2000), 452 bias incidents handled by the Boston Police Department were examined. McDevitt found

that only 19, or 4.2 percent, of the cases were appropriately identified as
bias incidents by reporting officers (Levin, 1992). Levin asserted that critics
of police-officer-reporting cite prejudice as the main factor influencing mis-
identification of bias incidences. Nolan and Akiyama (1999) conducted a series of focus groups with 147 police officers from four jurisdictions from the
northeastern, western, central, and southern regions of the United States.
Two precincts participated in bias crime reporting, and two precincts did
not participate. The results of the study pinpointed variables that affected
whether the *agency* and the *individual* reported a bias crime. The number
one factor affecting whether an agency participated in bias crime reporting
was "shared *attitudes/beliefs* about hate crime reporting" (Nolan & Akiyama,
1999, p. 120). The number one factor affecting individual reporting was
supportive organizational policies and procedures. The number two factor affecting whether an individual officer reported a hate crime was "individual *attitudes* and *beliefs* about hate crime reporting" (Nolan & Akiyama,
1999, p. 121).

Although the HCSA requires the federal government to collect data on
bias crimes, participation in the UCR is voluntary. Moreover, of those agencies that participate, 83 percent "reported 'zero' hate crimes occurred in their
jurisdiction" (Bureau of Justice Statistics, 2000, p. 13). More importantly,
McDevitt's research study involved interviews of police officers from "zero"
reporting agencies who reported "they had been directly involved in bias
crime investigations and had recorded them as such" (Bureau of Justice Statistics, 2000, p. 37). Specifically, 31 percent of the respondents who worked in
jurisdictions that reported "zero" hate crimes believe that their department
investigated one or more hate crimes (Bureau of Justice Statistics, 2000). Even
more interestingly, 37.1 percent of the respondents who worked in jurisdictions that did not report to UCR believed their jurisdiction had investigated
one or more hate crimes (Bureau of Justice Statistics, 2000).

Political influences and legislative differences. The definition of a bias crime
often varies from state/local jurisdiction (Bureau of Justice Statistics, 2000).
In addition, there is disparity across states in terms of what constitutes a
protected class. Minnesota, for example, includes gender, age, and national
origin in its legislation. Oregon protects based on "perceived" race, sexual
orientation, color, religion, national origin, marital status, political affiliation
of beliefs, membership or activity in or on behalf of a labor organization or
against a labor organization, age, physical or mental handicap, economic or
social status, or citizenship. In 2001, Perry noted that of the 50 states, only
21 included disability in their hate crime statutes.

Although the FBI has started moving away from the UCR, which collects
summary data, to the NIBRS, which collects incident-specific data, there is
much variability across states and jurisdictions as to which reporting system
is used (Bureau of Justice Statistics, 2000). As a result, crimes are reported

using either the UCR or the NIBRS system, resulting in significant variability in the data collected.

As mentioned above, people with disabilities are included in bias crime legislation in approximately 21, roughly half, of the U.S. states (Perry, 2001). Yet this doesn't appear to affect the reporting of bias crimes against people with disabilities. For example, the data from 1997 to 2004 were analyzed by state (FBI, 1997, 1998, 1999b, 2000, 2001, 2002, 2003, 2004; see Table 9.1). A total of 257 bias crimes committed against people with disabilities were reported during this time period. Twenty-two states reported no bias crimes, including Florida, Georgia, and Iowa, each of which has state-level bias crime legislation that includes people with disabilities. Conversely, California, Washington, and Wisconsin do not have bias crime legislation that includes disability, but each has reported at least one bias crime during this period. The largest number of crimes reported was from the state of South Carolina, with 48 (or 19 percent of the total) bias-motivated crimes from 1997 to 2004.

There also does not appear to be a pattern in the data by area of the United States. When comparing northeastern, southeastern, midwest, and western states, the southeastern states are the most puzzling. South Carolina and Tennessee were the only two states in the Southeast that reported any bias crimes against persons with disabilities during the period, yet South Carolina and Tennessee rank first and second in terms of the number of disability-motivated bias crimes compared to the other states. The top seven states reporting for the period were South Carolina (48), Tennessee and California (25 each), Michigan (23), Illinois and Virginia (13 each), and Texas (12). The fact that two of the top three reporting states are located in the Southeast when the other southeastern states did not report any bias crime incidents is curious. Additionally, of the top seven states, California does not have legislation allowing sentencing enhancement for bias crimes committed against persons with disabilities. From this analysis, there appears to be no pattern in terms of the disparity across states with regards to reporting.

CURRENT RESEARCH RECOGNITION OF BIAS CRIME INDICATORS

Among the factors that could affect police decision making, the recognition of bias crime indicators has been identified as one possible source of error in the bias crime data. Lane and Shaw (2008a) conducted a survey of 211 law-enforcement-officer participants in Florida. The participants were given a modified version of the Hate Crime Survey originally designed by Miller (2001), a survey consisting of 30 crime scenarios, 25 of which were bias crime scenarios and 5 of which were crime scenarios without bias crime indicators (Lane, 2006).

Table 9.1 Number of Hate Crimes Reported by State and Year

State	1997	1998	1999	2000	2001	2002	2003	2004	Total
Alabama	0	Np	Np	Np	0	0	0	0	0
Alaska	0	Np	0	0	0	0	0	0	0
Arizona	0	1	0	1	0	2	3	1	8
Arkansas	0	0	0	0	0	0	4	1	5
California	1	3	2	3	4	7	1	4	25
Colorado	0	1	2	0	0	0	0	0	3
Connecticut	1	2	0	3	2	0	1	0	9
Delaware	0	0	0	1	0	0	0	0	1
District of Columbia	0	0	0	0	0	0	0	0	0
Florida	0	0	0	0	0	0	0	0	0
Georgia	0	0	0	0	0	0	0	0	0
Hawaii	Np	Np	Np	Np	Np	Np	Np	Np	Np
Idaho	0	0	1	0	0	0	1	0	2
Illinois	1	5	3	1	1	0	2	0	13
Indiana	1	0	0	0	2	0	0	1	4
Iowa	0	0	0	0	0	0	0	0	0
Kansas	0	0	0	1	0	0	0	0	1
Kentucky	0	0	0	0	0	0	0	0	0
Louisiana	0	0	0	0	0	0	0	0	0
Maine	0	2	1	0	0	0	0	0	3
Maryland	0	0	1	2	0	1	0	0	4
Massachusetts	0	0	2	0	3	1	0	0	6
Michigan	0	2	0	0	7	1	0	13	23
Minnesota	0	0	0	2	1	3	0	1	7
Mississippi	0	0	0	0	0	0	0	0	0
Missouri	0	0	0	0	0	0	0	0	0
Montana	0	0	0	0	0	0	0	7	7
Nebraska	0	0	0	0	0	0	0	0	0
Nevada	0	0	1	0	1	1	0	0	3
New Hampshire	Np	0	2	0	0	3	1	0	6
New Jersey	0	3	0	1	4	0	0	1	9
New Mexico	0	0	0	0	0	0	0	0	0

(*Continued*)

Table 9.1   Number of Hate Crimes Reported by State and Year (*Continued*)

State	1997	1998	1999	2000	2001	2002	2003	2004	Total
New York	0	0	0	0	0	1	0	0	1
North Carolina	0	0	0	0	0	0	0	0	0
North Dakota	0	0	0	0	0	0	0	0	0
Ohio	0	0	0	0	0	0	3	1	4
Oklahoma	0	0	0	0	0	0	0	0	0
Oregon	1	0	0	2	0	0	1	0	4
Pennsylvania	0	0	0	0	0	0	0	0	0
Rhode Island	0	0	0	0	1	0	0	0	1
South Carolina	0	0	0	0	6	17	9	16	48
South Dakota	0	0	0	0	0	0	0	0	0
Tennessee	0	0	2	9	1	4	2	7	25
Texas	2	3	1	2	0	2	0	2	12
Utah	0	0	0	0	0	0	0	0	0
Vermont	0	0	0	0	0	0	0	0	0
Virginia	0	1	1	6	1	0	2	2	13
Washington	0	0	0	2	1	2	3	0	8
West Virginia	0	0	0	0	0	0	0	0	0
Wisconsin	2	0	0	0	0	0	0	0	0
Wyoming	0	0	0	0	0	0	0	0	0
Total	**9**	**23**	**19**	**36**	**35**	**45**	**33**	**57**	**257**

Lane and Shaw (2008a) modified the Hate Crime Survey from its original 20-item form to include 5 crime scenarios where the victim was a person with a disability and 5 items that did not have bias indicators to establish validity (Lane, 2006). The modified version included five bias crime scenarios for each of five protected categories: race/ethnicity, religion, sexual orientation, gender, and disability. Although gender is not recognized in the federal legislation as a protected category under the HCSA, it was kept in the modified version because of the similarities with disability in terms of perpetrator characteristics.

The results of the study showed that law enforcement officers agreed with categorizing a crime as a bias crime significantly less often when the victim was a person with a disability than if the victim was chosen because of race,

religion, or sexual orientation (Lane, 2006). Law-enforcement-officer participants rated the crime scenarios where the victim was chosen because of his or
her race on top, followed by religion and sexual orientation. Victims chosen
because of gender or disability were rated significantly lower by participants
(Lane, 2006). It's interesting that the crime scenarios for the Lane study were
rated higher for race and religion, as these two categories were the first two
groups included in the initial federal-level discussion about the need to track
the incidences of bias crime (Lawrence, 1999). Sexual orientation was included in the discussion about a year later (Lawrence, 1999). It's possible that
the less experience a law enforcement officer has investigating a disability-
motivated bias crime, the less likely he or she is to recognize the bias indicators, a conclusion that would be consistent with the findings of the McDevitt
survey of law enforcement officers (Bureau of Justice Statistics, 2000).

The results of the Lane and Shaw (2008a) study are limited because the
sample consisted of one law enforcement agency in Florida. However, the results provide interesting preliminary findings and warrant additional study
with a larger and more representative sample size to validate the findings
and increase the generalizability of the results (Lane & Shaw, 2008a).

LAW ENFORCEMENT OFFICERS' ATTITUDE TOWARD PERSONS WITH DISABILITIES

Lane and Shaw (2008b) also attempted to predict law enforcement officers' agreement with categorizing a crime against a person with a disability
as a bias crime based on the officer's attitude toward persons with disabilities.
The results of the study showed that law enforcement officers' attitudes toward persons with disabilities did not significantly predict their categorization of a disability-motivated crime as a bias crime (Lane & Shaw, 2008b).
However, it is possible that law enforcement officers' attitudes about hate
crimes and not disability would yield different results.

PERPETRATOR PROFILE

Theories of why people commit hate crimes can be seen to emerge in what
is known about the typology of offenders of bias crime. Hate crime offenders
tend to be white males between the ages of 13 and 24 (Anderson, Dyson, &
Brooks, 2002; McDevitt, Levin, & Bennett, 2002). Levin and McDevitt (1993)
initially suggested that offenders who commit bias crimes are motivated by
three factors that result in three separate typologies. They are the *thrill seeker*,
who is motivated by power and excitement; the *defensive*, who is motivated by
defending one's turf or resources; and the *mission*, who believes he or she is
on a crusade to rid the world of groups considered evil or inferior. In 2002,
McDevitt (Bureau of Justice Statistics, 2000) included *retaliatory* as a fourth

typology of hate crime offender. The retaliatory offender is motivated by a desire to avenge his or her group as a result of a perceived assault or degradation.

The two hate crime scenarios provided at the beginning of the chapter illustrate two of the four typologies, that of the *thrill-seeking* offender and the *mission* offender. The perpetrators of the bias-motivated crime committed against Eric Krochmaluk appear to have been motivated by power and excitement based on their treatment of him. For example, taping him to a chair, shaving his eyebrows, and so on are considered to be about power, and the perpetrator's history of violent crimes may also be motivated by a desire to seek excitement. The neighbors of Nicholas Steenhout appeared to believe they were ridding the world of an inferior or evil individual, based on their verbalizations of how he was punished by God and should be placed in a facility with other persons with disabilities.

The profile of the defensive individual who is motivated by protecting his or her turf or resources shows these individuals perceiving persons with disabilities as robbing their fellow citizens of resources. Recent advances in the civil rights legislation, such as the Americans with Disabilities Act (ADA), have made considerable modifications to the environment in the form of accessible parking spaces, wheelchair ramps, and accessible bathroom stalls, to name a few. Moreover, the ADA has resulted in an increase in the number of persons with disabilities working in competitive employment situations. It stands to reason, then, that a perpetrator motivated to defend his or her own turf could view persons with disabilities as a threat. This same scenario can be used to explore the retaliatory offender, who may perceive an increase in persons with disabilities in the workforce and other areas of society as an assault or degradation on citizens without a disability.

The examples of the thrill seeker and mission type offenders in the Krochmaluk and Steenhout cases, coupled with the feasibility of retaliatory and defensive offenders, appear to support the idea that perpetrators of crimes against persons with disabilities fit the existing typologies discussed in the literature. This idea is also supported by a simple comparison of the states with the highest number of hate groups. According to the Southern Poverty Law Center's Intelligence Report for 2007 (2007), the top six states with the highest number of hate groups are, in descending order, California, Texas, Florida, South Carolina, Georgia, and Tennessee. Of these six states, California, Texas, and Tennessee are in the top five states with the highest number of bias crimes committed against persons with disabilities. Of the remaining states that are highest in terms of disability-motivated bias crime incidents, Illinois, Michigan, and Virginia are in the top 20 states for the highest number of hate groups. Interestingly, Florida and Georgia are among the top five states with the most number of hate groups and yet no bias crimes against a person with a disability have been reported. Although there is some correlational evidence of a relationship between number of hate groups and disability-motivated bias crimes by state, it's possible that only those cases where the perpetrator clearly fits the one of the profiles is recognized by law enforcement and prosecuted.

Lane, Carmichael, and Shaw (2008) are conducting a qualitative and quantitative analysis of a sample of criminal case files where the victim was chosen because of his or her disability. The research questions are aimed at discovering whether the perpetrators fit one of the profiles of bias crime perpetrators or whether a different profile exists for persons with disabilities.

DIRECTIONS FOR FUTURE RESEARCH

The fact that little is known about hate crimes committed against people with disabilities means there are more questions than answers at this point. Merton's successive layers of error in crime data are currently being used by the authors of this chapter to serve as a framework to conceptualize underreporting. It makes sense, therefore, to organize questions within that framework.

The nature of some types of disability, such as intellectual and cognitive disabilities, might lead one to ask whether the person with a disability has the understanding or awareness that a crime has been committed and whether he or she is able to recognize the potential elements of bias motivation. Unless a crime victim with a disability is aware that a crime has been committed and that bias could be a motivating factor, law enforcement cannot be solicited and the elements of possible bias motivation communicated to an agency official or investigating officer.

If the crime victim with a disability is aware that he or she may have been the victim of bias motivation, as with the case of Nicholas Steenhout, the person with a disability may not report the crime if he or she has lost confidence that law enforcement officials at each level of the criminal justice system will prosecute the case. Future research should focus on interviewing persons with disabilities who have been the victims of a bias crime to discover what their experience was in interfacing with law enforcement.

Although the survey of law enforcement officers conducted by Lane and Shaw (2008a) should be replicated with a larger, more representative sample size to improve the generalizability of the results, future surveys should evolve beyond the Modified Hate Crime Survey. Disability is not a mutually exclusive category. In other words, to look at an individual as a victim because he or she is black or homosexual is fundamentally flawed. Future studies should look at the additive or subtractive quality that disability has when combined with other protected classes. For example, would a law enforcement officer believe that an African American homosexual is more or less like a victim of a bias-motivated crime than an African American homosexual with a disability?

CONCLUSION

Since the inclusion of persons with disabilities as a protected class under the HCSA in 1996, available FBI data through 2004 show that 257 cases have been reported from various states. A person with a disability is 350 times less likely to be the victim of a bias crime than an African American. One possible conclusion is that persons with disabilities are simply victims of bias-motivated crimes much less often than other protected groups. However, this statistic has been challenged by disability theorists who claim that it is inconsistent with other statistics on discrimination against persons with disabilities.

Persons with disabilities represent the largest minority group in the United States, with 20 percent of the population of 54 million Americans living with a disability. Research and historical accounts show that persons with disabilities have been discriminated against in almost every aspect of daily life throughout history, resulting in these persons having the highest rate of unemployment, residing in poverty, and experiencing criminal victimization at a rate that is as high as 10 times that of the general population. This evidence has been used to develop a series of hypotheses that support the theory that bias crimes against persons with disabilities are underreported in the United States.

A bias crime can go unreported if the victim is unaware that he or she has been the victim of a crime or does not understand that elements of the crime make it more serious in the view of society. However, even if a person with a disability is aware of the criminal victimization and understands the nature of bias motivation and its corresponding seriousness, refusal to investigate, charge, and prosecute a perpetrator for a bias-motivated crime if the bias elements are present may result in a lack of confidence within the disability community that law enforcement will do anything about the offense.

Law enforcement may also contribute to the underreporting of bias crimes. If law enforcement does not recognize the bias crime indicators, the case may not be prosecuted as a bias crime. Research shows that law enforcement officers may recognize the elements of a hate crime differently if the victim has a disability than if the victim was chosen because of membership in another protected category. Although the results are preliminary, further research in this area must be conducted. Additionally, misinformation about the importance of the relationship between the perpetrator and the victim in bias-motivated crimes could result in faulty conclusions. Research is currently under way to examine whether the perpetrator of disability-motivated bias crimes matches the existing profiles in the literature. The results of this research may answer some questions about perpetrator characteristics and the nature of the relationship between perpetrator and victim.

Finally, there is disparity in the state statutes across the 50 states in terms of whether disability is included in the statute and the definition of a disability. Clearly, disability-rights advocates should work to make sure disability is included in the statutes in all 50 states. Inconsistencies in statutes and reporting of crimes to the FBI further complicate the process of analyzing crime data.

REFERENCES

Albert, S., & Whetten, D. (1985). Organizational identity. *Research in Organizational Behavior, 7,* 263–295.

Anderson, J. F., Dyson, L., & Brooks, W. (2002). Preventing hate crime and profiling hate crime offenders. *The Western Journal of Black Studies, 26*(3), 140–148.

Bailey, A., Barr, O., & Bunting, B. (2001). Police attitudes toward people with intellectual disability: An evaluation of awareness training. *Journal of Intellectual Disability Research, 45,* 344–350.

Baladerian, N. (1991). Sexual abuse of people with developmental disabilities. *Sexuality and Disability, 9,* 323–335.

Block, R. (1974). Why notify the police: The victim's decision to notify the police of an assault. *Criminology, 11,* 555–569.

Bureau of Justice Statistics. (2000). *Improving the accuracy of bias crime statistics nationally: An assessment of the first ten years of bias crime data collection.* Washington, DC: Author.

Burgdorf, R. L. (2000). Assisted suicide: A disability perspective. In B. T. McMahon & L. R. Shaw (Eds.), *Enabling lives* (pp. 199–228). Boca Raton, FL: CRC Press.

Burger, W. R., & Youkeles, M. (2004). *Human services in contemporary America* (6th ed.). Belmont, CA: Brooks/Cole.

Cerulo, K. A. (1997). Identity construction: New issues, new directions. *American Review of Sociology, 23,* 385–409.

Federal Bureau of Investigation. (1997). *Hate crime statistics.* Washington, DC: U.S. Department of Justice.

Federal Bureau of Investigation. (1998). *Hate crime statistics.* Washington, DC: U.S. Department of Justice.

Federal Bureau of Investigation. (1999a). *Hate crime data reporting guidelines.* Washington, DC: U.S. Department of Justice.

Federal Bureau of Investigation. (1999b). *Hate crime statistics.* Washington, DC: U.S. Department of Justice.

Federal Bureau of Investigation. (1999c). *Uniform crime reports: Crime in the United States.* Washington, DC: U.S. Department of Justice.

Federal Bureau of Investigation. (2000). *Hate crime statistics.* Washington, DC: U.S. Department of Justice.

Federal Bureau of Investigation. (2001). *Hate crime statistics.* Washington, DC: U.S. Department of Justice.

Federal Bureau of Investigation. (2002). *Hate crime statistics.* Washington, DC: U.S. Department of Justice

Federal Bureau of Investigation. (2003). *Hate crime statistics.* Washington, DC: U.S. Department of Justice.

Federal Bureau of Investigation. (2004). *Hate crime statistics*. Washington, DC: U.S. Department of Justice.

Goffman, E. (1963). *Stigma: Notes on the management of a spoiled identity*. New York: Simon & Schuster.

Gove, W. R., Hughes, M., & Geerken, M. (1985). Are uniform crime reports a valid indicator of the index crimes? An affirmative answer with minor qualifications. *Criminology, 23*, 451–501.

Hiday, V. A., Swartz, M. S., Swanson, J. W., Borum, R. & Wagner, H. R. (1999). Criminal victimization of persons with severe mental illness. *Psychiatric Services, 50*, 62–68.

Hoffman, M. B. (2003). The case for jury sentencing. [Electronic version]. *Duke Law Journal, 52*, 951–1010.

Lane, F. J. (2006). Law enforcement officers' endorsement of the bias categorization of crime scenarios: A prospective study of differences between disability and other protected categories. *Dissertation Abstracts International* (UMI No. 3228769).

Lane, F. J., Carmichael, R., & Shaw, L. R. (2008). [A qualitative analysis of criminal case files of bias crimes committed against persons with disabilities in Illinois.] Unpublished raw data.

Lane, F. J., & Shaw, L. R. (2008a). *Law enforcement officers' agreement with the bias categorization of crimes committed against persons with disabilities*. Manuscript submitted for publication.

Lane, F. J., & Shaw, L. R. (2008b). *Law enforcement officers' attitudes towards persons with disabilities*. Manuscript submitted for publication.

Lawrence, F. M. (1999). *Punishing hate: Bias crimes under American law*. Cambridge, MA: Harvard University Press.

Levin, B. (1992). Bias crimes: A theoretical and practical overview. *Stanford Law & Policy Review, 4*, 165–171.

Levin, J., & McDevitt, J. (1993). *Hate crimes: The rising tide of bigotry and bloodshed*. New York: Plenum.

Lifton, R. J. (1986). *The Nazi doctors: Medical killing and the psychology of genocide*. Basic Books.

Luckasson, R. (1992). People with mental retardation as victims of crime. In R. W. Conley, R. Luckasson, & G. N. Bouthilet (Eds.), *The criminal justice system and mental retardation* (pp. 209–220). Baltimore: Paul Brooks Publishing.

Macfarquhar, N. (1999, February 17). 8 are charged in tormenting of learning disabled man. *New York Times*. Retrieved March 8, 2008, from http://query.nytimes.com/gst/fullpage.html?sec=health&res=9A01E7D7113AF934A25751C0A96F958260

Maclay, K. (2002, December 18). Flawed FBI reporting system undercounts disability hate crimes. *Campus News*. Retrieved December 18, 2002, from http://www.berkeley.edu/news/media/releases/2002/12/18 crimes.html

McDevitt, J., Levin, J., & Bennett, S. (2002). Hate crime offenders: An expanded typology. *Journal of Social Issues, 58*, 303–317.

McMahon, B. T., West, S. L., Lewis, A. N., Armstrong, A. J., & Conway, J. P. (2004). Hate crimes and disability in America. *Rehabilitation Counseling Bulletin, 47*, 66–75.

McNeil, J. (2001). Americans with disabilities. Current Population Reports: Household studies, no. 1997. Retrieved from http://www.census.gov/prod/2001pubs/p70–73.pdf

McPhail, B. A. (2002). Gender-bias hate crimes: A review. *Trauma, Violence, & Abuse, 3*, 125–143.

Miller, A. (2001). Student perceptions of hate crimes. *American Journal of Criminal Justice, 25*, 293–296.

Mishra, R. (2001, June 10). In attacks on disabled, few verdicts. *The Boston Globe.*

Muccigrosso, L. (1991). Sexual abuse prevention strategies and programs for persons with developmental disabilities. *Sexuality and Disability, 9*, 261–272.

National Council on Disability. (2000). *Harris survey of Americans with disabilities.* Washington, DC: Author.

National Institute of Justice. (1999). *Final report on the psychological and behavioral effects of bias and non bias motivated assault.* Washington, DC: U.S. Department of Justice.

National Organization on Disability. (2001, July 24) *Employment rates of people with disabilities.* Retrieved January 10, 2005, from National Organization on Disability online: http://www.nod.org/content.cfm?id=134.

National Organization on Disability. (2003, January 27). *The state of the union 2003 for Americans with disabilities.* Retrieved January 10, 2005, from National Organization on Disability online: http://www.nod.org/content.cfm?id=1293

Nolan, J. J., & Akiyama, Y. (1999). An analysis of factors that affect law enforcement participation in hate crime reporting. *Journal of Contemporary Criminal Justice, 15*, 111–127.

Nosek, M. A. (1996). Sexual abuse of women with physical disabilities. In D. M. Krotoski, M. A. Nosek, & M. A. Turk (Eds.), *Women with physical disabilities* (pp. 153–173). Baltimore: Paul Brooks Publishing.

Nosek, M. A., Howland, C. A., Rintala, D. H., Young, M. E., & Chanpong, G. F. (1997). *National study of women with physical disabilities: Final report.* Houston: Center for Research on Women with Disabilities.

One in a million? Tell it to the feds. (2002). *Berkeleyan.* Retrieved January 22, 2003, from http://www.berkeley.edu/news.berkeleyan/2003/01/22disabl.html

Oyez. (2000, June 26). *Apprendi v. New Jersey* 530 U.S. 466 (2000) Docket number: 99–478. Retrieved January 7, 2006, from http://www.oyez.org/oyez/resource/case/1218/

Perry, B. (2001). *In the name of hate: Understanding hate crimes.* New York: Routledge.

Reynolds, D. (2000, March 17). The torture of Eric Krochmaluk. *Inclusion Daily Press.* Retrieved March 8, 2008, from http://www.inclusiondaily.com/news/crime/krochmaluk.htm

Roeher Institute. (1995). *Answering the call: The police response to family and care-giver violence against people with disabilities.* Toronto, Ontario, Canada: Author.

Rubin, S. E., & Roessler, R. T. (2001). *Foundations of the vocational rehabilitation process* (5th ed.). Austin, TX: Pro-Ed.

Shapiro, J. P. (1994). *No pity: People with disabilities forging a new civil rights movement.* New York: Times Books.

Sherry, M. (2000). Talking about hate. *Bent.* Retrieved August 28, 2003, from http://www.bentvoices.org/culturecrash/sherry hatecrimes.htm

Sherry, M. (2003). Hate crime against disabled persons: One in a million? *IURD Developments, 13*, 3–4.

Smart, J. (2001). *Disability society and the individual.* Austin, TX: Pro-Ed.

Sobsey, D., & Doe, T. (1991). Patterns of sexual abuse and assault. *Journal of Sexuality and Disability, 9*, 243–259.

Sorensen, D. D. (2001). *Hate crimes against people with disabilities.* Unpublished manuscript.

Southern Poverty Law Center. (2007). Active U.S. hate groups. Retrieved March 8, 2008, from http://www.splcenter.org/intel/map/hate.jsp.

Steenhout, N. (2002, May 6). A confrontation. *Ragged Edge Magazine.* Retrieved March 8, 2008, from http://www.raggededgemag.com/extra/steenhout050602.html

Sullivan, P. M., & Knutson, J. F. (1998). The association between child maltreatment and disabilities in a hospital-based epidemiological study. *Child Abuse & Neglect, 22*, 271–288.

U.S. Census Bureau. (2004, March). *U.S. interim projections by age, sex, race, and Hispanic origin.* Retrieved January 6, 2006, from U.S. Census Bureau online: http://www.census.gov/ipc/www/usinterimproj/

Vash, C. (1994). *Personality and adversity: Psycho-spiritual aspects of rehabilitation.* New York: Springer Publishing.

Wilson, C., & Brewer, N. (1992). The incidence of criminal victimization of individuals with intellectual disability. *Australian Psychologist, 27*, 114–117.

World Health Organization. (2001). *International classification of functioning, disability and health.* Geneva, Switzerland: Author.

Young, M. E., Nosek, M. A., Howland, C. A., Chanpong, G., & Rintala, D. H. (1997). Prevalence of abuse of women with physical disabilities. *Archives of Physical Medicine and Rehabilitation, 78*(Suppl. 5), 34–38.

Zola, I. K. (1993). Disability statistics, what we count and what it tells us. *Journal of Disability Policy Studies, 4*, 9–39.

CHAPTER 10

PATHWAYS THROUGH HATE: EXPLORING THE VICTIMIZATION OF THE HOMELESS

Sandra Wachholz

In his brilliantly written novel *Midnight's Children*, Salman Rushdie (1983) suggests that when you have "city eyes" you overlook the human suffering of the homeless—"the beggars in boxcars don't impinge on you, and the concrete sections of future drainpipes don't look like dormitories" (p. 100). Tragically, it is not only with city eyes that individuals look upon the nearly three million people who experience homelessness within the United States in a given year (National Law Center on Homelessness and Poverty, 2007). For some individuals, this visual manifestation of destitution and oppression fosters only scorn and contempt (Cohen, 2001). They blame the homeless for their poverty and victimize them through hate-motivated actions simply because they are poor and without permanent residence. Accounts suggest that the homeless have been subjected to various forms of defamation, harassment, vandalism, and assault by those who see them as objects of fear and loathing—by those with "imperial eyes" filled with hate (Swanson, 2001; Wachholz & Mullaly, 1993).

Although there has been a long tradition of singling out the homeless for hate-motivated treatment and injurious acts, an extensive review of the literature reveals that their victimization has generally not been included in the social construction of hate crime and that few have sought to systematically study this behavior. Thus, while many have engaged in research designed to explore what it is like to be homeless, few have examined what it is like to be "regarded" as homeless. The absence of research in this area is of particular concern since it suggests that this form of victimization is not fully acknowledged as part of the dehumanizing, dangerous conditions endured by the very poor in this nation. Developing a more thorough understanding of the nature and extent of hate crimes against the homeless is of critical importance, as it can function to further underscore the pressing need for economic and social policies that address the macrolevel causes of homelessness, which include such structural forces as increasing imprisonment, eroding work opportunities, low wages, lack of affordable housing, de-institutionalization, and the dismantling of the welfare state.

Recognizing the need for research in this area, then, this chapter reports on the hate crime victimization experienced by 47 individuals over the course of their homelessness within a state in New England. In-depth interviews were conducted with the participants in order to provide a detailed, contextual account of (1) the nature and forms of their victimization; (2) how their victimization varied pursuant to, for example, race, ethnicity, sexuality, and gender; and (3) the strategies they used to avoid and prevent victimization. The research focused specifically on the participants' experiences with hate crime victimization in public and semipublic spaces (e.g., malls, churches, and restaurants). It is in these social spaces that the homeless are forced to carry out the private aspects of their lives, and it is where they encounter radically asymmetrical power relations and pervasive levels of hate.

The discussion of the hate crimes experienced by the participants is organized around four of the locations that configured into their routines of survival: panhandling places, resting places, toilet places, and sleeping places. These terms are taken from a discussion of a map that appears in Vanderstaay's (1992) book titled *Street Lives: An Oral History of Homeless Americans*. A homeless man created the map, and it delineates the various places within a city that are an important part of his daily efforts to stay alive and meet his basic needs while living on the streets. As the findings from this study demonstrate, the participants experienced movement within the four places discussed in this chapter as a process of navigating through hate.

METHODOLOGY

Semistructured, in-depth interviews were conducted to gather narratives about hate crimes against the homeless. Since legal definitions of hate crime are socially and politically contingent, this study was not limited to acts that violate criminal law (Perry, 2001). Instead, a sociologically meaningful definition was used to capture the broad array of hate-motivated acts perpetrated against the homeless. For purposes of this study, the concept of hate crimes against the homeless is defined as words or actions intended to harm or intimidate an individual because he or she is without an adequate, secure residence—in essence, homeless. This definition was discussed with each participant prior to the start of an interview. Following the lead of Dijkstra (2000), public space was defined as areas that have the characteristic of belonging to everyone. Semipublic space referred to areas that offer specific uses (e.g., purchase of gas, food, or clothing) and where it is generally illegal to discriminate against customers, therefore fostering public access, but without any guarantee that such space belongs to everyone.

The research design, interview guide, and interpretations of the data for this chapter were completed in collaboration with a group that advocates for the homeless. The group consists of individuals who are homeless or formerly homeless, and it engages in both direct service and political action on behalf of the homeless. The establishment of this collaborative relationship was the starting point for the research. It allowed the perspectives of the homeless to be incorporated into the production of knowledge about hate crimes. The director and staff of a nonprofit organization—which holds as its mission the goal of preventing bias, harassment, and hate violence—also provided valuable advice and support.

The interviews were completed in settings that were convenient to the participants and that also protected their privacy. As a way to learn about the participants' experiences with homelessness and thus contextualize their hate crime victimization, each interview began with the following question: "Tell me something about your life, generally what it has been like up to this point?" In *Beyond Nostalgia: Aging and Life History Writing*, Ruth Ray (2000, p. 78) notes that she always begins a life-history interview with this question as it helps her understand the respondents' narratives as well as their interpretive and evaluative strategies. It proved equally useful in this study, as it helped shed light on the violently fractured lives of the participants.

Sample

The interviews were conducted between 2002 and 2004 with a purposive sample of 27 males and 20 females. Forty-four of the individuals were homeless at the time of the interview, while the remaining three had relatively recent experiences with homelessness. Central to the recruitment process was the goal of generating a diverse sample so that it would be possible to explore how the participants' victimization experiences were shaped simultaneously by their status of being homeless as well as by factors such as age, race, ethnicity, disability, and gender. The salience of this goal was underscored by the majority of the female participants—they described their victimization as often being grounded in both homelessness and gender. As one woman lamented, "You're automatically called a homeless whore or a slut."

Among the 47 individuals who agreed to participate in the study, 9 were racial minorities, with Native Americans accounting for the largest percentage. Although the participants ranged in age from 18 to 65, the majority could be described as single, middle-aged men and women; their average age was approximately 30. The interviews were completed in five cities located in the southern and central regions of the New England state; racial minorities account for less than 10 percent of the state's population.

The forms of homelessness experienced by the participants reflect the variety of housing conditions that Watson and Austerberry (1986) include within their definition of homelessness. These authors suggest that homelessness must be understood along a continuum, where secure, tenured housing is at one end and literal rooflessness at the other. Within this definitional approach, the various forms of insecure, precarious housing conditions that fall between the two ends of the continuum, such as boarding homes, condemned rentals, and jails, are also included in the conceptualization of homelessness (Carlen, 1996). Reflecting this definition of homelessness, four of the participants identified themselves as homeless given that they were living in insecure, provisional housing. As one of the individuals explained, "I'm not saying that I'm sleeping on the street [like before], but I'm homeless. I feel homeless. It's not a permanent residence."

The overwhelming majority of the participants were living in shelters for the homeless at the time of the interview. However, almost two-thirds had experienced a variety of living conditions over the course of their homelessness. Their experiences included living in cars, tents, recycling bins, boxcars, abandoned buildings, carnival game boxes, and condemned trailers. Almost one-third had endured "couch surfing," which is a term that describes the process of sleeping on sofas in a broad array of homes. Their length of homelessness ranged from one week to 25 years; the average was approximately four years. Symbolic of the crushing weight of the structural forces of homelessness, well over half had experienced more than one period in their life without housing.

Panhandling Places

Although the participants were subjected to hate crimes throughout the contested landscape of public space, it was in panhandling places that they endured the most frequent victimization. There are presumably three reasons for this pattern. First, panhandling functions as an identification marker for homelessness and, therefore, those who engage in it are more readily identifiable targets for hate. Second, following Wagner's (1993) research on the homeless in North City, panhandling violates normative notions of work; as such, involvement in it presumably increases the chance of being labeled as deviant and brought into harm's way. Individuals may see panhandlers as intent on "making a livelihood off the hard-working citizen," as Stark (1992) underscores, even though the income generated from panhandling is generally very small, and individuals often turn to panhandling only after they have exhausted other economic resources (p. 350). Finally, the use of streets and sidewalks to make money defies conceptions about the types of space that should be used to facilitate financial exchanges and, for some individuals, this may also generate disdain for panhandlers (Gottdiener, 1985; Wright, 1997). Conceivably for these reasons, then, panhandling places were the sites where the homeless were most inclined to experience hate crimes. In general, it was white men from a diverse array of age groups who carried out these acts.

Among the participants, seven women and seven men indicated that they had periodically engaged in panhandling. Their panhandling behavior involved either "flying a sign," which refers to holding a cardboard sign, or "spraying"—asking for spare change, cigarettes, etc. Regardless of the panhandling technique, all of them provided myriad accounts in which they had been "categorized, inspected, dissected [and hurt]" by the public and city authorities (Wright, 1997, p. 39). These experiences left them keenly aware of the ways in which hate was being used to regulate how public space should be used and by whom. Jack, who said that he had been panhandling intermittently over the past 15 years since being written off by his family as "a bad apple, a bad guy," stated that he felt as if he was deemed as "out of place" when he panhandled:

> What I'm getting from the proprietors on the street is that y'all have your little space [homeless shelter] that we gave ya. Stay there, we don't want you to venture out of your circle. You venture out of your circle, you're in trouble.

The "trouble" that Jack and others encountered in panhandling places most frequently took the form of verbal assaults from individuals in moving cars. The mobility, spatial distance, and social isolation that cars provide seem to make them a particularly attractive mechanism from which to engage in hate speech. From the shelter and privilege of cars, then, individuals shout wounding words. For those who fly a sign near a street, the frequency of victimization from drivers and passengers is staggering. Ronald, who described himself as someone who had "done a lot of street time," noted that when he panhandles with a sign he may hear as many as 80 hateful comments over a four-hour period.

The most common form of hate speech directed against the participants who panhandled consisted of words linked to paid employment: "Get a job, fucking bum"; "Can you spell work?"; "You're living off tax payers, you bum." As one man recounted, "My street name seems to be 'Get a job.'" This discourse of hate, however, deeply saturated all of the public and semipublic places that were used by the participants, and it reflects the historical myth that the impoverished lack a work ethic. It is a language that seems to underscore Wagner's (1993) lament that if a person is poor and visible, "work status seems to become the primary public concern rather than hunger, illness, disease, or frostbite" (p. 69).

Among the women in the study who panhandled, the experience of being
the target of hate frequently included enduring sexually offensive or threatening comments. All of them described panhandling experiences in which
they had been called a "homeless slut"—words that reinforce the notion, as
Gardner (1995) argues, that public space is largely the realm of privileged
men. These women may have been particularly vulnerable to this form of
hate speech, as their involvement in panhandling, which is traditionally perceived as a masculine activity, violated the abridged agenda of behaviors that
women are expected to practice in public space (Gardner, 1995; Messerschmidt, 1997).

Many of the words and gestures that configured into the women's victimization left them feeling frustrated, angry, unsettled, and sometimes deeply
frightened. One young woman, who had been panhandling since the age of
12 after fleeing a sexually abusive home, talked at length about the degrading, offensive interactions she experiences with men when she "flies a sign":

> Like it's so frustrating . . . They'll like honk, they'll like be making gestures
> like a blow job. Yeah, yeah, oh all the time, constantly, constantly. One time
> this dude held money out a window, I got up, I walked right up to car, and
> I look down and in the corner of my eye I see his hand going and he's jack-
> ing off right there and he's all like you want it, and it was just a handful of
> change.

Her experiences with this type of victimization and other forms of hate
crimes linked to her identity as a homeless woman increased over time as
she aged on the streets. The two other young adults who panhandled while
growing up on the streets recounted a similar experience of maturing into
public hate. As children, they tended to arouse public pity and sympathy, but
as adults they became undeserving of such support. This pattern reflects the
historical distinction between the "deserving" and the "undeserving" poor
that was incorporated into the English poor-laws of the sixteenth century.
Under these statutes, individuals constructed as undeserving were singled
out for harsh treatment and sanction from their community (Katz, 1996;
Wagner, 1993).

While the hate speech directed at the homeless in panhandling places
presented a harm in its own right, it was often linked with other harms,
such as physical assault (Nielson, 2002). All of the panhandlers in this study
described multiple incidences in which assailants had combined degrading,
hurtful words or expressions with physical assault to communicate their hatred for the homeless and their desire, as one participant noted, to see the
homeless "off the streets." Most often, this assaultive behavior consisted of
throwing objects at panhandlers, again generally from the security of cars.
As one individual explained, "I've been hit in the face with a handful of pen-
nies. I've been hit in the face with a can of dog food . . . cups of coffee." As

another recounted, "The other day somebody threw a penny at my head . . . I got an ice cream cone thrown at me once."

Several men described being physically threatened by both male tourists and college students in a popular pub/port area within one of the cities. While this location was somewhat fruitful for panhandling, it carried with it the threat of unknowingly encountering a slightly intoxicated individual whose viciousness towards the homeless was fueled even further by alcohol. Describing such an encounter, one man stated, "We asked [four guys] for some change, to help a couple of homeless guys . . . And they were just college kids and they were drunk . . . They said, 'You guys are milking the system. We ought to kick your ass and teach you a lesson.' With the four of them approaching you, you split quickly."

Although relatively rare, there were accounts of assaults in panhandling settings that resulted in some level of physical injury. Sally, who almost always panhandles with her partner, Bill, was kicked in the face by a man one day when she was panhandling alone. Several people on the street witnessed the assault and called emergency services and the police on their cell phones. When asked why she thought he had kicked her, Sally stated simply that "he thought I was a piece of shit . . . Look, she's got a backpack, she's got filthy clothes, yeah, just shit.' One of the male participants, Tom, described an incident in which he was hit in the face with a closed fist when he was flying a sign. As he recalled, "And this guy comes up, got out of his car, bucked his chest at me, pushed me with his chest and called me a 'worthless piece of shit—get a job' and smacked me right in the face . . . closed fist punch—wham."

Both the men and women described an array of sophisticated victim prevention strategies that they use to avoid the harm that is all too often present in panhandling places. Several noted that when they make a verbal appeal, they carefully consider the tone and wording of their request so as not to anger, alienate, or frighten passersby. As Lankenau (1999) suggests, this effort transforms a request into a carefully orchestrated repertoire that functions to shield panhandlers from harm and increases the probability of a successful appeal. In turn, most indicated that to avoid escalating a situation and being at even further risk for harm, they actively work at concealing their emotions when someone lashes out at them. As such, they engage in what Hochschild (1983) refers to as "emotion work"—a process that entails managing one's emotions according to the requirements of a job. Finally, many employed friends from the homeless community to stand within hearing distance of them so that they could summon help if they encountered threatening behavior. This practice was referred to as "shadow work." Garry, who often "runs shadow" and uses a harp to communicate signals to the individuals he protects, explained that male panhandlers are frequently assaulted because they are homeless and begging. As he stated, almost every male panhandler gets hit or knocked down "every couple of weeks or so . . . that's why they want me. That's why they need someone to run shadow . . . I'm not a good beggar, but they love me to go with them, because I'm there."

The limited tolerance for the presence of panhandlers in public space, then, forced the homeless in this study to develop a complex and creative set of techniques to prevent victimization. As discussed in the following sections, they also employed a series of finely honed techniques to avoid being hurt in resting, toilet, and sleeping places. These resourceful actions stand in sharp contrast to the conventional notion of the homeless as helpless and disorganized, and they underscore the view that the homeless should not be pathologized as socially disorganized, disaffiliated, or disempowered (Anderson, Snow, & Cress, 1994; Snow & Mulcahy, 2001; Wagner, 1993).

RESTING PLACES

Public space is filled with what can be described as resting stations, examples of which include benches, steps, edges of planters and water fountains, walls, and railings (Bickford, 2000; Oriz, 1994). When the homeless in this study used these stations as resting places, they often encountered police and passersby who used hate-filled words, actions, and gestures to communicate the message that homeless people were undesirable and illegitimate users of such social space even though, by virtue of being homeless, they were "residents of public space" (Kawash, 1998, p. 320).

For many of the participants, resting accounted for a relatively small portion of their day. Several talked about the tremendous amount of time and energy they devoted to simply accessing and maintaining social service benefits. Patty, who is HIV positive and has spent a significant amount of time in search of appropriate health-care benefits and services, noted that she is "constantly always on the move for something. I'm on my feet all the time. I've been walking constantly because I have no truck . . . I mean I have 50 million things a day I'm doing, believe it or not."

Volunteer work, informal mutual aid within the homeless community, and waged labor also consumed a great deal of the participants' time. Well over half worked periodically in either part-time, casual jobs or in temporary day-labor positions; one in four was a volunteer in various nonprofit organizations. Their level of involvement in productive activities is similar to that found in other studies—and yet the homeless continue to be stigmatized as lazy (Rossi, 1989; Snow & Anderson, 1992; Wagner, 1994). Given this stereotype, by simply resting in public space, the homeless can arouse considerable anger among certain individuals who may view such behavior as a clear sign of lack of any work initiative (Wagner, 1994).

For many of the participants, then, activities such as sitting in public space or congregating with friends on sidewalks were all too often enmeshed with deflecting, ignoring, or responding to hate-filled words and actions. Similar to the participants' experiences in panhandling places, hate speech was the most common form of victimization in resting places, and it was also generally white men, from the security of cars, who engaged in these actions. There were, however, some very significant differences in the patterns of hate speech victimization in this setting.

For the female participants, resting in public space carried a more frequent risk of being the victim of direct, face-to-face hate speech victimization. Except for one, all of the female participants recounted incidents in resting places where individuals in close proximity to them had shouted sexually objectifying, hate-filled words such as "homeless slut" or "homeless bitch." In most instances, the perpetrators were men.

Mindy, who became homeless after fleeing an abusive husband, could find no safe place as a woman; she had escaped male abuse within her home only to be haunted by hate speech from men in the streets. While resting in parks or near food kitchens, as she explained, she commonly hears men say, "Go sell your body you disgusting bitch . . . You disgrace women." She also described feeling immensely pained by the hate speech and assault that was directed at a well-known homeless woman who was particularly vulnerable to victimization, given that she was suffering from mental illness. As Mindy explained, while resting in parks she has witnessed men yelling hurtful words at this woman while simultaneously throwing rocks at her—some the size of a fist.

Although the males in the study were also subjected to hurtful remarks through direct confrontations with passersby, they were more apt to experience what one male participant referred to as "distant hate." He described this phenomenon as hate-filled words, actions, or gestures that are used by perpetrators when their physical distance from the victim is sufficiently large enough to avoid retaliation. He noted that distance hate is usually employed from cars, but that individuals also engage in this behavior after they have walked past the homeless. As he explained, "It's generally when they've gotten far enough away to where they don't think I'm gonna come after them and beat 'em up or something, you know. There's fear." Overwhelmingly, men were cited as responsible for acts of distance hate.

The greater frequency with which the female participants were targets for direct, face-to-face hate speech from men reflects the gender hierarchies that permeate public space. In this realm, as Gardner (1995) laments, women are frequently subjected to male harassment and are "pawns for street commentary, targets of gaze, subjects of touches, lures for trailing and stalking, dupes for foolmaking—and victims of rape and violent crime" (p. 240). At their core, these forms of harassment and abuse are an expression of patriarchal entitlement (Nielsen, 2002). With respect to the victimization of the homeless women in this study, however, the perpetrators were not only asserting their masculine dominance, but they were also communicating the belief that homeless people should not be allowed to rest in public space and, in essence, be recognized as fellow citizens (Bickford, 2000; Perry, 2001).

For many of the racial minorities in the study, the hate speech they were subjected to frequently carried the message that public space was white space. Over half described instances in which individuals had shouted racial epithets that were punctuated by words that expressed a desire to end their presence in the community altogether: "Go back to where you came from, homeless scum"; "Homeless piece of shit, I'm calling immigration." Ironically, many of those who made hateful remarks to the Native American participants thought that they were of Hispanic origin and therefore shouted their wounding words in Spanish. Fred, one of the five Native American participants, noted that he was repeatedly victimized in this manner. As he stated, "I've had that done so frequently, I know a little bit of Spanish myself right now."

Resting places were also sites where the homeless encountered a significant amount of hate speech from the police; 10 men and 4 women described instances in which they had been the target of this form of victimization. Each of these individuals recounted derogatory statements leveled by the police about their status of homelessness that were interwoven with words such as *faggot, fag homo, bitch, bottom feeder*, and *white trash*. Terry, who noted that he was well-known among the local law enforcement officers as a member of the homeless community, provided a particularly chilling account of this pattern: "One [police officer] comes up from behind me and I was like, oh man, what did I do? And that's when he slapped me on my back and he was like saying all this stuff in my ear real quietly, calling me a punk, calling me a homeless bitch."

With few notable exceptions, the participants reported that they were most likely to encounter hurtful, hate-filled words from the police during routine examinations of their identification documents. In resting places, as they explained, the police consistently and systematically check their ID—a practice that was described as occurring so frequently that it appeared to resemble a form of petite apartheid. Speaking to the frequency of police checks, a participant explained, " They [the police] go to a lot of these places where people sleep and hang out . . . they check them frequently, like every day, sometimes three or four times a day." This heavy surveillance practice left many of the participants feeling angry, and it led to heated exchanges between the police and the homeless community.

Resting places were not only sites where the homeless were subjected to what Willokch and Slayden (1995) refer to as "credentialized" hate speech by officers of the state, but they were also forums where the homeless endured police brutality. Almost one-third of the participants indicated that they had been subjected to police use of excessive force—acts that they believe were driven by a disdain for the homeless and by a belief that the homeless were powerless to avail protection from the abuse. Overwhelmingly, the victims were male and, once again, the context for the abuse often surrounded interactions between the police and the homeless community that emerged from law enforcement surveillance practices. Sam, who started living on the streets at the age of 14, described the police as a tremendously significant source of danger. As he stated, "Out of all the people that I have dealt with in my entire life with being homeless, the most terrifying people to deal with on the streets are the police. They are brutal. They use excessive use of force. I have had the shit beaten out of me for nothing." Consistent with his concerns and accounts of police violence, the law enforcement department where he lived was under federal investigation for police brutality at the time of the study.

The fact that almost a third of the participants cited the police as perpetrators of hate speech and hate violence helps to dislodge, as Whillock and Slayden (1995) state, "the comfortable notion that hate is a pathological practice of 'others'" (p. x). The findings from this research, however, do not stand in sharp contrast to other studies on this form of criminality. There is now a growing body of literature that documents police involvement in hate crimes (Geller & Toch, 1996; Herek & Berrill, 1992; Perry, 2001). For example, in a study published by the National Coalition of Anti-Violence Programs (1998), the police accounted for 18 percent of the perpetrators of hate crimes against gays and lesbians. Clearly, then, the police play a relatively hidden but powerfully important role in removing the homeless from public resting space.

Although such factors as gender, race, and ethnicity shaped the forms of hate crime victimization the participants experienced in resting places, virtually all of them stated that the rate of victimization was largely driven by how easily an individual could be tagged as homeless. Tagging was most likely to occur if an individual could be linked to what Goffman (1963) refers to as stigma symbols—attributes, traits, or styles of conduct that reveal a stigmatized individual's true identity or condition.

The types of space that were frequently used by the homeless for resting, such as sidewalks and parking lots near soup kitchens, shelters, and social service agencies, functioned as stigma symbols that exposed their status. Individuals in this study were tagged as homeless and therefore brought into harm's way by virtue of, for example, sitting near a local homeless shelter—a space that clearly functions as a powerful stigma symbol. As one participant explained,

At least once a day someone says something [hateful] . . . especially when we're sitting out in front of the shelter at night when it's a nice, cool night. People drive by in cars, they know what the place is, they will yell, throw their fingers to us . . . calling us bums, homeless people, you're nothing.

To avoid tagging and possible hate crime victimization, some of the participants actively worked at avoiding stigmatized space. Stan, who had been living at a homeless shelter for approximately four years, indicated that to escape being identified as homeless he tried not to be seen anywhere near the shelter during the day. He also walked long distances each day as he was fearful that if he rested for too long in any one place he would be tagged as homeless. His daily journeys often covered large areas of the city. As he noted, "I might go up to the West-End promenade, East-End promenade, ya know, down to the port." He used movement between space, in essence, to avoid encountering the hate that operates through space.

Clothing and hygiene practices that conflict with middle-class appearance norms also function as highly significant stigma symbols that can trigger the tagging process and lead to hate crime victimization in virtually all of the settings that configure into the daily routines of the homeless. One of the stereotypes of the homeless is that they all wear shabby clothing and are unkempt (Lankenau, 1999). The participants in this study who violated appearance norms and conformed at some level to this stereotype were much more likely to be tagged as homeless and to experience hate crime victimization. Barry, who lived in a camp and often had difficulty accessing warm water for cleansing, noted that he was victimized by hate speech in resting places on a daily basis and felt that he was more likely to have this experience based on his appearance. Speaking to the frequency of his victimization he stated, "I encounter at least one asshole a day."

Almost all of the participants talked about how their appearance was subjected to what Gardner (1995) refers to as "inspection draw"—close public scrutiny. Thus, while it was natural for them to maintain their appearance, they also saw it as a means to protect themselves from failing inspection and thereby increasing the probability of being victimized. They were acutely aware of the association that has been culturally constructed between dirt and homeless people (Douglas, 1966; Lankenau, 1999).

Finally, various participants identified the mere act of sitting or standing in public space as a stigma symbol that could tag them as homeless and subject them to hurtful comments and threats. To avoid this detection, they used props, such as books, magazines, newspapers, and various religious items (e.g., the Bible or a yarmulke) to signal that they were involved in an activity and not simply resting. As Goffman (1963) suggested in *Stigma*, these types of strategies, which he referred to as "passing," are frequently employed by stigmatized individuals to mask their identity.

Both the frequency of victimization in resting places and the amount of energy required to avoid it left many of the participants angry and heightened their sense of displacement. Sam, who said that he was often the victim of hate speech in resting places because he was carrying the wrong plastic— a grocery bag and not a credit card—expressed this sentiment in poignantly clear words that reflect his sense of feeling unwanted and unwelcome. As he lamented, "I feel like I am losing my place on the planet . . . Why as a homeless person are you given no space at all?" His experiences and those of the other participants underscore that resting in public space, in quiet solitude and peace, is an act that is enmeshed in privilege.

TOILET PLACES

Although relatively few have sought to systematically study access to bathrooms, these are also a space where various power relations are reinforced and reproduced, and thus sites where the homeless in this study encountered hate. In this location, however, the perpetrators were no longer predominately "nasty white males in cars," but rather men and women from a broad array of socioeconomic backgrounds. This victim–offender pattern is important to understand for, as Perry (2001) explains, hate crime "is much more than the act of mean-spirited bigots. It is embedded in the cultural and social context within which groups interact" (p. 1; and see Bowling, 1993; Young, 1990).

Among the participants, almost one-third described instances in which hate-filled words and actions had been used to deny them access to semi-public bathrooms, such as those found in gas stations and fast-food establishments. All of these individuals were resoundingly clear that their victimization was based on the fact that they were homeless, and each provided detailed information to support his or her claim; they were not simply trying to use bathrooms that were private or "for customers only." Representative of this dynamic, one of the African American males in this study was called a "homeless ass boy" by a gas-station attendant who went on to indicate that he was tired of seeing him use the bathroom. This homeless person knew, with stinging clarity, that a racial and class line had been drawn between him and the bathroom.

The hate-filled words and incidents that the participants experienced in toilet places, however, is not surprising given the historical practice in the United States of restricting and segregating this space from marginalized groups. In this regard, the racial segregation of bathrooms up until the modern civil rights movement stands as one of the most poignant examples of how access to bathrooms has been used to maintain spatial boundaries between groups. Frequently, force and violence were used to carry out this objective (Cooper & Oldenziel, 1999).

Writing from a feminist perspective, various scholars have noted that limitations around women's access to bathrooms have placed restrictions on their full participation outside of the home. One of the rationales used historically to preserve the sexual division of labor has been the argument that women could not be hired because there were no female toilets. This excuse continues to surface as women seek access to, for example, elite cadet-training facilities and various other public service institutions. In this sense, access to bathrooms has been and continues to be used as a means to separate and rank women and men (Banks, 1991; Cooper & Oldenziel, 1999). Concomitantly, the establishment of executive washrooms, officer latrines, and faculty bathrooms also reflects a way in which bathrooms have been used to insure that groups from different hierarchical role-relationships remain distinct and separate from each other. These types of bathrooms are thought to provide a segregative punctuation to many institutional settings (Cahill et al., 1985).

Clearly, then, bathrooms have been used in ways that reinforce socially constructed differences and boundaries between people. The act of denying homeless people access to bathrooms seems to be yet another expression of this pattern. Among the homeless in this study, the suggestion that a bathroom was broken or closed for cleaning surfaced as a fairly common technique used to police the boundaries of toilet places. Mitchell Duneier (1999) also found this oppressive practice in operation during the course of his study of homeless street vendors in New York. As he notes:

> I personally witnessed Ishmael being told that the bathroom was being cleaned and could not be used, even after he had made a purchase. Though I had not bought anything, I got the key and entered the bathroom myself without receiving any warning, only to discover that it was empty. Many people who work outside on Sixth Avenue seem to be hassled in similar ways, even when they have made a purchase. The stories are repeated constantly. (p. 181)

Duneier (1999) speculates that some of the street vendors chose to pee in cups and in the streets because, among other things, it was easier than being denied access to a bathroom and enduring a hurtful rejection.

Thinly veiled rejections of requests to use a bathroom under the guise that the facilities are closed or broken are fairly easy to detect, as several of the participants in this study explained, but they are not emotionally easy to experience. Mary, whose monthly disability compensation of $520 left her able to afford only a condemned trailer on the housing black market, described feeling both angry and wounded by an incident in which she was told a bathroom she had previously used was no longer working. This incident occurred after her status of homelessness became apparent to the gas station attendant. As she explained,

> I went in there one day, and I was kind of dressed up that day and he let me use his bathroom, then he starts seeing me more and more around the area, and I wasn't quite as dressed up anymore, and now he won't let me use his bathroom. [He says], "The bathrooms are off-line." How does a bathroom get off-line? What did they do, disconnect the piping or something?

For Mary, there was simply no question that many toilet places were re-
served for more privileged groups in society and that disdain for the homeless created conditions where they were routinely unable to use them. Her
comment to the author of this chapter illuminates this sentiment: "And I bet
if you went there [to the bathroom], it wouldn't be off-line."

By far the most common strategy used to exclude the participants from
toilet space entailed the employment of the claim that homeless people routinely create dirty messes in bathrooms, particularly when they used them to
care for their bodies—for example, brushing their teeth and washing their
face. Almost all of the participants who had been warned out of bathrooms
were told they could not use a certain facility, as homeless people "trash"
bathrooms; not surprisingly, Duneier (1999) reports that the homeless men
in his study were also subjected to this hurtful accusation. Typically, the
message that participants were forced to endure was both patronizing and
hurtful. For example, Stan was told by the manager of a Burger King that
while it was *good* for the homeless to use toilets rather than the streets, "the
restroom, right, it's not for taking and making a mess and trying to wash
your face." As a homeless person, Stan was cast as someone who would dirty
and contaminate a bathroom; the weary airline traveler, however, who at-
tends to personal hygiene needs in an airport bathroom after a long flight,
washes in peaceful privilege

The belief that homeless people are summarily responsible for creating
uncleanly conditions in bathrooms seems to be an extension of the culturally
constructed association between dirt and homeless people. They are stereotyped as soiled, filthy individuals who will transfer their uncleanliness to the
spaces they occupy. As such, in battles to protect bathroom space from use
by the homeless, it would appear that people are employing hate-filled words
or action to maintain what they believe are the proper boundaries between
"good/bad, clean/dirty, pure/impure, and so forth" (Cooper & Oldenziel,
1999, p. 19).

For some of the participants, the accusation that they would dirty a bathroom was laced with words that made it simultaneously gendered and racialized. By way of example, one woman who sought to brush her teeth in a
gas station was told by the attendant that it wasn't a "hobo homeless bathroom for her to dirty," and she overheard this individual calling her a white,
homeless bitch. When confronted by the homeless woman about these harsh,
wounding words, the attendant stated simply, "Ma'am, this is not for homeless people—that's all I got to say."

Even when the participants had a history of using a particular bathroom
and were paying customers, if it was found in an exceptionally untidy state,
they faced the prospect of being accused of creating such conditions and
therefore being denied access to it. Jim, who often slept in tents and recycling
bins since getting laid off from his factory job, described an account of this

nature. As he stated, "Jane and I used to go in there [sandwich shop], use the bathrooms. When we had money, we would buy a coffee . . . One day the guy behind the counter goes, 'A hey man, you guys can't be using the bathroom, you trashed it' . . . I says, 'Who do think we are?'" Through this hurtful denunciation, Jim and his partner lost access to an exceptionally important resource, and one that was in short supply, given that there are very few public bathrooms in the cities that served as the sites for this research.

While using hurtful words and actions to deny homeless people access to bathrooms is a harm in its own right, it is particularly problematic given that it creates conditions where it is harder for the homeless people to maintain their hygiene, increasing their probability of hate crime victimization in other settings as they are more readily tagged as homeless. As one male participant bemoaned, "How you dress and look is how you are treated." If you don't look decent, as another fellow stated, "watch how you are treated." Fully half of the participants devoted some portion of their interview to a discussion of the hate crime victimization danger associated with failing to comply with middle-class appearance norms.

However, when the "going got tough" for the homeless in this study, many utilized clever strategies to gain access to bathrooms and to shield themselves from being warned out of them. Hiding one's identity, or "passing" in Goffman's (1963) terms, was the central mechanism they employed to carry out these objectives. To pass, they often engaged in behavior that was designed to signify that they were not homeless. Jill, who is a former elementary-school teacher and had fled a physically abusive husband, seemed particularly skilled at this maneuver. To gain access to bathrooms, as she explained, "[In hotels I] pretend that I'm waiting for someone or that I am inquiring about the conference upstairs. And I can do that—go into the bathroom, freshen up." By pretending to be attending a conference or visiting a friend, Jill was displaying what Goffman (1963) described in *Stigma* as "disidentifying" behavior—actions that served to mask her identity as a homeless woman.

Similarly, one of the female participants, Marge, utilized discourse about travel to pass as a tourist and thereby gain access to bathrooms in gas stations for her children when they were living in a car. She frequently drove to gas stations and asked for directions while her children washed and used the toilets; Marge would also talk to the attendants about fictitious travel experiences. As she noted, "I was always pretending that we were traveling to different places . . . So we just kind of played the game that we didn't live any different than anybody else." Chad, as another case in point, would periodically represent himself as someone who was seeking employment and would start to fill out a job application form before slipping into the bathroom.

Traditionally, the actions that the participants used to gain access to bathrooms have been categorized in the literature on homelessness as either stigma-management efforts or resourceful survival mechanisms (Anderson et al., 1994; Snow & Mulcahy, 2001). It is clear, however, that this behavior must also be understood as hate crime victimization prevention. They are strategies to avoid hearing the hate-filled words that Jim and his partner endured when they sought use of a bathroom to wash up: "Why don't you get a house!"

Sleeping Places

Simply put, the homeless sleep in public space because of their lack of private space (Mitchell, 1997; Wright, 2000). Among the participants in this study, approximately two-thirds had slept outside in, for example, cars, tents, boxes, and recycling bins. These individuals were forced to work hard, as Wright (2000) so evocatively noted, "to fit themselves into the never-world cracks of the city" (p. 29). In these cracks, however, many were subjected to the crushing weight of multiple forms of hate crime victimization. Approximately one-third of the participants who had slept outside reported being dislodged from their sleeping place by agents of social control (e.g., police, city workers, and state road crews).

Although residing in transitional housing shelters can shield the homeless from the hate crime victimization tied to sleeping outdoors, many of the individuals in this study expressed frustration about the conditions within the local homeless shelter and noted that these factors either inhibited or restricted their use of it. Fundamentally, then, like most shelters in this nation, it was not much of a shield. By far the most common set of complaints about the shelter included its noise, lack of privacy, and almost unbearable sleeping conditions. The men, in particular, described "sleeping rough" within this shelter as male residents are forced to sleep on floor mats only two inches apart from each other. This makes trying to get enough sleep one of the daily hardships of shelter life. John, one of the participants who periodically slept in the shelter, explained this challenge: "It takes a while to go to sleep. By the time you get to sleep, you are up again. Because they are snoring, talking in their sleep, and hollering." During the summer, he often found better sleeping conditions in carnival gaming boxes.

A number of the participants refused to sleep in the local shelter because it had too many rules and regulations, a common critique of transitional housing facilities (Bogard, 1998; Knowles, 2000; Liebow, 1993; Wagner, 1993). Their characterization of the organizational operation of the shelter, which they found oppressive, matched Goffman's (1961) description of a total institution—a place where like-situated individuals lead a formally administered life. For one young woman, residing in the shelter simply felt like being "in a jail." She preferred sidewalk sleeping, and its attendant risk of hate crime victimization, to the institutional social control of the shelter.

Finally, although this discussion is by no means an exhaustive examination of the issue, the fact that the shelter could not provide arrangements for individuals to sleep with or be near those they cherished—for example, husband or wives, partners, boyfriends, or girlfriends—locked several out of this living arrangement. To be together, Samantha and Henry slept in their car and during the New England winter nights had to "run the car a little bit, stay cold a little bit." Concomitantly, the shelter's inability to accommodate pets, particularly dogs, was a profoundly powerful deterrent to shelter use, and one that has also been found to keep battered woman from using safe house shelters (Ascione, Weber, & Wood, 1997; Flynn, 2000a, 2000b). One young woman said that she would never use a shelter, as that would mean separation from her dog, whose benefits to her knew few boundaries. As she explained, "They watch over you, they keep you company, they're your best friend, they don't *hate* you."

The conditions within the shelters in the research sites, and no doubt in all others within this nation, must be understood as contributing to the precarious situation in which many of the homeless have very few alternatives other than sleeping in public space. The act of appropriating public and semipublic space to sleep, however, exposes the homeless to individuals who use hate to facilitate their removal.

When the homeless in this study were moved from their sleeping places through hate, it tended to occur when they were occupying what Snow and Mulcahy (2001) refer to as prime space. This is one of three different types of urban space that the researchers discuss in their examination of how spatial control strategies employed against the homeless vary by differences in space. The researchers defined prime space as any realm that is used by the domiciled for residential, recreational, or navigational purposes; areas used for financial or entrepreneurial purposes are also part of this conceptualization of space. Marginal space, the second type, was identified as unused land that appears to be either abandoned or ignored, and transitional space, the third type, was described as land occupied by low-income, marginalized individuals who are, nonetheless, domiciled.

Not surprisingly, Snow and Mulcahy (2001) found that the homeless were most apt to encounter conflict with social-control officials when they used prime space to meet their essential needs (e.g., resting and sleeping)—a pattern not dissimilar from the findings in this study.

Most of the participants who slept outside camped in the marginal space of the city and were seldom asked to vacate their sleeping arrangements in this area. However, some had established tent encampments in prime space near roads, and these were the source of significant spatial contestations. These individuals slept near roads, as this space provided them with easy access to routes they used to traverse the city, and they utilized the landscaping along roads, particularly bushes, to shield themselves from the watchful eye of the police and public. As such, it was prime space for them as well, but sleeping in it was not without risks and dangers.

All of the men reported that they were angry about the loss of property they endured in roadside encampments when either city or state transportation crews appeared, without warning, and destroyed most of their belongings. They experienced this behavior as an act of vandalism and were certain, given the almost complete disregard for their dignity and property, that it was motivated by disdain for the homeless. Speaking to this sentiment, one man who had recently experienced having all of his possessions thrown away by a transportation crew said that the destruction of his property was deeply symbolic of societal hate and contempt for the homeless. Further to that point, he stated angrily, "They [public transportation workers] never have any respect for your property, never ask, 'Whose is this? Whose is that?' They just take it and dump it. I'm homeless, not worthless."

Typically, the road crews began their destruction of the camps by employing the power of law and suggesting, whether true or not, that the police were en route. This statement, of course, led to frantic scrambles among the men to salvage what they could before fleeing the site. Describing this scene, one man explained, "And so you make a choice, what do you take with you? You got seconds to get out of there so you usually grab the small backpack and your day pack . . . You got two seconds or you are going to jail." These flash-point moments, in which they lost their survival gear, created lasting financial hardships for the men, and some described them as emotionally painful. Reflecting on seeing all of his worldly possessions destroyed, one man stated, "I mean, I was hurt. You know I felt like dirt."

In addition to vandalism of their property, several men discussed incidents in which road-crew workers had also used hate speech and hate-motivated acts of violence to hurt them. One man reported that on two occasions a road crew employee had kicked him in the ribs as a method to rouse him. "It was a pretty good kick in the side," he lamented. Speaking to one of his experiences, he said that after being kicked he was then called a "homeless scumbag" and "piece of shit." Thereafter, the crew took most of his possessions.

Sleeping on sidewalks or within large parking ramps, also prime space, carried the specific risk of being hurt by those who use their cars as weapons or as a source of armor. Frank, who has been homeless since 1997 due to a physical illness, described several incidents where men had thrown glass bottles at him from their cars while he slept on a heating vent. On one occasion, a bottle hit him in the chest and then exploded against a wall. The drivers in the car shouted that they were going to kill him and called him a homeless bum. They drove past Frank several times—an experience that left him feeling like he had been terrorized.

While relatively few in number, several of the hate-filled experiences in other realms of prime space were at the hands of law enforcement. Three individuals described instances in which the police used tactics to dislodge them from prime space by demolishing their sleeping place and/or by forcing them to leave it without their possessions—acts that, once again, were described by the participants as forms of vandalism grounded in hate. Bob, whose illiteracy and limited level of formal education made it difficult for him to find employment that offered a living wage, explained that he had been forced to leave his sleeping places many times, and that he had suffered through both of the aforementioned police tactics. When the police find your sleeping spot, as he explained, "they ain't gonna *take* it down, they gonna *tear* it down [demolish it] . . . Nor do they give you the opportunity," as he countered, "to collect your property." He recited a warning from the police in which they specifically stated that if he collected his belongings, he faced arrest: "The only thing they'll do [the police], they'll give you a choice 'You can go back over to the tent and go to jail, now it's your choice.'"

One of the more haunting narratives about being removed from a sleeping place came from a man and woman who had been residing in a recycling bin used for cardboard boxes. Several hours before being interviewed for this chapter, they had been discovered sleeping in the bin by a police officer. Rather than being encouraged to assemble their sleeping bags and other items essential to survival on the streets, they were simply threatened with arrest and therefore fled empty-handed. For these individuals, the police officer's act of omission, not providing them with the time to gather their property, felt like an act of commission—vandalism. The timing of their loss was particularly tragic, as it was the dead of winter and they no longer had most of the items they were using to stay warm.

Marginal space, as noted, was often secure and safe for the homeless. However, one man was almost killed in his encampment by a group of male teenagers who called themselves "The Wrecking Crew," and were known to destroy homeless encampments. Adam and his partner, Frances, were sleeping when six young men, aged 13–18, woke them up and began to ransack their belongings. They hit Adam in the skull with a brick and with the jarring edges of a torn-up umbrella. Part of his skull was smashed, and he still has a rather large indentation in it. When Adam and Frances asked why they were being harmed, one of the teenagers replied, "Because we can."

As was the case with the participants' practices in the other spaces, they had developed a set of sophisticated hate crime prevention techniques to avoid being victimized in sleeping places. For example, to conceal the fact that they were homeless and sleeping in public space, several placed props, such as books, nearby when they slept to appear as if they had simply fallen asleep while engaged in an activity such as reading. They carried these props in their backpacks similar to the way in which some carry pepper spray or other weapons of defense to protect against victimization.

Developing a sleeping place that was somehow hidden from public view was by far the most common strategy the participants used to secure their sleeping arrangements and to shield themselves from hate crime victimization. In many instances, vegetation played an important role in this endeavor. One couple, for example, had established a safe campsite by burrowing deep into a large stand of Japanese knotweed, a bushy, invasive plant in New England that was originally introduced to hide outhouses. Concealed by the plant, they slept undisturbed in this place each summer.

As noted earlier, several of the men also used bushes and shrubbery along roadsides as a sleeping refuge. In one of the roadside encampments, known as "Camp Cal," the men had developed a furtive technique of carefully timing their entrance and exit from the bushes in order to keep their sleeping place secret. Camp Cal was in a particularly prized location as it was near a noisy highway overpass that functioned to drown out their voices and radios. Nestled in the protection of the bushes, the men felt, as one stated, "[that] they were right behind enemy lines." Indeed, given the level of hate crime victimization the participants were forced to endure in sleeping places, it is perhaps fair to suggest that in the burrows of their hidden living quarters, they were all behind enemy lines.

CONCLUSION

As Low and Smith (2006) underscore, public space is socially produced and is an expression of social power—a fact that is clearly brought to light through the voices of the homeless in this chapter. While many may assume that public and semipublic spaces are democratic venues where diverse people and activities are embraced, this assumption deserves close scrutiny, particularly in light of the victimization and suffering endured by the homeless as they traverse the spaces that are central to their survival.

The hate to which the homeless are subjected does much to reconfirm the dominant social–spatial hierarchical organization of public and semipublic spaces, and simultaneously reinforces the message that the homeless should not be recognized as fellow citizen. It creates, essentially, geographies of fear for those who lack housing. The streets are indeed mean, as Hagan and McCarthy (1998) have declared.

To curtail the hate the homeless are forced to endure, however, it is not enough to pass hate crime legislation—the heart of privilege must come under attack (Wright, 1997). The very best form of hate crime victim prevention for the homeless is housing, employment, and health-care justice. Essentially, the state plays a central role in molding the homeless population's vulnerability to hate crimes, and it is critical to framing a solution to this

220   The Victims of Hate Crime

suffering. As the United States spirals forward into even greater levels of inequality, one can only hope that the nation will eventually ready itself for heart surgery—to more fully share wealth, space, and privilege.

REFERENCES

Anderson, L., Snow, D., & Cress, D. (1994). Negotiating the public realm: Stigma management and collective action among the homeless. *Research in Community Sociology, 1*, 121–143.

Ascione, F., Weber, C., & Wood, D. (1997). The abuse of animals and domestic violence: A national survey of shelters for women who are battered. *Society and Animals, 5*(3), 208–218.

Banks, T. (1991). Toilets as a feminist issue: A true story. *Berkeley Women's Law Journal, 6*, 263–289.

Bickford, S. (2000). Constructing inequality: City spaces and the architecture of citizenship. *Political Theory, 28*(3), 355–377.

Bogard, C. (1998). The rhetoric of domination and its strategic use by homeless women. *Sociological Spectrum, 18*(3), 229–263.

Bowling, B. (1993). Racial harassment and the process of victimization. *British Journal of Criminology, 33*(2), 231–250.

Cahill, S., Distler, W., Lachowetz, C., Meaney, A., Tarallo, R., & Willard, T. (1985). Meanwhile backstage: Public bathrooms and the interaction of others. *Urban Life, 14*(1), 33–58.

Carlen, P. (1996). *Jigsaw: A political criminology of youth homelessness*. Buckingham: Open Press University.

Cohen, M. (2001). Homeless people. In A. Gitterman (Ed.), *Handbook for social work practice with vulnerable and resistant populations*. New York: Columbia University Press.

Cooper, P., & Oldenziel, R. (1999). Cherished classifications: Bathrooms and the construction of gender/race on the Pennsylvania railroad during World War II. *Feminist Studies, 25*(1), 7–36.

Dijkstra, L. (2000). Public spaces: A comparative discussion of the criteria for public space. *Research in Urban Sociology, 5*, 1–22.

Douglas, M. (1966). *Purity and danger: An analysis of the concepts of pollution and taboo*. London: Routledge.

Duneier, M. (1999). *Sidewalk*. New York: Farrar, Straus, and Giroux.

Flynn, C. (2000a). Animal abuse. In E. McLaughlin & J. Muncie (Eds.), *The sage dictionary of criminology* (pp. 8–10). London: Sage.

Flynn, C. (2000b). Women's best friend: Pet abuse and the role of companion animals in the lives of battered women. *Violence Against Women, 6*(2), 162–177.

Gardner, C. (1995). *Passing by: Gender and public harassment*. Berkeley: University of California Press.

Geller, W., & Toch, H. (Eds.). (1996). *Police violence: Understanding and controlling police abuse of force*. New Haven, CT: Yale University Press.

Goffman, E. (1961). *Asylums*. Chicago: Aldine Publishing.

Goffman, E. (1963). *Stigma: Notes on the management of a spoiled identity*. Englewood Cliffs, NJ: Prentice-Hall.

Gottdiener, M. (1985). *The social production of urban space.* Austin: University of Texas Press.

Hagan, J., & McCarthy, B. (1998). *Mean streets: Youth crime and homelessness.* Cambridge, UK: Cambridge University Press.

Herek, G., & Berrill, K. (Eds.) (1992). *Hate crimes: Confronting violence against lesbians and gay men.* Newbury, CA: Sage.

Hochschild, A. (1983). *The managed heart: Commercialization of human feeling.* Berkeley: University of California Press.

Katz, M. (1996). *In the shadow of the poorhouse: A social history of welfare in America.* New York: Basic Books.

Kawash, S. (1998). The homeless body. *Public Culture, 10*(2), 319–339.

Knowles, C. (2000). Burger King, Dunkin Donuts and community mental health care. *Health and Place, 6*(3), 213–224.

Lankenau, S. (1999). Panhandling repertoires and routines for overcoming nonperson treatment. *Deviant Behavior: An Interdisciplinary Journal, 20,* 183–206.

Liebow, E. (1993). *Tell them who I am: The lives of homeless women.* New York: Penguin Books.

Low, S., & Smith, N. (Eds.). (2006). *The politics of social space.* New York: Routledge.

Messerschmidt, J. (1997). *Crime as structured action: Gender, race and crime in the making.* Thousand Oaks, CA: Sage.

Mitchell, D. (1997). The annihilation of space by law: The roots and implications of anti-homeless laws in the United States. *Antipode, 29*(3), 303–335.

National Coalition of Anti-Violence Programs. (1998). *Anti-lesbian, gay, bisexual and transgendered violence in 1997.* New York: Author.

National Law Center on Homelessness and Poverty. (2007). *Homeless and poverty in America, 2007.* Retrieved from http://www.nlchp.org/haphia.cfm

Nielsen, L. (2002). Subtle, pervasive, harmful: Racist and sexist remarks in public as hate speech. *Journal of Social Issues, 58*(2), 265–280.

Ortiz, S. (1994). Shopping for sociability in the mall. *Research in Community Sociology* (Suppl. 1), 183–199.

Perry, B. (2001). *In the name of hate: Understanding hate crimes.* New York: Routledge.

Rossi, P. (1989). *Down and out in America: The origins of homelessness.* Chicago: University of Chicago Press.

Rushdie, S. (1995). *Midnight's children.* New York: Knopf.

Ray, R. (2000). *Nostalgia: Aging and life-story writing.* Charlottesville: University Press of Virginia.

Snow, D., & Anderson, L. (1992). *Down on their luck.* Berkeley: University of California Press.

Snow, D., & Mulcahy, M. (2001). Space, politics, and the survival strategies of the homeless. *American Behavioral Scientist, 45*(1), 149–169.

Stark, L. (1992). From lemons to lemonade: An ethnographic sketch of late twentieth-century panhandling. *New England Journal of Public Policy, 8*(1), 341–52.

Swanson, J. (2001). *Poor-bashing.* Toronto, Ontario, Canada: Between the Lines.

Vanderstaay, S. (1992). *Street lives: An oral history of homeless Americans.* Philadelphia: New Society Publishers.

Wachholz, S., & Mullaly, R. (1993). Policing the deinstitutionalized mentally ill: Toward an understanding of its function. *Crime, law and social change, 19,* 281–300.

Wagner, D. (1993). *Checkerboard square: Culture and resistance in a homeless community.* Boulder, CO: Westview.

Wagner, D. (1994). Beyond the pathologizing of nonwork: Alternative activities in a street community. *Social Work, 39*(6), 718–727.

Watson, S., & Austerberry, H. (1986). *Housing and homelessness: A feminist perspective.* London: Routledge and Kegan Paul.

Willoch, R., & Slayden, D. (Eds.). (1995). *Hate speech.* London: Sage.

Wright, T. (1997). *Out of place: Homeless mobilizations, subcities, and contested landscapes.* New York: State University of New York Press.

Wright, T. (2000). New urban spaces and cultural representations: Social imagineries, social-physical space and the homeless. *Research in urban sociology, 5,* 23–57.

Young, V. (1990). *The politics of difference.* Princeton, NJ: Princeton University Press.

ABOUT THE EDITOR

AND CONTRIBUTORS

Barbara Perry is professor of criminology, justice and policy studies at the University of Ontario Institute of Technology. She has written extensively in the area of hate crime, including two books on the topic: *In the Name of Hate: Understanding Hate Crime* (2001) and *Hate and Bias Crime: A Reader* (2003). She has just completed a book manuscript titled *The Silent Victims: Native American Victims of Hate Crime* (2008), based on interviews with Native Americans, and one on policing Native American communities. Dr. Perry continues to work in the area of hate crime and has begun to make contributions to the limited scholarship on hate crime in Canada. She is particularly interested in anti-Muslim violence and hate crime against Aboriginal people.

Walter S. DeKeseredy is chair of the American Society of Criminology's (ASC) Division on Critical Criminology and professor of criminology, justice and policy studies at the University of Ontario Institute of Technology (UOIT). He has published 13 books and over 70 scientific journal articles on a variety of topics, including woman abuse in intimate relationships and crime in public housing. He also jointly received (with Martin D. Schwartz) the 2004 Distinguished Scholar Award from the ASC's Division on Women and Crime and the 2007 inaugural UOIT Research Excellence Award. In 1995, he received the Critical Criminologist of the Year Award from the ASC's Division on Critical Criminology.

Ellen Faulkner has published in the areas of hate crime, antilesbian violence, hate propaganda, same-sex partner abuse, and reproductive technologies.

She is co-editor, with Dr. Gayle MacDonald, of *Victim No More: Women, Law, Feminism: Stories of Resistance from the Ground Up*, published in 2008. In 2006 she was awarded a standard research grant from the Social Sciences and Humanities Research Council of Canada (SSHRC) for her research project "Making Hate Crime: A Study of Police Work." Her research interests include critical criminology, policing, regulation and social control, violence against women and children, hate crime victimization, and qualitative research methods. She is an assistant professor of sociology in the Department of Sociology, Brock University, St. Catharines, Ontario, Canada.

Paul Iganski, PhD, is a lecturer in criminology in the Department of Applied Social Science at Lancaster University, England, and formerly Civil Society Fellow at the Institute for Jewish Policy Research, London. He is editor of *The Hate Debate* (2002); co-editor, with Barry Kosmin, of *A New Antisemitism? Debating Judeophobia in 21st Century Britain* (2003); and co-author, with Vicky Kielinger and Susan Paterson, of *Hate Crimes Against London's Jews* (2005). His most recent book is *Hate Crime and the City* (2008). He served as an expert witness providing written and oral evidence to the 2005–2006 UK All-Party Parliamentary Inquiry Into Antisemitism.

Silvina Ituarte is an associate professor in the Department of Criminal Justice Administration at California State University East Bay (CSUEB). She began teaching at CSUEB in 2003 after teaching at Kean University in New Jersey for eight years. While at Kean, Dr. Ituarte earned the honor of Professor of the Year in 2001 and served as director of the Criminal Justice major, director of Service Learning, and assistant chair of the Public Administration Department.

Martin Kim, BA, is a doctoral student at the Illinois Institute of Technology's Institute of Psychology in Chicago. He is working on his clinical psychology Ph.D. with an emphasis in rehabilitation. The focus of his clinical training is on neuropsychology, particularly pertaining to linguistic and cultural issues in the assessment of people who speak Spanish. In addition, psychosocial and forensic aspects of disability remain important areas of interest in his work.

Frank J. Lane, PhD, LCPC, CRC, is an assistant professor at the Illinois Institute of Technology's Institute of Psychology in Chicago. He has 10 years' experience as a rehabilitation counselor, program administrator, and rehabilitation educator and researcher. Dr. Lane's research interests include the criminal victimization of persons with disabilities, with particular emphasis on hate crimes committed against persons with disabilities. His current research projects are designed to answer research questions about the profile of perpetrators and issues related to the underreporting of disability-motivated bias crimes.

Helen Ahn Lim is assistant professor in the Department of Criminal Justice, California Lutheran University. Her research and teaching interests include hate crime, criminology, race, gender, white-collar crime, and theory.

Scott Poynting is professor in sociology at Manchester Metropolitan University. He is co-author of *Bin Laden in the Suburbs: Criminalising the Arab Other* (2004) and *Kebabs, Kids, Cops and Crime: Youth, ethnicity and crime* (2000), and co-editor of *Outrageous! Moral panics in Australia* (2007).

Linda R. Shaw, PhD, LMHC, CRC, is an associate professor and is the director of the Rehabilitation Counseling program at the University of Florida. She has 30 years' experience as a rehabilitation counselor, program administrator, and rehabilitation educator. Dr. Shaw is currently serving as president of the Council on Rehabilitation Education (CORE). She is a former chair of the Commission on Rehabilitation Counselor Certification (CRCC) Ethics Committee and a past-president of the American Rehabilitation Counseling Association.

Carolyn Turpin-Petrosino is associate professor of criminal justice at Bridgewater State College, Massachusetts. She has published several articles on parole decision-making, community policing, juvenile diversion, and most recently hate crimes. Her current projects involve antiblack hate crime patterns and the investigation of community responses to hate crime events. In addition, Dr. Petrosino is investigating the utility of ethical theories in policy analyses.

Sandra Wachholz received her Ph.D. from the Criminal Justice Center at Sam Houston State University in Huntsville, Texas. She is an associate professor in the Department of Criminology, University of Southern Maine. Her research focuses on barriers to justice for abused immigrant women, hate crimes against the homeless, and the gender-differentiated impacts of climate change. She complements her academic work with involvement in social justice organizations.

INDEX